D0040504

Marital Therapy:

Concepts and Skills
for Effective Practice

JOE H. BROWN
University of Louisville

CAROLYN S. BROWN
Greater Clark County Schools

BROOKS/COLE

THOMSON LEARNING

Australia • Canada • Mexico • Singapore • Spain • United Kingdom • United States

BROOKS/COLE

——————✳——————™

THOMSON LEARNING

Sponsoring Editor: *Julie Martinez*
Marketing Team: *Caroline Concilla,*
 Tami Strang
Editorial Assistant: *Catherine Broz*
Production Editor: *Kelsey McGee*
Production Service: *Buuji, Inc. /*
 Sara Dovre Wudali
Permissions Editor: *Connie Dowcett*

Manuscript Editor: *Buuji, Inc. / Alan DeNiro*
Cover Design: *Roy R. Neuhaus*
Cover Illustration: *Stock Illustration*
 Source / José Ortega
Print Buyer: *Vena M. Dyer*
Typesetting: *Buuji, Inc. / Carl Hokanson*
Cover Printing, Printing and Binding:
 Webcom

COPYRIGHT © 2002 Wadsworth Group. Brooks/Cole is an imprint of the Wadsworth Group, a division of Thomson Learning, Inc.
Thomson Learning™ is a trademark used herein under license.

For more information about this or any other Brooks / Cole products, contact:
BROOKS/COLE
511 Forest Lodge Road
Pacific Grove, CA 93950 USA
www.brookscole.com
1-800-423-0563 (Thomson Learning Academic Resource Center)

All rights reserved. No part of this work may be reproduced, transcribed or used in any form or by any means—graphic, electronic, or mechanical, including photocopying, recording, taping, Web distribution, or information storage and/or retrieval systems—without the written permission of the publisher.

For permission to use material from this work, contact us by
www.thomsonrights.com
fax: 1-800-730-2215
phone: 1-800-730-2214

Printed in Canada

10 9 8 7 6 5 4 3

Acknowledgments: **Chapter 1:** Excerpts from *The Good Marriage.* Copyright © 1995 Judith S. Wallerstein and Sandra Blakeslee. Reprinted by permission of Ticknor & Fields/ Houghton Mifflin Co. All rights reserved. **Chapter 8:** From *Evaluating Couples: A Handbook for Practitioners* by Mark A. Karpel. Copyright © 1994 by Mark A. Karpel. Used by permission of W. W. Norton & Company. **Chapters 3, 4, 5, 11:** From *Practice of Family Therapy: Key Elements Across Models,* 2nd edition, by S. M. Hanna and J. H. Brown. Copyright © 1999. Reprinted with permission of Wadsworth, an imprint of the Wadsworth Group, a division of Thomson Learning.

Library of Congress Cataloging-in-Publication Data
Brown, Joseph H.
 Marital therapy : concepts and skills for effective practice / Joe H. Brown, Carolyn S. Brown.
  p. cm.
 Includes bibliographical references and indexes.
 ISBN- 13: 978-0-534-52732-7
 ISBN- 10: 0-534-52732-9
  1. Marital psychotherapy. I. Brown, Carolyn S. II. Title.
RC488.5 .B763 2001   2001035438
616.89'156—dc21

Contents

✳

Preface

Three important reasons motivated the writing of this book. First, the book was designed to help entry-level marital therapists learn the concepts and skills necessary for effective practice. The skills and concepts selected for inclusion in the book are theoretically based and empirically tested; however, coverage of theoretical concepts and research associated with the skills is limited, because these areas are covered adequately in other texts.

The second reason for this book is related to current trends toward accountability and the requirements of mental health care. Because of such trends, therapists may well have to defend their very existence in the future. This can best be done through demonstrating skills with clients and being able to show through various measures that positive behaviors do, in fact, take place as a result of marital therapy. Still a third reason for the book is to provide a format that emphasizes skill acquisition and application. Each chapter includes an introduction, chapter objectives, information about the area, case examples, key points, and a marital skills inventory.

The book is based on our belief that beginning practitioners need to know how to work from a relational perspective, whether they are working with individual spouses or the marital dyad. When therapists are able to develop multiple views of the problem and select appropriate skills, they will be more likely to reach their goals. Thus, we have attempted to present both assessment and treatment skills in a logical order of the therapeutic process.

PART I: FOUNDATION OF MARITAL THERAPY

Chapter One begins with an overview of the normal developmental processes of marriage. The developmental perspective has become increasingly important to the field in recent years, and information concerning issues of the marital life cycle provides a necessary foundation for understanding the theory and practice of marital therapy. The marital relationship evolves as the needs and resources of individual members change over the cycle of family life. The first major task of the couple is for both spouses to function as a separate branch of the family system. Spouses must establish different relationships with families of origins; their roles as sons and daughters must become secondary to those of husband and wife. The birth of a child, or the decision not to have a child, requires spouses to reorganize to deal with new tasks. These new tasks may trigger underlying conflicts and challenge early resolutions. Couples who have been able to resolve conflict and have achieved a sense of intimacy without extreme cost to autonomy will be more likely to handle the challenges of midlife marriage and later life following retirement.

Chapter Two begins with a brief review of each of the therapeutic models: structural, strategic, transgenerational, behavioral, and solution-focused models. Differences in content and process between the models are emphasized in order to provide the beginning practitioner with a conceptual background from which to appreciate the challenge of integration. We also think that it is important for the student to attempt an integration of the various theoretical models that have much in common. To assist the reader, we have chosen to offer an example of how the various models might work with a specific case. As students begin to develop their own theoretical integration, they may wish to consult primary sources to broaden their conceptual base.

PART II: ASSESSMENT CONCEPTS AND SKILLS

Chapter Three provides detailed instructions on how to process a referral and structure a marital intake interview. Emphasis is given to the unique role of the marital therapist. This often helps to alleviate the spouse's anxiety regarding the therapeutic relationship and how to avoid unexpected events, which can confuse the spouses or cause negative feelings. There is considerable evidence to suggest that when the therapist and the marital dyad are in agreement regarding reciprocal responsibilities and similarity of expectations, harmony or stability is more likely to occur in their interpersonal relationship.

Chapters Four and Five provide guidelines on how to conduct an initial marital interview. Chapter Four illustrates skills for assessing marital problems. The reader will learn how to use circular questions and genograms to create multiple views of marital problems. Emphasis will be given to integrating marital assessment into the therapeutic process. The beginning practitioner will learn how to track both interactional and longitudinal sequences to understand how the marriage has evolved over time. This chapter is also designed to help the student gain a sense of direction in therapy by developing (with the couple) goals that fit the unique characteristics of their culture. Goals are developed from assessment data so that they fit each unique situation. The readers will learn to analyze hypotheses in order to: (1) prioritize areas of change, (2) make goals concrete and specific, and (3) build on existing strengths. Chapter Five provides specific considerations and guidelines for treatment recommendations, as well as indications and contraindications for individual and marital therapy.

PART III: TREATMENT CONCEPTS AND SKILLS

This section covers those systems concepts and skills that have demonstrated their effectiveness in treating marital problems. Each chapter breaks down complex skills into behaviors that can be easily learned. Guidelines for when to use each skill are provided so that the practitioner can develop a comprehensive treatment strategy. Case examples and learning activities emphasize skill acquisition and application.

PART IV: EVALUATION OF TREATMENT OUTCOME

This section covers basic concepts and skills for conducting evaluations, terminations, and follow-ups. This chapter helps the practitioner understand how to evaluate the couple while they are in therapy, with emphasis given to evaluating marital processes and outcomes from multiple perspectives. It also provides guidelines for conducting the final session. Once termination is agreed upon, the practitioner learns to plan transfer of learning and follow-up, since newly learned behaviors rarely generalize to other environments unless others support them. Follow-ups help the therapist to further evaluate behavior change and facilitate the couple's new behavior.

PART V: TECHNIQUES IN PRACTICE

The last section includes case studies of special populations to show some specialized techniques for families with special problems. Specifically, case studies related to marital infidelity, divorce, lesbian and gay couples, alcohol addiction, and chronic illness are included.

A FINAL NOTE

While we believe this book will promote learning, there are several issues the reader should consider. Clearly, this book can serve only as a guide; the beginning practitioner who uses it is obligated to use his or her own creative ideas in applying skills to specific marital problems. Technical concepts and skills cannot replace the personal dimension of therapy—genuineness, warmth, and concern. It is our purpose and hope that the readers will find the basic sets of concepts and skills helpful in meeting the needs of the couples they are serving.

ACKNOWLEDGMENTS

We thank the reviewers from a variety of academic institutions whose contributions in the form of suggestions, feedback, and comments were valuable to us as we wrote this book. The reviewers include Dr. Gary Bailey of Elon College, Dr. Cynthia Bishop of Meredith College, Dr. Clark Campbell of George Fox University, Dr. Bob Egbert of Southern Adventist University, Dr. Jo-Ann Lipford-Sanders of Heidelberg College, Dr. Thomas Millard of Montclair State Univeristy, Dr. Steven Rose of Louisiana State University, and Dr. Gerald Shapiro of San Francisco State University.

PART I

✳

Foundations
of Marital Therapy

1

✳

Dimensions of Marriage

CHAPTER OBJECTIVES

Upon completion of this chapter, the reader will be able to:

1. Describe characteristics of:
   - The couple system,
   - The effects of gender on marriage,
   - The effects of race and culture on marriage.

2. List the six stages of the life cycle and tell something about each.

3. List the nine psychological tasks of marriage and—given a case example—indicate:
   - Barriers to mastering the tasks,
   - Ways to overcome the barriers.

INTRODUCTION

Becoming married marks one of the most profound transitions an individual can undergo. A marriage represents not only the establishment of a new relationship but the creation of a new couple identity and a whole new set of social relationships with spouses, parents, relatives, and friends.

Marriage requires two individuals in a couple unit to renegotiate personal issues that they had previously defined individually, or that were defined by their parents. That is, they now have to negotiate when to eat, sleep, have sex, fight; how to celebrate holidays; where and how to live, work, spend vacations, and so on. Couples must renegotiate their relationships with parents, siblings, friends, and other relatives in view of the new marriage; this, to some degree, will affect all personal relationships. Carter and McGoldrick (1989) state, "This places no small stress on the family to open itself to an outsider who is now an official member of its inner circle. Frequently, no new member has been added for many years. The challenge of this change can affect a family's style profoundly; the tendency of members to polarize and see villains and victims under the stress of these changes can be very strong" (p. 210).

Every spouse enters marriage with a set of unspoken expectations, based largely on past experiences. Through their families of origin, they have observed how their parents related to each other, and this is often the model on which their expectations are built—expectations for how spouses relate to each other, how they express affection, how they handle conflict, how they spend free time, how they handle money, and so on. Expectations are further determined by gender and ethnic differences, and spouses often enter marriage with a set of assumptions of how the mate will behave based on these differences. If the therapist is to work effectively with couples, he or she must have an understanding of how the couple system functions (what the boundaries or rules are), what messages each spouse has brought from his or her family of origin, and what messages they bring to marriage related to their gender and ethnic backgrounds. Each of these areas will be discussed in turn.

THE COUPLE SYSTEM

The family system contains three key subsystems (marital, parental, and sibling) within the total family organism (Minuchin, Montalvo, Gurney, Roman, & Schemer, 1967). The marital subsystem is the first to form and is central to the functioning of the family. The marital subsystem's basic role is to provide mutual satisfaction of the couple's needs without compromising the emotional environment necessary for further growth and development of two maturing, changing individuals (Terkelsen, 1980). The marital subsystem is that part of a marriage that includes all the behavioral sequences that have evolved out of the partners' commitment to "love and cherish" each other. The marital subsystem does not include the role each partner plays with other members of the nuclear and extended family. In other words, the marital subsystem includes transactional patterns related to giving attention to one another, but does not include those transactional patterns concerning giving attention to their children.

Boundaries

The boundaries of a subsystem or system are "the rules of who participates and how" (Minuchin, 1974, p. 53), and many couple conflicts are related to boundary issues. An example of this is a couple who came to therapy because of daily conflicts about where the spouse went, when, and with whom. The therapist chose to explore with the couple what their rules were about relationships with others, and determined that the rules that formed this marital system's boundary were as follows:

1. The husband could make friends at work and occasionally made social arrangements with them that revolved around sports. Any other social activities had to include the spouse. He could not make any female social friends unless they were much older.

2. The wife worked part-time and could make friends at work, but saw them socially only infrequently. Such social occasions had to be announced in advance.

3. Although the wife's sister and her family lived only a block away, they and other relatives were always seen on a planned basis, the occasion preceded by arrangements made over the phone or through the mail.

4. The couple's social friends knew they were expected to call first rather than just drop in unannounced.

The couple had rules that formulated a system boundary that everyone understood. The rules were sufficient until they experienced tension in the relationship. Because the couple had established rules which limited their access to friends and relatives, they were dependent on each other to meet all their emotional needs. As the couple's needs changed, they had to evolve new rules to govern their system's boundary.

All couples evolve such rules, and each couple's boundaries vary in their degree of flexibility and permeability. Some boundaries may be too rigid (distant), and therefore make it difficult for the couple to adjust to new situations. Permeability of a system or subsystem's boundary refers to the amount of access spouses have across boundary lines. Some couples' boundaries are too permeable in that the boundary becomes diffused or ill-defined and allows too much access (or interference) from friends or relatives. Couples such as the one described above may have boundaries around their systems that are impermeable, limiting needed access to each other or the world outside the family.

GENDER DIFFERENCES

In working with a couple, it is imperative that the therapist understand gender differences, because such knowledge is essential in understanding the couple's relationship and in assessing characteristics that interfere with its effectiveness. Gender differences fall into three broad categories: physiological differences, role/rule differences, and differences in communication styles/emotional expression.

Gottman (1999) asserts that physiological gender differences are not noticeable in happy marriages. He adds, however, that in conflictual situations, males and females react in very different ways. While females are more likely to self-soothe or calm themselves in stressful situations, males tend to become more aroused and to maintain distressing thoughts. That is, if asked to calm down, women are much more able to do so than men. Furthermore, in a negative relational atmosphere, men are more likely to withdraw, while women are more likely to stay involved—to demand or complain (Christensen & Heavy, 1990). According to Gottman, these physiological differences are very relevant to assessment and treatment because dysfunctional relationships are characterized by chronic levels of physiological arousal and the inability to self-soothe or be soothed by one's partner. Some assessment questions concerning physiological gender differences would include:

1. In conflictual situations, what is the male's capacity to self-soothe (listen to his spouse, show interest, de-escalate the conflict, and so on)?

2. Does the wife attempt self-soothing techniques such as humor or affection?

3. Does the husband accept influence from his spouse?

A second area of differences is in perceptions or rules/roles for the relationship. At the most general level, all couples are influenced by patterns of socialization that lead to rules and roles governing the marital process. Gender-related rules and roles are the most fundamental of these patterns. Karpel (1994) classifies these into four categories: differences in socialization, differences in legal and economic status and power, differences involving childbirth and parenting, and differences in sexuality. In terms of socialization:

- Karpel (1994) notes that women give up more, for example, occupations and names, and McGoldrick (1989) asserts that married women have poorer health, lower self esteem, and lower job success than married men.
- The majority of domestic violence is perpetrated by men against wives;
- Boys are socialized to be active, aggressive, and competitive, while girls are socialized to be dependent;
- Men are socialized to argue their positions in order to meet their needs, while women are socialized to think of others' needs first;
- Women earn less money than men for comparable jobs; and
- Mothers are more likely to be given custody of children in a default situation than fathers.

Obviously, even in situations where couples strive for equality, socialization and economic factors remain a reality. Karpel (1994) asserts that the challenge for couples is to deal with gender differences in ways that are acceptable to both spouses. This means that each person must be respected and that each is committed to work for fairness in the relationship.

Goldner (1988) has also argued that gender is an important variable to consider in family therapy. Because gender influences marital interaction processes, it should be a fundamental element in marital assessment. Hare-Mustin (1978), in her pioneering work on gender, begins the assessment process by asking the following gender-related questions:

1. Could role inflexibility regarding tasks be related to the problem?
2. Have generational coalitions developed as a result of disempowerment in the marriage?
3. Can disempowering stereotypes ("nag," "passive-aggressive") be relabeled to account for the context of powerlessness?
4. Can the female therapist model more egalitarian relationships with males (husband), and can male therapists affirm female (wife) strengths within the family?
5. What are rules around the female's (wife's) personal development and autonomy outside the family?
6. What will the husband and wife each need from the therapist in order to feel understood and accepted?

A third issue involves gender differences in communication styles and emotional expression. In cases of marital conflict, gender difference is often the core issue to be identified. For example, Jacobson, Holtzworth-Monroe, and Schmaling (1989) have found that women often complain more than men about their current relationship. Indeed, women often desire greater involvement and closeness with their husbands, while husbands prefer to maintain the status quo and create greater autonomy and separateness for themselves. Moreover, women are more likely to seek therapy and push for an egalitarian relationship, whereas men are less likely to seek therapy and are inclined to maintain traditional gender roles.

Gottman (1999) refers to a situation in which a couple differs on how emotions should be expressed as a meta-emotion mismatch, and indicates that a mismatch is typically related to gender stereotypes. Women are more likely to want intimacy and believe that expressing feelings will lead to intimacy, while men are more likely to think expressing feelings is a waste of time, wanting to quickly solve the problem instead. Such a mismatch leads to emotional withdrawal and precludes the positive affect that is necessary in an effective relationship. In order to assess a couple's expression of emotions, Gottman asks them to think about how they have responded to various emotions. Here are some sample questions:

1. When you were growing up, how did members of your family express anger?
2. What kinds of things made you sad? How did you deal with sadness?

3. How did your parents show love to you when you were growing up? How did you show love to them?

4. How did you express happiness when growing up? How did you know when other people were happy?

Even if partners recognize and discuss the differences in their philosophies of expressing emotion, it does not necessarily follow that either partner will change his or her way of dealing with feelings. It will, however, help them develop a better understanding of why they respond as they do, and make minor changes that, in some cases, promote a more positive relationship.

The couple's understanding of how gender relates to the presenting problem should dictate whether the therapist addresses gender directly or indirectly. When couples are not ready to address gender differences directly, the therapist should refrain from direct confrontation and address the issues in more indirect ways. For example, couple problems might be an opportunity to explore the impact of gender on the couple's developing relationship. In such cases, the couple can examine the "norm" the husband or wife aspires to, and the consequences in the relationship of changing it (Sheinberg & Penn, 1991).

Marital partners may be highly sensitive to gender issues if they feel criticized. For example, a husband may be sensitive about being labeled "chauvinistic," and a wife may be sensitive about being labeled "just a housewife," when a therapist begins to explore issues of sex-role stereotypes. Therapists should maintain a curious but optimistic position as they explore patterns of behavior related to gender. Gender issues should be freely explored as part of the couple's developmental assessment.

THE EFFECTS OF RACE AND CULTURE

In assessing the couple's life cycle issues, it will be important to account for the effects of race and culture. Regardless of how the therapist conducts an assessment, it is important to acknowledge and respect differences between the therapist and couple. Then, couples can be invited to teach therapists about the significant parts of their cultural identity. In this case, the therapist's role is similar to that of an anthropologist who lives with people and understands them while being a participant in the process. Such a role is in contrast to that of a scientist who treats people from a distance.

It is normal for couples from different cultures to experience problems. Differences in closeness–distance issues, sex roles, and boundaries are often based on cultural differences. With these couples, the focus on culture is an important part of assessing the couple's life cycle development.

In some cultures, the couple are seen as two separate individuals, while in others, their identities are merged. Carter and McGoldrick (1989) elaborate:

Western values of privacy and individualism conflict with Indian values of collectivity and family-centeredness. In the context of separation, less acculturated families view adolescent and young adult struggles around independence as disloyal cutting off from the family and culture. When Asian Indians speak of respect, they mean obedience to the family and culture. Similarly, it is difficult for them to comprehend that some aspects of the Western ideal of love includes separation and independence from the family of origin. For Asian Indians, the concept of love includes loyalty and control. (Mukherjee, 1991, p. 82)

When exploring cultural differences, the therapist begins to ask how culture relates to the problem. What personal beliefs of each spouse seem to be perpetuating these differences? Are each spouse's beliefs about himself or herself constrained by each person's heritage? What lessons did each spouse learn from his or her family? How have those lessons impacted expectations and behaviors in marriage? By getting answers to these questions, the therapist can begin to understand the cultural life cycle development of the couple.

Today, many couples experience differences in religion, ethnicity, race, and social class. Because of such differences, couples enter marriage with different expectations and interpretations related to their dissimilar backgrounds. It should be noted, however, that even when backgrounds are similar, individual families differ. That is, each family has its own culture, and people tend to enter marriage with expectations, roles, and beliefs that they developed in their own families of origin. For instance, Betty came from a family that celebrated every event—birthdays, Easter, Valentine's Day, and so on—by giving and receiving gifts. Birthdays were particularly special, and the "birthday person" got to select a favorite meal or favorite restaurant, received many cards, and received a nice gift. Bob, on the other hand, came from a family that gave gifts only at Christmas time. When Betty's birthday came and went, with no gift or celebration, she was extremely disappointed and felt that Bob didn't care about her. Bob did not understand why she was making such a fuss about it.

In happy times, cultural differences may be overlooked or even appreciated. When the couple is stressed, however, problems may be intensified. For instance, a person from a very open, expressive family is likely to be even more open and expressive in times of conflict, while a person from a closed, nontalkative family is likely to be less communicative under stress. The communicative partner becomes very frustrated with his or her mate's distance, leading to false assumptions, which exacerbate the problem.

An important aspect of therapy is allowing couples to converse about rituals in their families of origin. This helps each spouse to understand the other's heritage and serves as a starting point for developing their own shared rituals as a couple. In fact, in every marriage, the partners have to develop a shared meaning for various events (Gottman, 1999). They have to first understand the meanings each spouse gives to certain activities or situations, and at the same time develop new rituals meaningful to the new unit they have formed. In fact, Gottman asserts that each couple creates their own unique "culture" by creating a "shared meaning" system. The degree to which they can develop such a system and feel that their dreams are supported by each other is predictive of whether the marriage will flourish or fail.

Understanding partners' backgrounds, expectations, and needs is only part of the picture. It is also important to recognize their "place" in the family life cycle and the kinds of pressures and stresses related to that stage.

THE LIFE CYCLE OF A FAMILY

Just as all individuals follow a predictable sequence of development from birth to death—with particular tasks related to each stage—a family has a developmental sequence. Being aware of the stages, understanding that transitions between stages are marked by increased stress, and knowing that each stage brings specific developmental tasks allows the therapist to predict change and times of disruption. It also helps to normalize some of the stress in the family at various stages.

The first detailed description of the family life cycle from a systemic point of view occurred in Jay Haley's 1973 book *Uncommon Therapy*. Haley outlines the therapeutic techniques of Milton Erickson across six stages of the family life cycle. Haley highlights the notion that some things are likely to occur at points of transition between stages. More recently, Betty Carter and Monica McGoldrick (1999) edited a popular book entitled *The Expanding Family Life Cycle: Individual, Family and Social Perspectives*. Carter and McGoldrick suggest six stages: (1) leaving home—single young adults, (2) marriage—new couple, (3) families with young children, (4) families with adolescents, (5) launching children and moving on, and (6) families in later life. They propose that problems are a result of an interruption of the family life cycle and indicate that the goal of therapy is to get the family back on track. This book provides a review of the family life cycle, and offers clinical suggestions for working with couples at each developmental stage.

Perhaps the greatest contribution of Carter and McGoldrick is their conceptual vision of the nuclear family as a three-generational system that reacts to pressures from generational tensions as well as developmental transitions. Carter and McGoldrick use a vertical and horizontal axis in their model to describe this interactive process (see Figure 1.1).

Anxiety can be transmitted both vertically and horizontally. It is transmitted vertically across the generations through emotional triangulation, family expectations, and myths. It is transmitted horizontally through changes in the developmental life cycle, either through expected events such as getting married, or unexpected events such as an illness, job loss, or death. When a certain amount of stress results on both axes, a crisis in the system often follows.

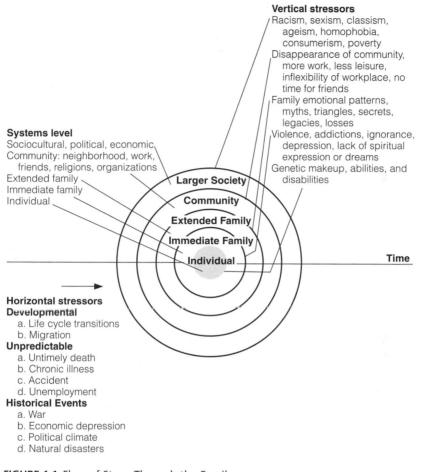

Vertical stressors
Racism, sexism, classism, ageism, homophobia, consumerism, poverty
Disappearance of community, more work, less leisure, inflexibility of workplace, no time for friends
Family emotional patterns, myths, triangles, secrets, legacies, losses
Violence, addictions, ignorance, depression, lack of spiritual expression or dreams
Genetic makeup, abilities, and disabilities

Systems level
Sociocultural, political, economic,
Community: neighborhood, work, friends, religions, organizations
Extended family
Immediate family
Individual

Larger Society
Community
Extended Family
Immediate Family
Individual

Time

Horizontal stressors
Developmental
   a. Life cycle transitions
   b. Migration
Unpredictable
   a. Untimely death
   b. Chronic illness
   c. Accident
   d. Unemployment
Historical Events
   a. War
   b. Economic depression
   c. Political climate
   d. Natural disasters

FIGURE 1.1 Flow of Stress Through the Family

SOURCE: From Betty Carter & Monica McGoldrick in *The Expanded Family Life Cycle*, 3/e. p. 6. Copyright © 1999 by Allyn & Bacon. Reprinted by permission.

   The level of stress on both axes is much greater for couples today than for those of past generations. The increasing divorce rate, the women's movement, and technological revolutions have had profound impact on marriages through-out the life cycle. The vast amount of change produced by these events puts a great deal of stress on the marriage of today. A loss of a job or an illness often precipitates new crises that send couples to therapy. However, if therapy focuses only on the symptom or the interactional patterns at the time of the crisis, the therapist may be missing information about relationship patterns transmitted through previous generations' struggle with developmental hur-dles—patterns that may be contributing to the current crisis.
   It should also be noted that many marriages, particularly remarriages, are complicated and more stressful because they involve individuals and families

who are simultaneously experiencing different stages of the family cycle. For instance, mates who each have children from a previous marriage may have a child of their own. They are not only dealing with their marital relationship, but with being new parents and also parenting older children with different parents. Therefore, the therapist should be aware of the couple's vertical stressors (messages from families of origin) as well as their developmental stage and the psychological tasks to be mastered at each stage.

PSYCHOLOGICAL TASKS OF MARRIAGE

When parents are familiar with typical behaviors for children at different ages and stages, they can better understand and respond to behaviors which they may perceive as undesirable (for example, the tendency for a two-year-old to say no). Knowing what to expect allows one to respond more appropriately. Similarly, if couples are aware of typical developmental tasks of partners in a marriage, they can respond to conflictual situations with less emotion.

Premarital counseling provides an opportunity to acquaint couples with stressors in most marriages, such as in-law struggles, money disagreements, and conflicts about time with friends. However, very few couples seek such counseling and often seem confident that they will not experience the usual difficulties. Even so, there is value in knowing the kinds of predictable difficulties that have to be negotiated in most marriages and in also knowing that they can be negotiated successfully and do not mean that the marriage is over. Gottman (1999) reports that in his research on marital satisfaction, a large drop in satisfaction occurred after the birth of the first child. It is helpful for a couple to understand that such a change is not unusual and that they are not alone. Therefore, rather than thinking of divorce, they recognize it as a temporary situation and work on ways to develop more positive affect.

In her book *The Good Marriage: How and Why Love Lasts* (1995), Judith Wallerstein outlines nine psychological tasks that must be negotiated in every successful marriage. The formulation of these tasks is described in a preliminary report of a longitudinal study of fifty happy marriages (Wallerstein, 1993). Tasks that must be addressed at the outset of marriage must continue throughout the life cycle and be redefined and resolved over the years. These early tasks are continually joined by new tasks, which may trigger conflicts and challenge earlier resolutions. For most people, marriage begins during young adulthood; therefore, the early tasks of marriage may likely conflict with some of the initial tasks of adulthood. According to Wallerstein, a successful marriage promotes maturity and consolidates sexual identity.

1. Consolidating Psychological Separation and Establishing New Connections with a Family of Origin The beginning family commences with the marriage and continues until the first child is born. It is becoming increasingly difficult to become a couple in our rapidly changing society.

Sociological shifts, including the changing role of women and the development of contraceptives, have produced later marriages. The U.S. Census Bureau (1996) reports that the median age of first marriages rose from 20.8 for women and 23.2 for men in 1970, to 24.5 for women and 26.7 for men in 1994. In addition, the percentage of nuclear families (married couples with children under 18) shrank from 40 percent in 1970 to 25 percent of all households in 1996. Only about 50 percent of American children live in nuclear families (Carter & McGoldrick, 1999, p. 13.)

Even though many people are deciding to marry later, there appears to be an optimal range for coupling. Ahrons (1999) notes that women who marry before the age of 20 are twice as likely to divorce as those who marry in their twenties. Likewise, those who marry in their thirties are fifty percent more likely to divorce than those who marry in their twenties. Monica McGoldrick (1980) suggests that "while it may be better to marry later than sooner, those who fall too far out of the normative range on either end are more likely to have trouble making the transition" (p. 95).

The first major task of the family is for both spouses to function as a branch of the family system. Spouses must establish different relationships with extended families; the role of son or daughter must become secondary to those of husband and wife. The degree to which a couple is able to develop intimacy and independence often depends on how each spouse has developed a separate personal identity in his or her own family. Spouses who have failed to develop a solid autonomous relationship in the family of origin will often either withhold themselves emotionally or develop an intense couple relationship that takes precedence over their own personal interest (Meyer, 1980). One must become a separate "self" before joining with another to form a couple.

Spouses who have failed to develop a separate "self" in their own family remain dependent on their extended family. Often a spouse will develop pseudo-independence from his or her family (Bowen, 1978). More specifically, Bowen notes that a spouse will often distance himself or herself from the family of origin to avoid emotional intensity; yet the unfulfilled need for closeness leads the individual into a marital relationship that is likewise reactive. When the tension in the marital relationship reaches a certain level of intensity, the spouse may again remove himself or herself emotionally. Thus, emotional cutoff can result from the family's need for togetherness and the spouse's unresolved closeness with his or her family of origin.

According to McGoldrick (1999, p. 247), there appear to be a number of other factors that make marital adjustment during this beginning phase more difficult:

1. The partners come to the marriage with marked differences in power, socioeconomic status, or career options;
2. One spouse is financially dependent on the other because of lack of employment or job skills;
3. The husband tries to isolate the wife from work, friends, or family to control her financially or to intimidate her physically;

4. The couple meets or marries shortly after a significant loss;

5. The wish to distance from one's family of origin is a factor in the marriage;

6. The family backgrounds of the spouses are significantly different (religion, education, social class, ethnicity, the ages of the partners);

7. The spouses come from incompatible sibling constellations [birth order];

8. The couple resides either extremely close to or at a great distance from either family of origin;

9. The couple is dependent on either extended family financially, physically, or emotionally;

10. The couple marries early (before age 20) or late (after age 35);

11. The couple marries after an acquaintanceship of less than six months or more than three years of engagement;

12. The wedding occurs without family or friends present;

13. The wife becomes pregnant before or within the first year of marriage;

14. Either spouse has a poor relationship with his or her siblings or parents;

15. Either spouse considers his or her childhood or adolescence to have been an unhappy time;

16. Marital patterns in either extended family were unstable;

17. One or both partners believe implicitly or explicitly that men's rights, needs, or privileges should predominate in marriage, and that women should serve the needs of others.

Another difficulty is reflected in the common cultural/religious expression "and then they are one." Often repeated in marriage ceremonies, this phrase is based on the assumption that one can become complete by "fusion" with another person. Bowen (1978) suggests the contrary. He writes that couples who are fused have failed to differentiate from their families of origin and do not feel free to develop a separate intimate relationship with another. They fear to accept differences in the other because this would be too great a threat to their own poorly developed "self."

When two people are fused, they often fail to take responsibility for themselves in the relationship. In a fused relationship, each spouse feels that his or her happiness is the other's responsibility and often blames the other for the problems in the relationship. It is common for a spouse to feel that if his mate would change his or her behavior, the problem would go away and they would be happy. When spouses blame each other, they are failing to take responsibility for themselves and the relationship.

Couples who are fused also have trouble negotiating in the relationship. Negotiation means that each spouse must give in to some degree. A spouse who is fused in the relationship often fears that "giving in" means "caving in" and risking the fearful emotion of losing one's identity. Thus, fusion inhibits couples from sorting and resorting priorities and developing spoken and unspoken rules about all the little ways they wish to live together. Moreover, such couples even have difficulty resolving mundane issues such as whether the toilet seat should be up or down, who puts the dishes away, or who takes out the trash. Such minor issues become identity struggles.

The resolution of major and minor issues in this initial stage of family life can establish major patterns that will endure over the life cycle. All couples must decide how to deal with conflict, how control and feelings are handled in the family, who is responsible for whom, and under what conditions. Couples must also develop rules for closeness, cooperation, and specialization. Each spouse must know what is important to the other and appreciate the other spouse's feelings even when they are different. Couples who receive premarital counseling might have a headstart toward mastering the initial tasks of marriage, because they will have been exposed to common areas of conflict and will have had some opportunity to discuss these. The ability to appreciate differences in the other person, however, can come only when a person has developed an autonomous identity, and an autonomous identity can come only when a person is emotionally independent of one's parents. The following case illustrates the first psychological task of the couple.

A young couple sought counseling after three years of marriage because the wife was convinced that her husband was having an affair. The wife had met her husband when she was 15, and married him the next year. She was attracted to his "free wheeling," independence, and charm. Two months before her marriage she lost her older brother, who was living at home. Her father had died when she was ten years old. The husband was the youngest of seven children and was attracted to her "affection and warmth," something he did not receive in his own family. Married when both were still in their adolescence, neither had time to develop a separate sense of self. After the first year of marriage, the characteristics that had attracted them to each other had become the problem. The husband showed his independence by spending more time with his friends. He spent little time at home and rarely consulted his wife about financial and household decisions. The husband complained that his wife was "smothering" him. She asked too many questions and criticized him constantly. When a problem arose, the husband would withdraw and the wife would pursue with frustration. Each blamed the other for their unhappiness. In the second year of marriage, the problems were compounded when they had a child. The wife reported that she had bad feelings about herself during adolescence and that she often depended on her older brother for help. When her older brother died, she expected her husband to take care of her. The husband reported that his family showed little affection. When conflict occurred, each seemed to go his or her own way. The therapist attempted to show how patterns in the extended families were carried over into marriage and that each spouse was responsible for his or her own happiness. As each spouse began to take more responsibility for their own selves, the couple was better able to resolve issues of closeness and distance.

In this case, each partner was attempting to complete himself or herself through the other. Each spouse's role and the patterns of communication in their extended families contributed to their inability to develop a relationship as a couple. It is also common for people to marry shortly after the loss of a parent or other family members. When the wife lost her father and brother, she expected her husband to take their place. However, such desires are unrealistic, and often lead to disappointment and failure to appreciate the spouse for what he or she is. When a couple cannot successfully negotiate their own needs, they will often move from a dyad to a triad by having a baby. However, if a couple cannot resolve their differences before the arrival of a baby, they will have even more difficulty in doing so afterwards.

2. Building Togetherness and Creating Autonomy Building togetherness and creating autonomy is critical to developing a psychological identity for the marriage. Construction of an identity is often absent or is very weak in distressed marriages. In happily married couples, togetherness is not created at the expense of autonomy or each spouse's efforts to meet their individual needs.

Judith Wallerstein (1995) states:

> Building this new identity of "the marriage" is a multifaceted task that draws on complex developmental achievements in both partners. It is important in this connection to recall the extent to which adolescent identity is "me"-centered. The central drama of adolescent development involves establishing a separate identify from the family of origin. But building a new shared identity within the marriage requires a shift from the "I" of the emancipated adolescent and the young adult to the solid and lasting "we" of marriage. It is the new expanded identity of feeling part of the "we-ness" of the couple that establishes and consolidates modern marriage, more so perhaps than the legal bond, which can, after all, be legally broken on demand. The marriage that commands appropriate loyalty, that is worth defending, and that requires continued hard work and sacrifice is based on a willingness to part to some degree from the narcissism of the "I," delegating an important portion of the narcissistic investment in an overarching identity built on the melding of two separate selves. This process differs significantly from that of narcissistic investment in the other in lieu of oneself, as was once expected of women after marriage. (p. 645)

A marital identity helps couples cope with life's inevitable frustrations and problems. The new identity is built on mutual respect and the primacy of the relationship with each other. Relationships with friends and coworkers need to be changed or terminated if they compete with the spousal relationship. How do partners resolve personal and work issues? Marriage requires that couples together resolve a variety of issues (for example, money, sex, and recreation) that they had previously defined individually. Couples must also decide about which family traditions and rituals to keep and which traditions to develop for themselves (Carter & McGoldrick, 1989).

Closeness and togetherness within a marriage require sacrifice and putting the interests of the relationship ahead of individual interests. To maintain a satisfying relationship, it is critical that partners understand and communicate that understanding of the partner's position. Specifically, this involves listening to how the partner expresses him or herself, and then responding with empathy and warmth. Being aware of tone of voice, repetitiveness of speech, nonverbal gestures, and the verbal content of the partner's message can help spouses understand each other. For example, the rate of speech may indicate discouragement or excitement. Differing tones of voice, blushes, and stammers can provide indications of the partner's emotions.

The nature of marriage is always evolving since marriage requires individuation and separation from one's family of origin. Nichols (1987) states this as follows:

> The ideal in an ongoing relationship would be a situation in which the mates' discovery that expectations were not being met would lead to a sharing of thoughts and feelings, an improvement in communication, and a workable solution of any conflict that was present between them. Weathering the often inevitable disillusionment does not always lead to a reworking of the contract between the spouses. Sometimes one or both of the mates will alter their expectations without discussing their thoughts and feelings with the other. This kind of unilateral approach may lead to a strengthening of the marital relationship, as can be the case when unrealistic personal expectations are replaced with more realistic and mature expectations. Conversely, such an approach may simply conceal disappointments or resentments and set the stage for future difficulties, as when the disappointment and related feelings are retained on an unresolved basis. (p. 29)

Other challenges to the couple's completion of psychological tasks during the early stages of marriage are brought forth by changes in the marital relationship and the partners' needs and resources. The therapist must assess the nature of a couple's commitment and determine if this commitment will maintain as needs and expectations change. Partners need to reorganize and work together to meet their changing needs. The specific problems of autonomy and togetherness during this period vary considerably with the couple and their situation.

Consider the following case:

> Maurice and Lucy came to marital therapy because they were concerned about tensions between them. Married ten years, both complained that they spent little time together and had little money to go out. Maurice reported that he would try to take Lucy out on occasion but she did not

enjoy it because she did not want to spend the money. Maurice would then become upset because he thought she did not want to be with him and would spend more time with his friends, while Lucy would spend time with her parents. After two sessions, the therapist helped Maurice and Lucy to find areas of their life (going for a walk, gardening, taking trips to the library) that they could share without spending money. Both felt that the time together helped them feel closer to each other.

Maurice and Lucy found that being together more gave them strength to deal with life's inevitable frustrations and conflicts. It also gave both spouses a sense of autonomy in which they could establish their own roles and create an identity for the relationship, thereby reducing the tension.

3. Becoming Parents This psychological task begins with a decision to have a child. It is believed that this task will be completed more successfully if partners have completed the two previous psychological tasks of the marital life cycle. Couples who have achieved a sense of intimacy without extreme costs to autonomy, and have been able to resolve conflicts, will be more likely than others to accept their roles as mother and father.

The transition to the parenting role often begins with the decision to have children. It appears that women are much more ambivalent than men about having children, and today, an increasing number of couples are agreeing to remain childless. The decision to have children is compounded by the changing role of women in our society. Furthermore, pregnancy forces the couple to deal with expected changes in lifestyle. Women also fear that the spouse will not share childrearing responsibilities (McGoldrick, 1980). Parenting roles are easier when couples have at least a year of courtship before marriage and ample time after the marriage to prepare for having a child.

When a couple has a child, the three automatically form a triangle. The mother becomes close to the child. If the mother gets too involved with the child, the father will often distance himself by getting more involved with his work. The husband often feels that the wife spends a disproportionate amount of time with the new member of the system. In some instances in which distance exists, however, the baby may serve to bring the couple closer together. The baby, then, can play a key role in monitoring the distance in the marital triangle.

Wallerstein (1995) states that

The marriage also changes during this period. Some find child rearing too great a burden, and they run from the responsibility. But in a good marriage, the man and woman share new feelings of tenderness and pride and willingly make sacrifices for their children. They also share their resentment and fatigue. Most parents most of the time accept the sacrifices as necessary, fervently hoping that it will be worthwhile in the long run. The adults' partnership is reinforced by the funny, poignant antics of the children and by their shared concern. The memories of these years will sustain the couple when the children have grown and left home. (p. 72)

As the child grows, parents must establish rules that maintain safety and parental authority and still encourage growth. Both partners must make psychological and physical space (independence) for the growing child while protecting the couple's relationship. The couple must work together to provide the child support. Accordingly, they must provide adequate opportunities for the child to be himself or herself, to experiment, and to make mistakes. Too little time or engagement with the child equates with distance (the couple has no time for the child). Too much involvement with the child equates with excessive closeness (the couple uses the child to fill a vacuum) (Carter & McGoldrick, 1980).

Spouses sometimes are involved in so many activities that they do not have space or time for their child. Likewise, children who fill a vacuum in the couple's relationship may not be able to adequately develop a sense of autonomy. If a couple has already developed an intimate relationship and can resolve their conflicts, then the couple will be able to provide a favorable environment for support and autonomy of the child.

When spouses have not fulfilled their own goals, they often concentrate on the child. Those couples are denying their own problems and focusing on the child's problem. In such cases the child picks up the conflict and senses that he or she should be close to one of the parents. To keep the child "out of the middle," the couple must unite to support the child and put their disagreements on the "back burner."

The young child's development has a profound impact on the marital relationship. Women who have landed a career often experience a great deal of frustration when they have spent most of their time around adults, and now find their world made up of children. Many husbands, however, are still able to maintain adult contacts on the job. Haley (1973) found that the women at this stage often desire more involvement in the adult world and often feel "discontented and envious" of their husbands. Under such conditions, the marital relationship often deteriorates until the husband and wife can negotiate child-rearing and adult activities outside the home. Take the following case:

> Steve, 32, and Melba, 29, sought therapy for their three-year-old, Jackie, who was born four months prematurely. Jackie had frequent severe temper outbursts when she did not get her way. She was conceived shortly after the mother had a miscarriage and both parents reported that Jackie was often "sickly." Steve reported that he had no difficulties with Jackie, whereas his wife stated that she could not handle her. Steve felt that Melba should handle Jackie more effectively. In the first session, Jackie sat close to her mother. Melba reported that she worried about Jackie and was afraid to allow her to play outside because "she would get hurt." While Melba agreed she had difficulty controlling Jackie, it also became clear to the therapist that she would not let her husband share in the parenting. Melba reported that Steve did not understand Jackie. In subsequent sessions, both indicated that the marriage deteriorated shortly after the birth of Jackie and the death of Steve's father. Steve reported that he

began spending time either at work or with his mother, who had never accepted his marriage to Melba.

In this case, the mother became overinvested in the child, while the father became overinvolved with his work and his mother. A fragile bond characterized the early phase of their marriage. Steve would feel that he was betraying his mother when he became close to his wife. Also, the death of Steve's father as well as his wife's miscarriage added further stress to their young relationship. With the birth of the baby, Steve responded by moving further away from his wife while Melba moved closer to the needy infant. Steve and Melba stayed connected through Jackie's misbehavior, which eventually brought them to therapy.

4. Coping With Crises The fourth task, coping with crises, is associated with the couple's development over time. Some crises are relatively minor, but others can have a major impact on the marriage. When a husband loses a job, the family must make temporary adjustments, but the birth of a handicapped child may redefine the couple's relationships with other family members. A couple may rely on each other for support or withdraw to handle the stress alone.

As discussed earlier, there are predictable stresses (life cycle transitions) as well as unpredictable stresses such as job loss, illness, birth of a handicapped child, and death. The combination of these stresses that are transmitted across generations (attitudes, expectations, taboos) often place the family in crisis. In such cases, spouses often become anxious or angry and turn to their partner for support. Spouses will often ask, "Do you still love me if I can't work?" or "Will you care for me if I'm ill?"

A crisis in the marriage often occurs when the demands are greater than available resources to cope with these demands. A stressor is thus seen as a life event which produces change in the couple's relationship (McCubin & Patterson, 1983). For example, the death of a child may produce anger and guilt in each spouse, which produces additional needs and anxiety. Unless the couple has a history of successfully coping with stress, each spouse will feel that the other "doesn't understand" or will feel that the other is "not available" when needed. In such cases partners often feel alone in the relationship.

In short, it is not the crisis or stress that is the problem, but the way in which the couple manages it. Successful marriages experience as much stress as distressed marriages; but instead of going their separate ways, they are emotionally available to each other. Moreover, they seek and appreciate the emotional support they receive from each other. In such cases, crises may help the couple to have a closer relationship.

Wallerstein (1995) suggests five steps for coping with crises in a marriage. Couples who cope effectively do the following: (1) They maintain perspective and try to understand how the crisis will affect the marriage and other family members; (2) They avoid blaming each other for the problem; (3) They have fun and don't allow the problem to dominate them; (4) They do not feel persecuted or helpless; and (5) They intervene early with serious crises (drinking, depression, and so on). A couple is more likely to take these steps if they have established a strong marital bond.

Consider the following example:

> Geoff and Julie presented themselves for therapy three months after Geoff sustained a broken leg in an auto accident. Eighteen months of rehabilitation was necessary before Geoff could return to work. Julie worked part-time as a paralegal and stayed home to raise their four-year-old child. Since Geoff was not working, Julie felt she should return to work and reduce their financial burden. Geoff was opposed to this and wondered if Julie would still love him since he could not provide for her economically. He also wondered if Julie thought he was "less of a man and father" because he could not work. The therapist helped Julie reassure Geoff that he was still "number one" with her and that she did not resent going back to work. Further discussion brought them closer together and helped them understand each other's needs.

In this case, because of his accident, Geoff felt vulnerable and believed he had lost his manhood and role as father. This crisis required them to renegotiate the "we-ness" in their marriage. When Julie was able to assure Geoff that she understood and that he was "number one" with her, he felt her support and their relationship was strengthened.

5. Making a Safe Place for Conflict   The fifth psychological task is learning to resolve conflicts since problem solving and conflict resolution are critical to marital satisfaction. Couples must learn how to express their disagreements in a safe manner. In healthy marriages, partners see validity in the partner's concerns, whereas in distressed relationships, conflict is expressed in the form of contempt and personal attacks that often lead to divorce.

When partners attack each other, conflict is likely to escalate, leading to increased anger and frustration. Escalating arguments often lead to verbally abusive comments and personal attacks. Coercive comments such as, "All you think of is yourself" or "I'm not your slave" over time violate safety and trust and lead to deterioration of the relationship.

Healthy couples are able to take responsibility for the conflict and preserve the well being of the relationship. In healthy relationships, spouses respect each other's character and are less likely to negatively interpret the other's behavior. The couple's sense of togetherness and shared interests are stronger than those forces (negative comments, threats) that serve to destroy the relationship. The couple can freely express their anger without worrying about whether the marriage will dissolve.

Couples who are able to develop rules for handling conflict protect their closeness and promote growth in the relationship. Rules are "spoken" or "unspoken" expectations for how conflict should be played out. Couples are better able to handle conflict and disagreements when the rules are clearly specified. Rules allow partners to withdraw from conflict when conditions are no longer safe.

Couples thus promote safety if they can recognize when a conflict is getting out of control and call a "time out" as needed before resuming the discussion. Withdrawal stops unproductive arguments and protects the relationship against destructive attacks.

Consider the following case:

> Bob and Debbie had been married for only six months but had developed a pattern of intense conflicts that escalated in personal attacks on the other. Both reported to the therapist that they didn't have a safe way to talk about their differences and that they didn't want to repeat the same patterns as their parents. Each worried that this pattern would lead to separation and divorce. Both agreed that they needed to find a time to share feelings when they were less stressed and that each needed to take more responsibility for his or her behavior instead of blaming the other when things did not go their way.

Personal attacks and intense conflict can destroy a marriage. Bob and Debbie found that they were repeating the same patterns as their parents. They had to learn to take responsibility for getting control over their conflicts and provide a safe place to discuss differences, rather than blaming each other for their problems.

6. Exploring Sexual Love and Intimacy The sixth task requires the couple to develop a lasting sexual relationship. A good sexual relationship is an expression of affection and a strong marriage. According to Wallerstein (1995), sexual expression affects all aspects of the couple's relationship. She states that:

> A harmonious sex life adds powerful new strands to the relationship and affects all other domains of the marriage. As a couple finds sexual pleasure together, their perceptions of and fantasies about each other expand. Their shared erotic experiences, the memories they have created, and their new physical ties profoundly change their self-images. A good sexual relationship strengthens self-confidence, affirming a man's pride in his manhood and a woman's pride in her womanhood. The ability to give and receive sexual pleasure is a mature dimension of adulthood. Achieving it together is not only a source of individual pride but an affirmation of the couple's unity and commitment. . . . (p. 186)

Wallerstein further notes that a healthy sexual relationship requires communication about the couple's physical relationship. Sexual intercourse requires vulnerability where partners let the other know what they desire. Each partner must trust the other and overcome the fear of rejection. When couples are able to overcome such fears, they are able to find satisfaction and fulfillment in their marriage.

The completion of this task cannot be fulfilled if there are unexpressed issues that affect the relationship. Expression of desires requires each partner to risk being rejected, while avoidance of key issues such as money or intimacy creates distance and dissatisfaction. When partners can communicate openly about their expectations and desires, they are able to feel accepted and may improve their physical relationship. When the couple communicates about this sexual relationship, the therapist can help them explore other areas of their relationship including trust and intimacy.

Completion of this task requires that the couple communicate verbally and nonverbally about their desires. Healthy couples are able to share their desires and expectations and look for ways to please each other. The couple works as a team where each partner gives and receives pleasure in the relationship.

Consider the following example:

> Joe and Wanda had been married for seventeen years. Both in their early forties, they came to therapy because they were unhappy about their sex life. Neither felt the other understood his or her sexual needs, but both reported that they had difficulty discussing such issues. Both felt the demands of work and caring for aging parents and their sixteen-year-old son. The therapist helped the couple to see they were expecting too much of themselves and each other. After several sessions, each felt more comfortable expressing needs for intimacy with each other. Both agreed that they needed to be more patient with each other and block out more time to be together.

Joe and Wanda learned that when they could talk about their needs, they were better able to satisfy each other. Both found that when their expectations became more realistic and clearer, their sexual relationship was less stressful and richer.

7. Sharing Laughter and Keeping Interests Alive Fun, play, and humor are important traits of healthy marriages. Couples often report that they are no longer friends and no longer enjoy doing things together. Couples who can laugh together are better able to manage boredom and routine. Shared humor and fun also help couples handle stress and achieve intimacy.

Couples commonly report that they had fun when they were first married but stopped making time for fun (for example, going out to eat, or seeing a movie) over time. Work and childrearing responsibilities often take precedence over fun and personal enjoyment, and couples often report being too tired to go out. In cases such as this, couples should be encouraged to maintain the fun and playfulness of their relationship.

Fun and humor help to strengthen the bond in the marriage. Couples who are able to enjoy each other share positive feelings more frequently, manage conflict better, and maintain a shared vision for the future. This type of bond helps couples weather the stressful or conflictual times in the marriage. Healthy couples not only have fun together but they have individual interests as well.

They allow each other to pursue their own interests and spend time with their friends.

Consider the following case:

> Enoch and Ariel have been married for twelve years and reported to the therapist that the fun had gone out of their lives. During the first years of marriage, they belonged to an athletic club and frequently worked out together and then went to dinner or a movie. Five years ago, they had their first child and began spending less time having fun with each other. After a while, they noticed that their life together was less enjoyable. Over several sessions the therapist helped them to understand the importance of preserving fun in the marriage. Both agreed that they needed to start setting one time aside each week for a date. In addition, they agreed to alternate weeks for organizing an activity to ensure more variety of activities.

In this case Enoch and Ariel recognized the importance of restoring fun in their relationship. Setting aside one night a week for a date, with both spouses taking responsibility for planning the activities, helped build more interest and excitement into the relationship. The distinctiveness of a good marriage lies in the energy and excitement of their lives.

8. Providing Emotional Nurturance In healthy marriages, each spouse provides nurturance and support to the other. This task requires that each partner provide emotional support that is "safe for dependency, failure, disappointment, mourning, illness, and aging—in short, for being a vulnerable human being" (Wallerstein, 1995, p. 239). Marriage should provide a "safety zone" where partners receive comfort and nurturance to protect them from the daily demands from the outside world.

Unless partners feel safety and relief at home, they are not likely to provide emotional support to each other. Partners will not open up with each other unless they feel some degree of emotional safety. Without this safety, partners will be unlikely to express their real beliefs, dreams, values, and concerns, and will instead hide what they are really thinking and feeling. In such cases, the deeper and more intimate parts of the relationship often go unexpressed (Markman, Stanley, & Blumberg, 1994).

In healthy marriages partners are encouraged to openly express their feelings. Partners tend to listen to one another and accept one another's feelings. Satir (1967) suggests that when spouses are free to express themselves, they feel valued and loved. Moreover, such freedom of expression allows partners the important opportunity to support each other in times of stress.

Open communication and emotional support require that the couples speak in first person and express their real feelings, and that the partner be receptive to these feelings. Each partner, then, is free to express himself or herself knowing that he or she will receive emotional support from the other. In such cases, the therapist should help the couple clarify and alter their values so that they can communicate openly. Rules should be flexible, and differences in feelings, opinions, and desires should be valued and accepted. Satir (1972) notes that when couples provide emotional support to each other, they are communicating acceptance of each other, thus improving self-esteem.

When couples provide nurturance and support for each other, each experiences increased self-esteem. Studies have consistently shown that partners who do not receive emotional nurturance feel more isolated and experience emotional problems (depression, anxiety, and lower self-esteem) (Notarius & Markman, 1993). When partners are able to support each other, they are able to build a trusting relationship where each party can count on the other.

Consider the following case:

> Ron and Carla were referred for therapy because Ron felt Carla did not understand the demands of his job. When Ron came home, he expected Carla to stop what she was doing and listen to him. Carla had often just returned from the child care center with their two children, feeling exhausted, but thinking she should get dinner ready and attend to the children's needs. She also felt "helpless" because she did not know what to say to Ron when he complained. Over time she felt guilty because she didn't know how to support him. Therapy helped Ron and Carla to find a better time to confer with each other than when they first arrived home. Ron was able to describe the kind of nurturance and support he needed from Carla, and Carla was able to describe what she needed for herself. Ron and Carla learned that they could become closer by providing comfort to each other.

Ron and Carla understood the need for comfort and encouragement in their relationship. When Ron and Carla were able to provide this comfort, they were able to provide safety from the stresses and disappointments that all couples must endure—and thus master a major psychological task of a healthy marriage.

9. Preserving a Double Vision Remembering old memories while dealing with current realities constitutes the ninth task. It requires each partner to remember the loving aspects of the relationship while confronting daily issues and demands. Healthy couples are able to remember images of when they first met and how they courted each other. Couples who share stories with each other, and with friends and family, solidify their relationship (Wallerstein, 1995).

Wallerstein (1995) further states:

> When these feelings become a part of daily life, they help to mute the inevitable disappointments that occur in every relationship. The powerful memories provide a reservoir of past indulgence on which people can draw when things look dark. Beloved recollections of a better past soften the blows of the present. When a couple who have never idealized each other encounter disappointment, they have a bitter sense of déjà vu. They have a hard time forgiving each other for failing, because they have no reason to hope; they conclude bitterly that this is all there was and all there can be in the relationship. (p. 324)

Healthy couples often do a number of things to maintain positive memories. Sharing personal dreams and goals through videos, photo albums, or old yearbooks often brings back positive images. Some partners discuss core values and write a mission statement for their marriage. This helps the couple to focus on the meaning of life and death and helps the couple to remember what is important in their relationship. Attention can be focused on positive events in the marriage and the partner's good intentions and positive behaviors. Remembering when the couple first fell in love and the ensuing courtship helps partners to cope with stress and daily problems.

One of the ways couples celebrate their relationship is to develop rituals. These may include simple things such as regular goodnight kisses or daily time after work to relax together and discuss the day's events. They may also include activities such as "once a week or month dates," special celebrations for anniversaries, returning to a particular place that conjures up special memories, and so on. Returning to a honeymoon site (or going on a honeymoon if that stage was skipped), renewing vows, and other similar rituals help maintain and enhance the strength of a relationship.

The need to recall past images is probably greatest at midlife when life becomes routine. This is often a time when spouses are reexamining their marital relationship. Spouses may find they have nothing to talk about because all their past discussion has focused on the child(ren). In some cases, couples will argue about old issues that were put aside when the children arrived. In such cases, it is important for couples to recall the early years of their marriage and the positive memories they had of each other, as well as to establish new rituals which are appropriate to that developmental stage.

> Bryce married Candy after his wife died of cancer, leaving him with two young children. Together, they had a third child who suffered from learning disabilities and experienced much difficulty in school. Rearing the three children was challenging, but they worked together. When the three children were gone from home, however, conflicts arose frequently because of Candy's continued overinvolvement with the children. In therapy, the therapist helped Bryce and Candy refocus on their marriage, the positive feelings they had initially, and the satisfaction of having worked together to rear the children. Because of limited funds, they had not gone on a honeymoon and one of Candy's tasks was to present a honeymoon plan to Bryce. The couple was also instructed to take turns planning a night out each week and surprising the other. Through the memories of positive aspects of the marriage, as well as planning new events and rituals, Candy became less involved with the children, and the couple's bond became stronger.

Couples can often cope with the present when they are able to maintain positive memories from the past. For instance, the first author worked with a couple who were able to resolve their differences about finances because they were able to remember a time when they had no money. They were able to openly discuss ways they tried to save money and how they supported each other at the time. By remembering the past, this couple was able to resolve the current financial and emotional problems in their marriage.

CONCLUSION

Marriages can succeed when couples are able to negotiate psychological tasks that are the foundation of the relationship. Essential to any successful relationship is the couple's ability to separate from their extended families and create their own identity in their relationship. If they choose to have children, they must have skills to include these additional people, while still protecting the marriage. Throughout the marriage, the couple must have skills to deal with inevitable crises and conflicts, establish a pleasurable sex life, and keep interest alive in the relationship. A mature relationship requires the ability of each partner to provide emotional nurturance to the other and to draw on positive images to cope with current pressures.

KEY POINTS

- Marriage requires couples to renegotiate their relationships with parents, siblings, and friends.
- Couples must successfully complete a set of psychological tasks for a good marriage.
- Early tasks that are addressed at the outset must be redefined throughout the marriage.
- Couples who fail to complete early tasks will have difficulties in the latter stages of the life cycle.
- Early task mastery requires resolving conflicts between individual and couple needs.
- During parenthood, the couple must reorganize to care for the child while still protecting the marriage.
- The couple must provide a safe environment to deal with the inevitable stresses and disappointments of life.

MARITAL SKILLS INVENTORY

Please check when you have completed these procedures.

_____   Assess the couple system.

_____   Assess the effects of gender.

_____ Assess the effects of race and culture.

_____ Assess the psychological tasks of the marriage.

_____ Help the couple consolidate psychological separation and establish new connections with family of origin.

_____ Build togetherness and create autonomy.

_____ Demonstrate skills for coping with crisis.

_____ Make a safe place for conflict.

_____ Explore sexual love and intimacy.

_____ Provide emotional nurturance.

REFERENCES

Ahrons, C. R. (1999). Divorce: An unscheduled transition. In E. A. Carter & M. McGoldrick (Eds.), *The expanded life cycle: Individual, family, and social perspectives* (3rd ed.). Needham Heights, MA: Allyn & Bacon.

Bowen, M. (1978). *Family therapy in clinical practice.* New York: Aronson.

Carter, E. A., & McGoldrick, M. (Eds.). (1989). *The changing family life cycle: Framework for family therapy* (2nd ed.). Needham Heights, MA: Allyn & Bacon.

Carter, E. A., & McGoldrick, M. (Eds.). (1999). *The expanded family life cycle: Individual, family, and social perspectives* (3rd ed.). Needham Heights, MA: Allyn & Bacon.

Carter, E. A., & McGoldrick, M. (Eds.) (1980). *The family life cycle: A framework for family therapy.* New York: Gardner Press.

Christensen, A., & Heavy, C. L. (1990). Gender and social structure in the demand/withdraw pattern of marital conflict. *Journal of Personality and Social Psychology, 59,* 73–81.

Glick, P. C., & Norton, A. J. (1977). Marrying, divorcing and living together in the U.S. today. *Population Bulletin 32/5.* Washington, DC: Population Reference Bureau.

Goldner, V. (1988). Generation and gender: Normative and covert hierarchies. *Family Process, 17,* 17–31.

Gottman, J. M. (1999). *The marriage clinic: A scientifically based marital therapy.* New York: Norton.

Haley, J. (1973). *Uncommon therapy.* New York: Norton.

Hare-Mustin, R. (1978). A feminist approach to family therapy. *Family Process, 17,* 181–194.

Jacobson, N. S., Holtzworth-Monroe, A., & Schmaling, K. B. (1989). Marital therapy and spouse involvement in the treatment of depression, agoraphobia, and alcoholism. *Journal of Consulting and Clinical Psychology, 57,* 5–10.

Karpel, M. A. (1994). *Evaluationg Couples.* New York: Norton.

Markman, H., Stanley, S., & Blumberg, S. L. (1994). *Fighting for your marriage: Positive steps for preventing divorce and preserving lasting love.* San Francisco: Jossey Bass.

McCubbin, H., & Patterson, J. (1983). Family transitions: Adaptation to stress. In H. McCubbin & C. Figley (Eds.), *Stress and the family* (Vol. 1). New York: Brunner/Mazel.

McGoldrick, M. (1980). The joining of families through marriage: The new couple. In E. A. Carter & M. McGoldrick (Eds.), *The family life cycle: A framework for family therapy* (pp. 93–120). New York: Gardner Press.

McGoldrick, M. (1999). Becoming a couple. In E. A. Carter & M.

McGoldrick (Eds.), *The expanded family life cycle: Individual, family, and social perspectives* (3rd ed.). Needham Heights, MA: Allyn & Bacon.

Meyer, P. (1980). Between families: The unattached young adult. In E. A. Carter & M. McGoldrick (Eds.), *The family life cycle: A framework for family therapy* (pp. 71–92). New York: Gardner Press.

Minuchin, S. (1974). *Families and family therapy.* Cambridge, MA: Harvard University Press.

Minuchin, S., Montalvo, B., Guerney, B., Rosman, B. & Schumer. (1967). *Families of the slums: An exploration of their structure and treatment.* New York: Basic Books.

Morsback, H. (1978). Aspects of Japanese marriage. In M. Corbin (Ed.), *The couple.* New York: Penguin.

Mukherjee, B. (1991). *Jasmine.* New York: Fawcett Crest.

Nichols, W. C. (1987). *Marital therapy: An integrative approach.* New York: Guilford Press.

Notarius, C., & Markman, H. J. (1993). *We can work it out: Making sense of marital conflict.* New York: Putnam.

Satir, V. (1972). *People Making.* Palo Alto, CA: Science & Behavior Books.

Sheinberg, M., & Penn, P. (1991). Gender dilemmas, gender questions and the gender mantra. *Journal of Marital and Family Therapy, 17* (1), 33–44.

Terkelsen, K. (1980). Toward a theory of the family life cycle. In E. A. Carter & M. McGoldrick (Eds.), *The family life cycle: A framework for family therapy.* New York: Gardner Press.

U.S. Census Bureau. (1996). *Annual Demographic Survey, March Supplement.* Revised September 26. Contact (pop@census.gov).

Wallerstein, J. (1993). *The psychological tasks of marriage.* Paper presented at Harvard Medical School Couples Workshop, Boston, MA.

Wallerstein, J. (1995). *The good marriage: How and why love lasts.* New York: Houghton Mifflin.

2

✳

Models of Marital Therapy

CHAPTER OBJECTIVES

Upon completion of this chapter, the reader will be able to:

1. Describe major concepts and skills from models of marriage and family therapy.

2. Describe differences in content and process of each of the models.

3. Integrate concepts from various models and apply them to a case.

INTRODUCTION

The intent of this chapter is to assist the beginning practitioner in discovering theoretical concepts and skills from which to begin practicing marital therapy. Although models of marital therapy appear dissimilar, they also share many similarities in practice. Practitioners often start out from a particular theoretical position "but eventually discover the validity of theoretical concepts from other approaches and the usefulness of other people's techniques" (Nichols & Schwartz, 1991, pp. 512–513).

This chapter begins with a brief review of each of the models of marital and family therapy: structural, strategic, transgenerational, behavioral, and solution-focused. Differences in content and process between the models are emphasized to provide the beginning practitioner with a conceptual background from which to appreciate the challenge of integration. Examples of how various models might work together are provided and related for specific cases. An example of theory integration is offered in hope that it will give structure to the reader's creativity.

Case Study

Tim and Patty entered therapy to end their marital conflict. Both spouses were in their mid-thirties and had been married for twelve years. The couple had one child. Tim was a teacher and Patty was employed as a decorator. Patty had an unhappy childhood and married after becoming pregnant at the age of 16. Her mother blamed her for the pregnancy and consequently made her feel guilty. Patty felt "grateful" to Tim for marrying her and taking care of her. She reported that most of her life was devoted to making things easy for him. However, shortly after they were married, she realized that Tim often placed his own needs above hers. He spent a great deal of time at work and was unavailable to help her with the baby. Their relationship soured early in their history and settled into a compromise of roles for each that kept conflict from surfacing. The compromise was characterized by minimal tolerance of differences. Patty subjugated her individuality to Tim's needs. It was not done without bitterness, however, which of course created ill feelings toward Tim. She begrudged his requests; rather than dealing with them directly, however, she devoted more of her energy to her baby. Tim was not straight with Patty about where he stood and instead punished her for "tying him down." Each feared that to be one's self, someone would get hurt. Since Patty felt in a powerless position, she used crying to get Tim's attention. Crying got his attention, but it did not lead to intimacy; rather, Tim often discounted her by suggesting her problems were "insignificant" and that "she was acting like a child." Her crying frightened him but he would not admit it. He would often withdraw and shortly thereafter return and make sexual advances as his way of "making up." Patty responded to his advances while still resenting them.

STRUCTURAL MODEL

The structural model encompasses both a conceptual model of families and an applied model of intervention with couples and families. It emphasizes the active and organized wholeness of the family system. Structural therapists focus on the interactions of family members to determine the structure of the marital relationship. Emphasis is placed on how, when, and to whom spouses currently relate in an effort to understand, and then to change, the structure of the marriage.

The theory and technique of the structural model is closely associated and identified with master therapist Salvador Minuchin. In the late 1960s, Minuchin and his colleagues developed their therapeutic approach at the Wiltwych School, a residential institution for delinquent boys from New York City. The structural approach was influenced also by the problem-solving approach of Jay Haley (1976) and the network therapy of Ross Speck (Speck & Attneave, 1973), who were associated with Minuchin after he moved to the Philadelphia Child Guidance clinic in the early 1970s.

Therapeutic Assumptions and Concepts

The practice of the structural model is grounded in some basic theoretical concepts that give meaning to the skills. Among the key concepts are the following:

The Family as a Multibodied Organism In the structural model, the client is the family, and a problem with one spouse is seen as a symptom for the marriage. The structuralist assumes that problems or symptoms are created and/or maintained by interactional or structural problems within the marriage.

The Function of Subsystems The family system contains three key subsystems, the first of which is the *marital subsystem*. It is the first to form and provides mutual satisfaction of the couple's needs without compromising the autonomy of each spouse.

The Characteristics of Marital Boundaries The boundaries of the marriage are "the rules of who participates and how" (Minuchin, 1974, p. 53). In some cases, the boundaries that protect the marriage are too permeable and permit interference by other family members, friends, and coworkers. For example, when a husband and wife argue, a child will often experience some distress. If the couple allows the child to interrupt, and the couple's disagreement goes unresolved, the boundaries protecting the marriage are weakened, and the couple does not learn to work out their own problems. Alternatively, the boundaries may be too rigid, thus making it difficult to respond to new situations (e.g., no one responding to the child).

The Effects of Enmeshed and Disengaged Behavior Between Spouses The concept of boundaries is closely related to the concept of enmeshed behavior in the structural model. Minuchin (1974) describes an axis at the ends of which couples have extremely diffuse or permeable boundaries. When boundaries are too permeable, spouses are enmeshed at the expense of their own autonomy, not learning to work out their problems. At the other end of this axis are couples who have rigid boundaries and are disengaged from each other. Spouses in this case are too autonomous, maintaining their separateness at the expense of mutual support.

Evolution of Change The couple must develop transactional rules and patterns to meet the needs of each new stage of the life cycle. Each stage of the life cycle brings with it a new set of needs. For example, the couple that experiences the birth of a child has different needs than the couple whose child has just left home. In each case, the couple must develop patterned interactions or structures that meet their needs at their developmental stage. In the first example, they must develop a set of functional behaviors to protect their young relationship; in the second case, the couple must redefine their relationship.

Problems in Boundaries, Alignment, and Power Family dysfunction often resides within the dimensions of boundary, alignment, and power (Aponte & Van Deusen, 1981). If boundaries are diffuse, spouses are stuck together and have little personal autonomy; the spouses are not permitted to be different. If boundaries are too rigid, spouses are disengaged and have little contact with each other. This often leads to alignment problems in which couples detour conflict through others, such as in-laws and children.

In some cases, spouses will attempt to triangulate the therapist; that is, each spouse will attempt to get the therapist to side with him or her against the other partner. Problems in alignment often are related to boundary definitions: for example, a cross-generational coalition—such as a husband and his mother coalescing against his wife—can be an alignment problem (husband and mother against wife) and a boundary problem (mother crosses the boundary of the marital subsystem) (Brown & Christensen, 1999). Boundary and alignment problems are closely related to power problems: a cross-generational coalition between father and son against the wife (mother) reduces the power (control) the parents have over their son.

Therapeutic Skills

Joining Minuchin (1974) states that through joining with the couple, the therapist becomes an "inside the system" agent of change. The methods therapists use to join the marital partners appear to be much like those used with family and friends. The therapist tries to get on the "same wavelength" with the couple through being attentive and responsive to the couple. Joining pervades the therapeutic process and conveys to the couple that the therapist is working with them. The three aspects of the joining process are accommodation, tracking, and mimesis.

Accommodation Accommodation is a skill that requires the therapist to adopt the couple's style, pace, and unique characteristics. The therapist must modify his or her own behavior to match the couple's values, culture, and language. The therapist must also engage the couple and be responsive to their needs, as well as respect the couple's rules for interactions or structure. For example, if the husband is the family spokesperson, then the therapist accommodates to the couple's structure by initially addressing the couple through the husband.

Tracking Tracking a couple's communication is similar to the relationship techniques derived from client-centered therapy (Rogers, 1961). In such cases, the therapist attempts to "listen with a third ear." The therapist listens and then responds to feelings that the couple may not understand. The therapist uses metaphors for marital transactions that are as diverse as "you are indebted to each other," or "you're her memory." The therapist's use of metaphor helps a couple perceive situations differently by tracking what the couple actually says and reframing it as process, such as the way the couple communicates with each other.

Mimesis Mimesis is a therapeutic skill in which the therapist appears similar to the couple through imitation of style, nonverbal behaviors, and idiosyncrasy. The therapist may practice mimesis with a spouse (perhaps adopting the same body posture) as a way to align him or herself with that person. Mimesis creates the impression that the therapist is similar to the couple.

Focus Focus refers to the therapist's choice of which pieces of information to target. This might be related to the couple's presenting problem. If the couple is concerned about inability to resolve conflict about in-laws, the therapist may want to track problems in this area.

Enactment Enactment occurs when the therapist requires the couple to replay an actual interaction to determine the function of the problem. The therapist may ask the couple to "talk to each other about the problem," or "continue to discuss the problem you had in the car this morning." The therapist's instructions must be direct: "Tell your wife what you would like for her to do when you come home." According to Minuchin and Fishman (1981), enactment consists of three movements: (1) the therapist observes dysfunctional areas to emphasize, (2) the therapist focuses on an area of the relationship, and (3) the therapist suggests alternative ways to interact. In the first movement, enactment evolves out of efforts to join and accommodate the family, while in the second movement, the focus is on a specific interactional pattern or problem area. In the third movement, the therapist alters the couple's interaction by building intensity, unbalancing, complementarity, reconstructing reality, and boundary marking. A brief description of each follows:

Intensity Intensity refers to pressure created by the therapist to effect a meaningful impact on the couple. One way to build intensity is by encouraging the couple to continue their interaction longer than the couple would normally feel comfortable doing so. The therapist might also manipulate space by moving the husband and wife closer to each other. Or, the therapist might continue to repeat the message ("You have the resources to handle this situation"). The therapist may also build intensity by not accepting the couple's message (insisting that the couple can resolve their conflict).

Unbalancing Unbalancing refers to the therapist's attempts to alter the balance of power within the couple. The therapist may use unbalancing to align or affiliate with a spouse who is in a one-down position. The therapist may support the wife ("I agree with you") to alter the husband's position and structure of the relationship, or might use his or her power to support the husband ("She needs to be convinced of your position"). In such cases, the therapist is agreeing with the spouse to alter interaction patterns in the relationship.

Complementarity Complementarity is a technique therapists use to show how spouses serve reciprocal and complementary functions. A wife who is overly organized and in control of situations may have a husband who is very disorganized and unconcerned. Couples evolve roles, often without conscious awareness, to maintain a balance and keep the couple functioning. Regardless of a spouse's characteristic (lazy, strict, organized), the other spouse may have a complement (less lazy, less strict, less organized) to balance the system.

Reconstructing Reality Reconstructing reality refers to the therapist's effort to reinterpret the couple's view of the problem. Spouses often blame each other and fail to see how their actions affect each other. The therapist might relabel a husband's "jealousy" as "caring" for his wife. The therapist may also use universal constructs such as aging or growing wiser to reconstruct the couple's view of the relationship.

Boundary Marking Boundary marking indicates a series of steps that lead to altering the couple's boundaries. As the marital therapist accommodates to the couple, he or she observes specific behaviors or interactions that assist in identifying the structural boundaries of the relationship. The therapist can mark boundaries by: (1) rearranging the seating, (2) reframing the problem, and/or (3) challenging belief systems.

THERAPEUTIC PROCESS

In the session with Tim and Patty, the structural therapist joins by discussing the couple's outside interests. The therapist looks for strengths in the system as well as patterns of interaction. As the patterns become evident and hypotheses are formulated, the therapist becomes directive, asking the couple to participate in specifically designed enactments. For example, Tim and Patty are asked to sit together and discuss a family activity. The therapist nudges them to be direct and honest with each other. Patty is asked to talk about the needs of the baby and how much time is dedicated to caring for the child. She is encouraged to ask Tim for help. When Tim begins to respond and she tries to interrupt, the therapist interrupts her interruption and directs Tim to continue. Suggestions are made regarding ways that Tim and Patty can alter their roles (for example, Tim needs to spend more time helping with the baby, and the couple needs to spend more time doing things as a couple). The therapist shares personal stories that demonstrate an empathy with the family's struggle. As Patty's powerless position becomes more evident, the therapist works to strengthen the therapeutic bond with her, pointing out her strengths and acknowledging her good intentions.

The structural therapist relies heavily on in-session interventions to produce behavioral changes. These changes are thought to stimulate cognitive and perceptual changes as well. By aligning with each spouse, the therapist helps the couple reorganize so that the couple's subsystem is strengthened with appropriate boundaries.

STRATEGIC MODEL

Jay Haley (1976) defines strategic therapy as therapy in which the therapist designs specific approaches or strategies for each prescribing problem. Symptoms or problems are viewed as formal communications between family members. Specific goals are set to alleviate these symptoms. Problems often occur when a family is stuck in a particular stage of life.

Strategic therapy is based on the work of communication theorists at the Mental Research Institute (MRI), including Jay Haley, Don Jackson, Paul Watzlawick, and Gregory Bateson. Haley worked with Salvador Minuchin at the Philadelphia Child Guidance Clinic, and assisted in the development of the structural model. Both Haley and Minuchin were concerned with problems and interactional patterns that precipitate and maintain the problem.

Theoretical Assumptions and Concepts

The strategic therapy model shares similar constructs with the structural therapeutic model. According to Stanton (1981), both approaches view the couple in the following adapted ways:

1. Spouses interact within a context. Problems and functions must be considered within the interactional context in which they occur.

2. Problem couples are seen as being "stuck" at a particular stage within the family life cycle. The couple has difficulty making the transition from each stage of the family life cycle to the next.

3. **Symptoms** are system-maintained and system-maintaining. A marital system works to maintain homeostasis in interactional patterns, and symptoms serve to maintain this system.

4. Emphasis is on the present rather than on the past. The couple's history is not so relevant, since dysfunctional behavior is maintained by current interactions.

5. Insight is not a necessary prerequisite for change. Problems cannot be alleviated through understanding alone, because ongoing interactional processes maintain the problems.

Strategic therapists are concerned principally with five interrelated concepts: (1) symptoms, (2) metaphors, (3) power, (4) sequence of interactions, and (5) hierarchy.

1. *Symptoms.* Strategic therapists place primary emphasis on symptoms, which they see as a way to maintain balance in the marital system. Symptoms can be a way of communicating metaphorically within the marital system. A wife's depression may be a way of conveying her unhappiness in a marriage. Strategic therapists are much more symptom-focused than are structural therapists, and both are more symptom-oriented than are transgenerational therapists (Stanton, 1981). Strategic therapists assume that symptoms characterize the ways couples interact with each other. Symptoms are more likely to occur when couples are making a transition to a new stage of the life cycle.

2. *Metaphors.* Symptoms may be metaphors for describing some aspect of the family system. A metaphorical message usually contains an explicit element (for example, "I can't sleep"), as well as an implicit element (for example, "I want you to be more attentive to me.") A symptom may be a report on an internal state, and also a metaphor for another internal state: a wife's headache may be expressing more than one kind of pain.

3. *Power.* Haley (1976) describes the power struggle between two people not as a question of who controls whom, but rather of who defines the nature of the relationship and by what means. Haley notes that "when one person communicates a message to the other, he is by that act making a maneuver to define the relationship" (Haley, 1963, p. 8). Any message has elements of both "command" and "report." When a wife says to her husband, "The toilet is leaking and there is water on the floor," she is reporting on the toilet, but also may be requesting him to fix the toilet or clean up the floor. If he refuses, he is engaging in a power struggle with his wife.

4. *Sequence of Interactions.* The strategic therapist places special emphasis on the sequence of interactions. In assessing the problem, the therapist should begin to look for sequential patterns of behavior. Does one spouse accuse the other of being neglected? Does one spouse feel that the other spouse does not care what is going on? When one spouse speaks, does the other spouse interrupt or reject what is being said? By assessing the sequence of interactions around the presenting problem, the therapist gains information useful in developing a strategy to alleviate the problem.

   Once spouses have expressed their views on the problem, the therapist should get them to interact with each other about the problem. The therapist may want to see if the husband and wife can discuss the problem without turning to the therapist. The therapist should be careful not to be central to this interaction; instead, he or she should get family members to talk to each other.

5. *Hierarchy.* Hierarchy begins to emerge once the sequence of interactions maintaining the problem has been identified. In functional families, parents are responsible for their children. However, in dysfunctional families, the hierarchy may be violated. For example, when conflict between

a husband and wife increases, a wife may get closer to her son—a cross-generational coalition that undermines the parent's role.

Therapeutic Skills

Strategic therapists are concerned primarily with those skills that alter the sequence of interactions maintaining the problem. Therapeutic skills are designed to alter repetitive sequences that are maintaining the problems. The strategic therapist maintains control of marital therapy through the use of tasks or directives. Tasks can be overt (telling a spouse how to behave), or they can be covert (nonverbal behavior or silence).

Haley (1976) lists three reasons for giving tasks to family members. First, tasks are one way to get people to behave differently in therapy. Second, tasks increase the salience of the therapist. If a task or directive is given for the couple to complete during the week, then the couple must decide whether they are going to comply with the therapist's directive, and what they will say to the therapist the next session. Third, if the couple completes or fails to complete the task, the therapist has gathered useful information.

Each therapeutic skill involves three distinct components: task selection, task construction, and task delivery (Bross & Benjamin, 1983). The selection and construction of a therapeutic task is determined by the nature of the couple and the therapeutic style. In most cases the therapist must convince the couple that they should follow the directive or task. However, getting the couple to complete the task is often based on the nature of the task and the relationship the therapist has with the couple (Haley, 1976). There may be little payoff for the wife making a request from her husband if there is little expectation that it will be met. In such cases, the wife must feel that the therapist is on her side.

Straightforward tasks are used if the therapist expects the couple to be cooperative and comply with the directive. If the couple is likely to follow through on the therapist's suggestions, it is easiest to simply suggest some straightforward tasks. The purpose of such tasks is to change the sequence of interactions in the relationship. For instance, when one partner complains that the other partner never wants to go out or do anything, the therapist may give them a straightforward task of planning a date for the next week.

Haley (1976) offers several suggestions to therapists for getting couples to follow their tasks or directives:

1. *Discuss all the things the couple has done to try to solve the problem.* By this device, the therapist can avoid making suggestions that already have been tried before. The therapist should lead the couple to the final conclusion that "everything has been tried and nothing has worked." At this point the therapist is in a position to offer the couple something different from what they have experienced before.

2. *Ask spouses to discuss the negative consequences if their problem is not handled now* (that is, what is going to happen if this problem is not resolved?).

Aversive consequences will probably be different for each spouse. Nevertheless, examining the negative consequences of the problem for each spouse emphasizes the intensity of the problem. It is important for the therapist to emphasize those consequences and to project what might happen if the problem is not resolved.

3. *Assign a task that is reasonable and easily accomplished.* In order to ensure that the couple can complete the task at home, it is necessary to get the couple to complete the task in the session.

4. *Assign a task to fit the ability and performance level of the each spouse.* Avoid tasks that are not too difficult. It is important for the couple to experience some initial success.

5. *Use your authority to get the couple to follow the directive/task.* Sometimes the therapist must use his or her knowledge and expertise to get the couple to comply. It is important for the therapist to accept the role of expert, rather than asking the couple what they think they should do.

6. *Give clear instructions.* Everyone should know what his or her responsibilities or role should be.

The authors have used the following straightforward directives/tasks in their own clinical work:

- A wife who had difficulty separating from her parents was asked to visit her parents unannounced and talk about something that would meet with their disapproval.

- A conflictual couple was asked to return to a place, such as a restaurant or park, which had been pleasant during their courting period. The task focused on positive experiences and changed the affect of the relationship.

- A couple living with their parents was having difficulty moving out. They were asked in the session to plan how they would move out and present the plan to the parents the next week.

- A couple who had little contact with each other were asked to have a meeting in which each spouse presented his or her view of the problem.

The therapist congratulates couples for completing tasks. For couples who have not completed the tasks, the therapist finds out why, and asks the couple to complete the task or a similar one in the session.

Paradoxical Directives Paradoxical directives can be given when straightforward directives and tasks do not work. In such cases, "psychology" must be genuine and avoid sarcasm. In other words, the therapist must have some empathy for the family's need to develop the symptoms to preserve their collective stability.

Weeks and L'Abate (1982) list five types of family transactions that point to the appropriateness of paradoxical directives/tasks:

1. *Fighting and bickering.* Couples relate to one another primarily through fighting and bickering. Spouses are at odds regardless of the issue. Spouses are highly volatile and reactive. Straightforward directives/tasks are ineffective with this type of marriage.

2. *Non-cooperativeness and failure to complete assignments.* The couple is not as expressive as the spouses in a couple that fight with each other. Spouses may cooperate verbally but undermine each other nonverbally. Spouses generally act out their aggression through other means, such as drinking, drugs, or work. Spouses will often agree to complete homework assignments but fail to take personal responsibility when they have left the session.

3. *Continuation of the problem regardless of the intervention.* The couple fails to respond to any type of intervention. The therapist often feels discouraged with this type of couple because he or she sees little change.

4. *Separation and polarization.* This pattern is characteristic of couples whose children can easily separate them. Adolescents are especially effective in challenging or separating their parents.

5. *Disqualifying one another.* Spouses contradict or disqualify each other's statements. Spouses show no support of each other and fail to set limits for the children.

Peggy Papp (1980) (adapted; appearing in Brown & Christensen, 1999, pp. 96, 98) describes three steps in giving a paradoxical directive:

1. Clearly explain how the symptom benefits the family from an interactional perspective (for example, "Your husband's depression makes you [wife] feel needed.")

2. Encourage the family to continue their behavior because a change would mean a loss of benefits to the family (Stanton, 1981). If the family complies with the therapist's directive, it allows the therapist to maintain control and is a first step toward change. Likewise, if the couple fails to comply with the directive, they must discontinue the symptomatic behavior. Thus, both compliance and non-compliance may produce change in the family's interactional pattern.

3. Restrain the family as it begins to improve to keep the paradox working. Here, the therapist is suggesting that change may not be beneficial. The therapist may be saying, "I recognize that things are better, but do you really want to improve this rapidly? There may be some benefits to slowing down." The therapist must be sincere and not take credit for the change. The therapist must also be genuine and empathic toward the family to help them preserve their collective stability.

This process can be illustrated with a high-conflict couple to whom the therapist described the benefits of their behavior ("Arguing seems to bring you closer together.") Next, the therapist prescribed the symptom ("I want you to take one hour each night to argue.") The couple was urged to continue their same pattern of arguing (talking at the same time, blaming each other for their problems, not listening). In the next session, the couple reported that they had not complied with the therapist's directive and in fact, reported some improvement. The therapist celebrated this change, restraining the couple and questioning whether they wanted to give the arguing up since they may "need this time together." It is important in such cases for the therapist to express both concern and hope for the couple.

Jay Haley (1976, pp. 72–74) outlines eight stages (adapted; appearing in Brown & Christensen, 1999, pp. 97, 98) he considers important when giving paradoxical directives:

1. *Defining a therapeutic relationship.* The therapist must join with the family to establish a trusting relationship. The trust between the therapist and family allows the therapist to give a paradoxical directive in a way that still shows concern for the family.

2. *Defining the problem clearly.* The problem should be clearly and concretely defined. Weeks and L'Abate (1982, p. 75) ask the following questions, which are useful in defining the problem: "Who is involved in the problem? Where does the problem occur? How frequently does the problem occur? What happens when you experience this problem?" It is important to identify the sequence of events that maintain the problem.

3. *Setting goals.* Goals should be stated in concrete terms so everyone will know whether the goals have been achieved. Goals can be established by asking family members how they would like things to be after treatment ("What would you be doing after we have finished?"). The therapist must make sure that the goals are reasonable and set an appropriate time period for their accomplishment.

4. *Designing a plan.* All homework tasks should be provided at the end of the session. A directive to any member should be stated clearly and connected to the other family members in the system. The therapist should make sure the client has understood the directive. The therapist should present the task with an authoritative voice if he or she wants the family member or members or both to resist him (Rohrbaugh, Tennen, Press, White, Raskin, & Pickering, 1977). If the therapist wishes the client to perform the task, he or she will need to encourage the client to complete the task.

5. *Disqualifying the current authority on the problem.* The authority is generally a spouse or other family member who is trying to help solve the problem (Haley, 1976). In some cases, the authority may be people outside who have influence on the family. Unfortunately, family members often attempt to do more of the same to solve the problem. Thus, those who attempt to solve the problem may be an obstacle to its resolution. Consequently, the person who is attempting to solve the problem is actually maintaining it and must be disqualified.

6. *Giving a paradoxical directive.* Paradoxical directives or tasks should be designed to fit the client's special interest (Weeks & L'Abate, 1982). The directives should play to the client's style, values, and abilities if possible.

The authors have found that written directives can be phrased in language that appeals to special types of clients, such as lawyers or doctors. The directive or task should be tailored to the family member's schedule so that the task does not occur spontaneously.

7. *Encouraging symptomatic behavior to occur.* When improvement occurs, the therapist should restate the rationale and encourage the client to continue to follow the directive. If the client fails to comply, the therapist should be solemn and suggest that the client is not cooperating. The therapist should avoid behaving in a way that the family might view as insincere or sarcastic (Stanton, 1981). The therapist should then request that the client continue the symptomatic behavior. The therapist should not back off if the family is resistant, or he or she will lose credibility.

8. *Avoiding taking credit for change.* If improvement occurs, the therapist should avoid taking credit for it. If a task does not produce the desired result, the therapist should accept responsibility for the failure. If the therapist accepts credit, he or she risks a relapse for the client who is acting to please the therapist.

Pretending Strategic therapists often use absurdity or fantasy to alter entrenched patterns of problem behavior. The therapist may ask the wife to pretend to be upset by the husband's behavior while the husband must guess whether she is pretending or is actually upset. Pretending is designed to break up patterns of dysfunctional behavior resulting from the confusion and therefore the couple must find other ways of interacting.

Positive Labeling and Connotation A positive connotation may be given to the spouse to alter the other spouse's views of him or her. A positive label for "jealousy" could be "caring," and a new label for "anger" could be "desiring attention." Positive labels give family members a different way to think about the problem, so that it can be resolved. Positive connotation requires the therapist to attribute "positive motives to clients" (Stanton, 1981, p. 376). Couples then have the opportunity to identify their strengths and abilities, making the problem more amenable to change. The therapist should be cautious not to relabel violent or destructive behavior.

Brief Therapy in the Strategic Model

Brief therapy was pioneered at the Mental Health Institute in Palo Alto, California and is described in the book *Change: Principles of Problem Formation and Problem Resolution* (Watzlawick, Weakland, & Fisch, 1974). Brief family therapy is a step-by-step approach lasting a maximum of ten sessions. In the problem-focused interview, the therapist can ask the following questions: What is the problem? Who did what the last time the problem occurred? When is the problem likely to occur? When did the problem first occur? (Hoffman, 1981). Once the problem is identified, the therapist examines the couple's attempted solutions to assess which interactions were unsuccessful. In many cases, the couple's attempts to resolve the problem are worse than the problem itself. Goals are set to resolve the specific problem, and paradoxical suggestions and symptom prescriptions are used to assist spouses in reaching their goals. All resources are used to maintain the desired changes in the couple's behavior.

Therapeutic Process

In the case of Tim and Patty, the therapist asks, "What do we need to work on?" or "What would need to happen for you to be successful here?" Patty begins to explain something about Tim's behavior, focusing primarily on her own frustration and helplessness. The therapist does not accept the couple's initial definition of the problem. Rather, the therapist redefines the presenting problem from an individual condition (Tim's neglect of Patty) to an interaction problem that can be alleviated (Tim caring for the baby with Patty's support).

The therapist next looks for sequential patterns of behavior. Do spouses interrupt each other? When this happens, what happens next? The therapist is attempting to identify the sequence of interactions surrounding the presenting problem. In the initial session as Patty speaks, she begins to cry. Tim looks the other way. Patty becomes more emotional and Tim puts his head down. Both report that they interact in this way whenever the problem is discussed. When the therapist asks Tim how he might respond to Patty's requests, he reports that "I don't know what to do. I can't be at home all the time." The therapist now requests that Patty state her requests for help with the baby, so that Tim can respond.

As the therapist helps the couple to interact differently in the session, he begins to attribute positive motives to each spouse. Problem behaviors are relabeled to have more positive meaning. For example, a positive label for Patty's emotional behavior is "caring" and Tim's "nonresponsiveness" is relabeled as "overwhelmed." These new labels can help the couple with a new way of thinking about the problem, so that it can be resolved. Further interaction with the therapist might lead to a list of attempted solutions focused on specific requests from Patty without crying.

As the session concludes, the strategic therapist often assigns a task for the next week. Since Tim and Patty seem compliant, the therapist assigns a straightforward task. Patty is to make a specific request for Tim's help without crying, and without reminding him that he never helps her. Both are to keep a record of the number and type of requests and frequency of compliance. This will help the therapist assess the couple's ability to change.

BEHAVIORAL MARITAL MODEL

Early models of behavioral marital therapy were based on social learning (Thibaut & Kelly, 1959) and operant principles or rewards partners exchange with each other (Patterson & Reid, 1970). More recent models focus on cognitions and attitudes (Jacobson, 1981). The combination of social learning theory and cognitive theory led to the development of cognitive-behavioral marital therapy. These therapists believe that changing cognitions such as expectations and beliefs are critical to helping couples achieve satisfaction in their marriage.

Theoretical Concepts and Assumptions

Positive Reinforcement Positive reinforcement occurs when an event follows a behavior that increases the probability of that behavior's recurrence. If the husband agrees to hang up his clothes, such behavior is more likely to occur if the wife compliments or recognizes (positively reinforces) this behavior. Likewise, the therapist is more likely to increase positive couple interactions by complimenting each spouse or recognizing their progress. It should be noted that an event is *only* reinforcing when it *increases* the behavior it follows. Couples often come to therapy when they are receiving a low level of positive reinforcers (compliments, smiles, hugs, touches). Often behaviors that were once reinforcing are no longer satisfying ("We have just grown apart.") In many cases, low levels of positive reinforcers are coupled with high levels of aversive or punishing behaviors. The result is a distressed marriage in which both spouses are dissatisfied.

Extinction Extinction refers to the reduction or elimination of a behavior through the removal of a reinforcer. In many marriages, behaviors (attention) that were once reinforced (affection) are ignored, and attention continues to decrease until it is extinguished. Presenting complaints such as "He doesn't notice," "He doesn't care," or "I can't seem to get his attention" are indications that behavior is being ignored or extinguished (Patterson & Reid, 1970). Therapeutic efforts in these cases may begin by getting spouses to stop ignoring and instead attend to desired behaviors in the other spouse.

Reciprocity Reciprocity is a concept derived from social learning theory that refers to the equitable exchange of rewarding behaviors between spouses. Spouses often reinforce each other at an equitable rate that maintains the behavior of both parties (Patterson & Reid, 1970). Reciprocity is often conditional on other aspects of the relationship, and does not necessarily mean that spouses will immediately reciprocate. The expectation that one's spouse will do so immediately is often disappointing and leads to further conflict in the relationship (Stuart, 1980).

Coercion Coercion refers to attempts by either spouse to control the other partner's behavior with negative reinforcement. For example, a wife may attempt to control her husband's behavior by complaining that he never pays attention to her. Her complaints become louder when her husband continues to ignore her. As the wife's complaints become more aversive, the husband reluctantly pays attention to end the unpleasant interactions and the requests by his wife. Unfortunately, the husband's behavior is negatively reinforced, while the wife's unpleasant requests (yelling) are positively reinforced by his paying more attention to her. Coercion may also produce a negative cycle of interaction that leads the husband or wife to withdraw (leaving the room or house) to avoid coercive behavior of the other. Such cycles may lead to a low exchange rate of rewards that may result in a low level of satisfaction in the relationship (Gurman & Kniskern, 1978).

Unresolved Conflict Regardless of the ratio of rewards and punishments, un-resolved conflict will affect it. Whereas a positive ratio of positive-to-negative behaviors is critical, ongoing conflict will greatly reduce satisfaction in the relationship. Jacobson (1981) says:

> Maintaining a high ratio (rewards/cost) is not much of a problem for cou-ples during the early stages of a relationship, particularly given a large degree of initial attraction. Reinforcing value is at its peak, fueled by the novelty inherent in the exchanges and shared activities. Couples ensure during these periods that the contacts are as positive as possible. None of the costs inherent in a long-term commitment has been realized as yet. (p. 559)

The daily burden of unresolved conflict is the single most probable cause of marital failure (Mace, 1979). Couples are often not able to resolve conflict because they lack skills for problem solving and communication. Descriptions of these areas appear in the next section.

Observable Behavior One of the cornerstones of behavioral marital therapy is emphasis on observable behaviors. The behavioral therapist is primarily interested in decreasing the couple's general complaints ("He or she doesn't care about me," "He or she doesn't respect me," or "I'm not happy in the mar-riage"), to more specific behavior and objectively verifiable behaviors ("When I ask my husband to spend time with me, he ignores me.") As the couple pre-sents these complaints, the therapist asks questions, as well as models how the spouses should communicate with each other. It is important to note that this type of assessment is indistinguishable from treatment intervention in behav-ioral therapy (Jacob, 1976). Each question helps the couple focus on observ-able behaviors. The behavioral therapist focuses primarily on two types of observable behaviors: (1) problematic behaviors that each partner would like changed, and (2) ways that these problematic behaviors currently are rein-forced in the relationship. Behavioral therapists attempt to assess these observ-able behaviors through a wide variety of verbal, psychological, and behavioral variables (Goldfried & Sprafkin, 1974).

Cognitive Behaviors Cognitive behavioral therapists have recently empha-sized the role of cognitions (thoughts, beliefs, expectations) in marital interac-tions. Cognitions can be both antecedents (triggers) or consequences of behavior. How do spousal expectations influence spousal behaviors? Cognitive behavioral therapists help couples monitor their thoughts and expectations and the influence of their thoughts and expectations on how the spouses interact with each other. Unrealistic expectations of a spouse ("You promised we could spend time together when your assignment was over") often lead to aversive behaviors (anger, personal attacks). Such behaviors should be viewed in light of spousal expectations, not just spousal interactions. Thus, it may not be the complaint (spending more time) that is the problem; rather, it may be the underlying expectation that is the issue. Assessment of cognitions is essential if the therapist is to fully understand problem maintaining patterns and the potential for change in the relationship.

Therapeutic Skills

Creating an Atmosphere of Change Couples often come to therapy feeling hopeless, blaming each other for their problems. They often are not ready to hear what the therapist has to say. Moreover, a spouse may feel pressured or threatened into seeking help. Thus, the atmosphere is one of bitterness, mistrust, distance, and anger. This is not an atmosphere where change can easily occur. When the therapist attempts to make change, he or she often is seen as aligning with one spouse against the other. The therapist must overcome these obstacles and create an atmosphere where change can occur.

The behavioral marital therapist defines the relationship to create a proper climate. The therapist avoids immediately focusing on the presenting problems and goals. Rather, the therapist focuses on the history of the couple's relationship (Jacobson & Margolin, 1979). The therapist attempts to alter the couple's mood by replacing negative perceptions with positive pictures and images. When couples can remember the good times (courtship, honeymoon) they had together, they are more likely to view their disagreements from a more positive perspective.

Establishing a Contract for Change Another strategy for creating an atmosphere for change is to work together to establish a contract that the couple will follow the therapist's advice and will commit to do what the therapist instructs. Contracts are written agreements between spouses stipulating specific behavioral changes. Spouses state the exact behaviors they want increased and stipulate what they will provide for the other in exchange. Stuart (1980) gives an example of a contract that offers each partner several choices, any one of which would produce satisfaction in the spouse. One side of the agreement states that the wife would like the husband to . . . and gives six choices. The other side states what the husband would like the wife to do and also includes six choices. The bottom of the contract states that the couple will do as many of the things requested as is comfortably manageable, ideally at least three or four times weekly.

The contract establishes the framework within which the therapist instructs the couple to collaborate (Jacobson, 1981). The therapist is able to establish a contract by first viewing the problem as resolvable. Next, the couple sets expectations about what is going to happen in the session. The therapist should explain his or her role, and discuss how he or she plans to work with the couple. This process permits the therapist to connect with each spouse, thereby building a foundation for communication between the spouses.

Behavioral Exchange Practice Behavioral exchange practice is based on the principle of social exchange (reciprocity), in which each spouse "gives" in order to "get" behaviors they want from the other. Behavioral exchange appears to work best when both parties possess resources (that is, reinforcement potential valuable to each other). When both partners have equal or nearly equal resources (for example, friends and skills), spouses are more likely to negotiate a solution to their problem. But when one spouse has control over most of the resources, negotiation is difficult.

Behavioral exchange consists of two basic procedures. First, one or both spouses identify positive behaviors. Spouses are encouraged by the therapist to identify behaviors they wish to see more frequently. "I want you to pay more attention to me," might mean, "I want you to talk to me when you first come home." Second, the therapist attempts to increase the frequency of the positive behaviors (Jacobson, 1981), with the goal of producing more satisfaction in the relationship by extinguishing undesirable behavior and reinforcing desirable behavior.

The therapist may start the exchange process by asking each spouse to make three specific requests from the other. A wife may request that her husband (1) pick up the children from school on Monday and Wednesday, (2) ask her about her day in the evening, and (3) call her if he is going to be late. A husband may request (1) that when his wife makes a request, she won't yell, (2) when there is an argument, she won't go to her mother's, and (3) that she won't "put him down" in front of others. When spouses replace desired behaviors for undesired behaviors, reciprocal behaviors will serve to reinforce both spouses positively, and thus lead to a more satisfying relationship.

Cost/Benefit Analysis Cost/benefit analysis is a variation of behavior exchange. Weiss and Perry (1979) ask couples to conduct a cost/benefit analysis to help partners determine how much effort they should expend for each other, and to help them decide what behaviors each considers important in the other. Couples are asked to examine the "Benefit Exchange Sheets" (Weiss, 1978), which contain lists of potentially pleasing behaviors taken from the Spouse Observation Checklist. The Benefit Exchange Sheet is divided into twelve categories (e.g., companionship, affection, and consideration).

Each spouse is asked to rate each item as being "beneficial" or "costly" on a 5-point scale. Some spouses may focus only on a particular area, such as parenting or communication. Cost-benefit analysis works best when benefits and costs are equitable for both spouses. The exercise provides opportunity for negotiation of differences.

After spouses have completed the cost/benefit exercise, they complete a weekly client assignment sheet that lists: (1) what each spouse will do, and (2) when the spouse will complete it. Thus, each spouse's assignment sheet becomes a contingency contract, whereby desirable behavior is contingent upon the other spouse's desirable behavior. If one partner agrees to make reasonable requests without yelling, the other spouse will comply with the request. If one spouse fails to do his or her part, the other spouse has the choice not to meet his or her obligation. Thus, if the cost/benefit exchange is successful, each spouse is maximizing his or her benefits, and, at the same time, minimizing the costs.

Caring Days On caring days, each spouse makes a special effort to please the other by engaging in a significantly greater number of caring behaviors than the other spouse expects (Paolino & McGrady, 1978). Stuart (1980) asks spouses to make requests that they would like to receive from one another, and to carry out from eight to twenty of the requests made by the other partner on a daily basis. For example, a spouse may request breakfast in bed, hugs in the morning, body massage, calls at work, and so on. Spouses are to carry out the requests, independent of the other's actions to demonstrate commitment. Each spouse is asked to record the number of instances of caring, and type of caring behavior, he or she offers each day and how it was experienced. It is assumed that caring days will increase positive feelings between partners.

Requests should be concrete and stated in positive terms (Stuart, 1980). Requests should avoid major problem issues, and focus on specific behaviors that can be emitted each day. For example, a negative complaint ("You only care about yourself") could be stated in positive and specific terms ("Tell me I look attractive"). Frequent responses are likely to produce positive interactions. Requests should avoid conflict because conflict will not be resolved until there is improvement in the relationship: "Therefore, if the couple has been having arguments over when to turn off the television set and go to bed—one wishing to watch the late show through to the end, while the other wishes to retire much earlier—this would not be an acceptable item to include on the list" (Stuart, 1980, p. 201).

The therapist can model appropriate requests such as "Please fix the coffee," or "Tell me I'm nice to be around." Stuart says that caring lists should contain eighteen items and be open-ended so that spouses can modify their lists. Each item on the list should be thoroughly discussed so that both spouses are clear about the request. Each spouse is asked to emit five behaviors each day. Caring behaviors exhibited by one spouse should not be contingent on whether the other spouse responds in a positive manner; otherwise, each spouse would emit a caring behavior only when the partner responds in a positive manner, in which case neither partner would be taking responsibility for the relationship. Caring days help to rebuild trust and commitment in the marriage.

Using Symbols Stuart (1975) also encourages couples to use symbolic events, places, objects, or rituals that hold special meaning to the couple. These symbols help the couple to recall more pleasant times in their marriage, and create a more favorable climate for treatment. The therapist will often ask a couple to return to a special place (for example, a restaurant or park) that has special meaning to the couple. Some couples take a second honeymoon or celebrate a special anniversary. Regardless of the activity, the importance lies in the symbolic meaning it holds for the couple.

If couples lack important symbols or rituals, the therapist must help them create new ones. If a couple has not had a courtship or honeymoon, the therapist will spend time with the couple planning one. When planning the honeymoon, the therapist can work with the couple to create new activities that are pleasing to both partners. If this is successful, the therapist will encourage the couple to continue developing new activities and rituals.

In the process of developing new activities, couples learn what is especially pleasing for each spouse. This in turn helps them establish "reinforcement reciprocity," in which rewarding behavior replaces coercive behavior (Nichols, 1984). The structure exchange of caring behaviors provides an opportunity for trust, and trust is the foundation for intimacy and long-term commitments to one another.

Conflict Resolution and Communication Skills in conflict resolution and problem solving are a set of well-developed strategies for dealing with disagreements when they arise (Stuart, 1980). Problem solving/conflict resolution has proven effective in treating marital conflict (Jacobson & Margolin, 1979). Problem solving/conflict resolution has two distinct phases: problem definition and problem solution. The phase of problem definition is designed to define operationally the critical issue or problem. For example, "You don't come home after work" provides a clearer definition of a problem than "You don't care about me." The important advantage of defining a problem in operational terms is that it is more likely to lead to an effective response to the problem.

Once the issue or problem has been defined operationally, efforts are directed toward resolving the problem. The resolution phase emphasizes behavior change rather than insight. Couples are given a set of instructions or cues for the acquisition of more effective problem-solving behaviors. To ensure focus on the solution, couples are taught to generate alternative solutions through brainstorming (Goldfried & Davison, 1976). Couples are asked to brainstorm as many solutions as possible, without criticism. In addition to contributing his or her own ideas, each spouse is encouraged to suggest how the ideas of the other spouse can be turned into better ideas and how two more ideas can be combined into still another idea (Osborn, 1963). When alternatives have been proposed, the advantages and disadvantages of each alternative can be considered.

In the process of determining the best course of action, couples are encouraged to predict the likely consequences of each course of action, and consider the utility of these consequences in dealing with the problem (D'Zurilla & Goldfried, 1971). Couples are taught that the solution should be equitable and involve some change on the part of each spouse. Couples should also be assisted in selecting behaviors for exchange that require equal time and effort.

Once a solution has been selected, an agreement should be made that specifies the selected behavior. The agreement should help to verify the behaviors of each spouse and should include the specific conditions of the exchange. It should include who will do what, when, how often, and in what location; the consequences; and what happens when a spouse does not follow through on an exchange (Harrell & Guerney, 1976). The actual exchange behaviors should be sufficiently reinforcing to ensure maintenance of the desired behaviors.

Problem-solving/conflict-resolution skills are facilitated by communication skills training. Although communication training is common to systems (Satir, 1967), relationship therapy (Rogers, 1951), and psychoanalytic approaches (Ables & Brandsma, 1977), the behavioral approach to communication training is unusual. Jacobson (1981) states:

> First, it utilizes a systematic method of training adapted from other skill training paradigms in behavior therapy. . . . Second, the communication training tends to be change-oriented rather than expression-oriented. That is, whereas most approaches to communication training focus on communication per se (i.e., the expression and reception of feelings), behavior therapy teaches couples how to communicate in order to facilitate the resolution of conflict. (p. 574)

Modeling The first step in helping a couple to communicate more effectively is to demonstrate, or model, the appropriate communication skill to be learned. That is, the behavior therapist shows each spouse what the response looks like or how it sounds. Modeling has been effective in teaching clients information-seeking behavior (Krumboltz, Varenhorst, & Thoresen, 1967), reducing feelings of alienation (Warner & Hansen, 1970), and improving attitudes toward drug abuse (Warner, Swisher, & Horan, 1973).

The process of modeling or demonstration often consists of the therapist's providing live or symbolic models—for example, on audiotapes or videotapes—who show in sequential steps the specific behaviors necessary to solve the problem (Hosford & deVisser, 1974). Taped or filmed models have been successfully used for problem solving (Hansen, Pound, & Warner, 1976). Since the models are being used only to demonstrate the desired behaviors, there is no opportunity for interaction between the models and the spouses. The taped models, however, may help to stimulate discussion in the desired direction. Such discussion may prevent rote imitation by the spouses. If new behaviors are to be effective, spouses need to learn a variety of responses for a particular problem situation.

The therapist may also wish to develop models for each of several sessions. For example, the therapist could develop tapes that teach each spouse to: (1) listen, (2) express a compliment, (3) express appreciation, (4) ask for help, (5) give feedback, or (6) express affection (Goldstein, 1973). Each skill could be modeled and practiced during a session if the spouses' skill levels allowed. Each modeling sequence could thus represent a closer approximation of the final behavior.

Instruction Once the couple has attended to and understood the model behavior, the therapist should provide instructions before the couple begins practicing the new behavior. The therapist can focus attention on the relevant and essential aspects of the model's performance. The instruction may be spoken or written by the therapist, or it can be provided through an audio or video-tape recorder. If each spouse knows how to follow instructions, the therapist need not go through a lengthy shaping process (Gelfand & Hartmann, 1975). The therapist might say, "Watch how I show appreciation to your husband," and then model the appropriate behavior, adding, "Now I want you to show appreciation for something your husband has done recently."

The therapist is now essentially serving as a coach who prompts specific behavior for the couple to try out. Instructions generally are broken down into "do" and "don't do," with the therapist giving numerous specific examples. Instructing a wife to give feedback to her husband, the therapist might say, "Look directly at your husband and tell him how it makes you feel when he doesn't call to say he will be late coming home. Don't just accuse him of being inconsiderate."

The therapist might discuss the importance of giving feedback at appropriate times, for example, "when you have time to sit down" or "when you are not so angry"—since a spouse may know *what* to say but not know *when* to say it. By going over the demonstration, the therapist can pinpoint behaviors emitted by the model spouse and discuss why such behaviors can serve as a cue to the other spouse to emit specific behavior.

Practice Having received instructions on what to say and do, the couple is ready to practice the behavior. Practice is an essential part of the learning process, since one learns by doing. By practicing or role-playing the behavior, the couple is able to try out new behavior without the risk of failure. In addition, practice allows each spouse to anticipate difficult encounters and handle them more effectively.

Before practicing or role-playing a new behavior, the couple must be prepared. Both partners must accept the idea that practice would be an appropriate way to develop new relationships or problem-solving behaviors. If either spouse shows resistance to this idea, the therapist can provide examples of the usefulness of practice. The crucial point is that each spouse must feel that he or she is not just learning a role that is artificial and unusable. Consequently, the role-playing situations should be as realistic as possible and should include verbal responses with which each spouse feels comfortable.

Feedback When each partner has practiced the sequence of skills, both must receive feedback on their performances. Knowledge of one's performance provides an incentive for improvement. Information received about poor performance can be helpful in improving positive performance.

Several factors influence the effects of feedback on learning. Feedback is more effective when it is solicited or agreed upon prior to practice. When a spouse denies or disagrees with feedback from the therapist, feedback was probably not solicited or agreed upon prior to practice. Feedback should also describe rather than evaluate the spouse's response. The therapist's statements of feedback should avoid judgment or blame. Finally, in some cases, the therapist may wish to reinforce a spouse's response and at the same time prompt similar responses. By prompting similar responses the therapist is encouraging the generalization of the behavior to other situations.

Therapeutic Process

Both Tim and Patty reported that they received little attention and affection from each other. Their reports were confirmed by responses to the Dyadic Adjustment Scale (DAS) and the Marital Precounseling Inventory, on which each spouse recorded his or her daily activities. The therapist elicited agreement from both Tim and Patty to work on improving their marriage. He then reviewed their courtship, having them discuss what attracted them to each other and what was happening during the time of their courtship. This created a more positive mood and willingness to cooperate. He then got the spouses to commit to following his instructions, and they began with behavioral change practice. One day was established as "caring day" and each person was to do something special for the spouse on that day.

The therapist also worked with Tim and Patty on conflict resolution skills. They worked on ways the baby could have time with Tim as well as Patty. This was done through brainstorming ways both parents could be involved, evaluating consequences of these alternatives, and choosing one or more which seemed acceptable to both. They agreed that Tim would spend at least 1–2 hours each night playing with and caring for the baby, thereby giving Patty some time to do other things.

Communication skills were dealt with also, since neither Tim nor Patty tended to express feelings. They practiced ways to give compliments, express appreciation and affection, and ask for help. First, the therapist modeled the situation, talked about how and when to perform the behavior, provided an opportunity for the couple to practice through role-playing, and gave them feedback. Both Patty and Tim learned how to say positive things to each other as well as how to request changes in the other person's behavior. Because they were experiencing more positive feelings, it was easier for each to compromise with the other.

TRANSGENERATIONAL MODEL

Transgenerational/Psychodynamic Model

Psychodynamic approaches to family or marital therapy include both systems thinking and analytic thinking. Such approaches are often referred to as transgenerational therapies. They have also been referred to as "extended family" therapy and may include members across generations in the therapy, or at least, will conceptualize families in terms of images, ideas, perspectives, and dynamics that may be passed from generation to generation. These theorists hold that difficulties often are rooted in experiences from the family of origin.

Two major theorists who follow the psychodynamic or transgenerational model are Murray Bowen and Ivan Boszormenyi-Nagy. Many other theorists who have developed various models were trained in the psychoanalytic model and have been influenced by it.

Therapeutic Assumptions and Concepts

The marital therapist who operates from the psychodynamic model combines concepts from both the analytic model and systems theory. Some of the major assumptions and concepts from this model follow:

Past Experiences Affect the Present To tell a couple that is having difficulties that these may be attributable to relationships from the family of origin may seem incredible. In fact, a partner who comes from a conflictual family or an unhappy family may wish to sever all ties with that family, believing that he or she can start over and not be affected by past relationships. However, one of the major assumptions of psychodynamic theory is that for a person to resolve a current problem in his or her marriage, he or she must explore and try to resolve issues from early relationships. These early influences affect and help to explain current difficulties. Therefore, the therapist may work with the spouse individually, with the focus of helping him or her deal with issues brought from the family of origin. While the therapist may see the person individually, the therapy is thought of in a systemic way; in other words, how a spouse's individual issues affect the relationship.

Nuclear Family Emotional System The nuclear family emotional system includes those living in a household as well as extended family. Even though a couple lives with each other and there is no one else living in the household, it does not mean that the couple is independent emotionally. In fact, the emotional system includes all extended family, whether they are living or dead, and whether they live close by or far away. Bowen (1978) would say that even when the therapist works with a couple, the extended family are very much a part of the process because the couple has to deal with all the emotions, beliefs and images that he or she brought to the current relationship.

Differentiation To be healthy, a person must differentiate self from others and differentiate feeling processes from intellectual processes. Differentiation refers to a person's ability to free him or herself from emotional entanglements. All people have an emotional system and an intellectual/rational system, and the differentiated person is able to keep these systems separate. That is, he or she feels his or her own feelings, and even though there may be sensitivity to feelings of others around, he or she is not swept into them. In another sense, the differentiated person has a strong sense of self, is comfortable with that self, and can make choices based on reasoning rather than emotions.

The opposite of differentiation is fusion, which is a tendency for emotions to overtake reasoning. Statements such as, "She is distraught and not herself" reflect a lack of differentiation or ability to separate emotions from reason. This is problematic in a relationship because couples that are operating only on emotions are unable to solve problems.

When a couple is fused, they do not have a sense of self separate from the couple bond. Bowen refers to this as a pseudo-self versus a solid-self. The person with a solid-self has clearly defined beliefs, opinions, and ideas developed through intellectual reasoning; conversely, the person with a pseudo-self makes choices on the basis of emotions. He or she is controlled by emotional pressure, and is unaware of the inconsistencies resulting when trying to conform to all the different expectations from family and friends. Because the person with a solid-self has rationally and consciously made choices about beliefs, he or she accepts responsibility for behavior, and can be much more flexible than the person with a pseudo-self.

Bowen says that individuals tend to marry mates with similar degrees of differentiation to their own. Therefore, the partner who left his family of origin with a pseudo-self tends to marry a wife who also has a pseudo-self. When fusion occurs, the couple cuts off emotionally from their families of origin, each looks to the other for stability, and neither feels comfortable making choices or decisions. Such instability is likely to lead to emotional distance, conflict, projection of the problem onto one or more of their children, or physical or emotional dysfunction in one of the spouses (Becvar & Becvar, 2000).

Bowen indicates that persons become more and more undifferentiated through the process of passing unproductive family processes from generation to generation. For instance, the person who has not differentiated from his family of origin may become cut off emotionally, then become fused with a partner, and eventually pass on this unproductive family process to his children, who will in turn become undifferentiated, and then become fused with a mate. A fused couple that has children will often project the problem onto one or more of the children through triangulation.

Triangulation Triangulation occurs when anxiety in a dyad is increased beyond a comfortable or tolerable level. This involves a third person in an attempt to achieve some kind of resolution for anxiety. However, the triangles actually work against resolution. A person who is differentiated does not need to bring in a third party to reduce tension. Consider the case of Pamela and Ralph who came to therapy after one year of marriage. Pamela came from a very enmeshed family, and was particularly close to her mother, who helped her make all decisions. Ralph came from a family with somewhat rigid boundaries and reported that he did not feel particularly close to his parents or his siblings. His siblings were scattered across the county, and his parents lived about 500 miles away. The couple had recently bought a new house, and Pamela was quite concerned about furnishing it well. She had sought her mother's advice, and her mother had suggested that she purchase good quality furnishings. Ralph disagreed, saying that they were not in a position to buy expensive furniture, and that they should buy furniture gradually. Arguments over this occurred frequently, and Pamela's response was to talk with her mother. When she talked with her mother, she felt better and felt more justified in her position; however, time with Ralph became more and more uncomfortable because it was filled with conflict. Consequently, Pamela began spending more time with her mother, and Ralph began spending more time with friends from work. Although both spouses could contain their anxiety by being away from each other, the real problem—how to spend their money—was not reaching an agreeable solution, and the marital relationship was deteriorating.

Pamela's tendency to seek out and actually need her mother's advice and approval when she and her husband could not agree suggested that her level of differentiation was low. A person with low differentiation has difficulty establishing one-to-one relationships without including a third person in anxiety-provoking situations, and this is a hindrance to establishing a marital bond.

Transmission Parents who are undifferentiated transmit this on to their children through the family projection process. Spouses who are fused are often anxious and experience marital conflict. Then one of the mates attempts to seek stability and assurance by triangulating the child, who is hoping the parent will provide him or her some stability and assurance. An example of this is the case of Bill and Martha, who married shortly after high school—both had very negative relationships with their parents. It was the unconscious hope of each that the other person would provide what was missing in his or her life. When neither spouse was able to fill the gap in the other's life, conflict arose. The conflict was very anxiety-provoking, and Martha tended to avoid this tension by getting involved with the daughter. As she spent more time with her daughter, age 10, her daughter became less and less involved in age-appropriate activities and chores. As her daughter began to exhibit more dependency on her mother, Martha became even more protective, stating that her daughter was unable to do things on her own. When the focus shifted from the parent's conflict and rested on the child's problems, the triangle became more stable. That is, tension was reduced; however, the couple remained fused and the child was brought into the emotional process, preventing her from developing a self of her own.

There are also examples of couples that have several children, with the children showing different levels of differentiation. That is, one may have a very strong sense of self and low emotional reactivity, while another sibling may have a very poorly defined sense of self and high emotional reactivity. This may occur when one child is chosen as a way of diffusing tension. For instance, a parent may select a child who is handicapped or tends to be ill often and needs help, or a child who is already less sure of himself. The tension may consistently be projected onto that child. When much of the family anxiety is directed toward the child, the parents are more able to have a conflict-free marriage.

Another of Bowen's concepts about differentiation concerns multigenerational transmission. He theorized that an undifferentiated couple will have children who are undifferentiated, and that each subsequent generation will move toward an even lower level of differentiation, resulting in emotional problems. Kerr (1981) gives a case example of a mother who felt insecure in interpersonal relationships and manifested this by focusing on any sign in the child that might indicate similar insecurity. As a result, she increasingly related to the child as if he were insecure and the child began acting more and more in a way that confirmed the mother's diagnosis. Once the process was in place, both the parent and child played roles that continued it. In this way, the mother's undifferentiation was transmitted to her child.

Emotional Cutoff Emotional cutoff refers to the way persons deal with their attachments to their families of origin at the point of separation. In a very undifferentiated family, with a high level of triangulation, the separation process becomes more difficult. There will likely be what Bowen calls unresolved emotional attachments that may be handled various ways. Some persons attempt denial, some isolate themselves, some develop a pseudo-self. None of these attempts will be successful until the person can develop a sense of self. Some individuals run away from their families of origin and deny their unresolved emotional attachments. Sometimes, these attachments appear as disengaged families; however, with a closer look, it may be apparent that the person is in fact emotionally dependent on his or her family of origin. Bowen (1976, p. 84) argued that "the more intense an individual's cutoff with the past, the more likely the individual is to have an exaggerated version of his parental family problem in his own marriage, and the more likely his own children are to do a more intense cutoff with him in the next generation." Emotional cutoff, then, cannot be confused with the person who truly speaks from an "I" perspective of what he or she really believes.

According to Bowen, in an ideal marriage, partners have reached a high degree of differentiation, and can be emotionally intimate without losing a sense of self. This couple, when they have children, will rear the children to be their own persons without forcing them to be whatever the parents want them to be. Family members rely on themselves and succeed or fail according to their own efforts. This does not mean that the family is uncaring; it does mean that each person in the family accepts responsibility for his emotions, rather than blaming them on someone else.

Invisible Loyalties No couple or family starts out with a clean slate. Rather, each partner brings into the marriage the heritage of past generations of families. Fair parental behavior creates loyalty in the children; however, unfair demands or an extreme sense of obligation may produce an "invisible loyalty," in which the child continues to try to pay off a debt to parents, often to his or her own detriment. Invisible loyalties provide a major link between generations. Relationships in the new family will be built on these potentially unconscious invisible loyalties, that are a bond to the family of origin of each spouse, as well as the families of origins of previous generations. Each couple enters marriage with a ledger containing both a legacy and a record of an individual's accumulated merit. This record combines what one is due as a parent or as a child, as well as what one merits or deserves. The legacy comes simply from being born of particular parents, and from taking on a role accorded to the child in the family. The loyalty is more than just a feeling of owing parents something for raising them. It is related to loyalties, legacies, and unhealed wounds in the history of the family.

For example, Melanie came to therapy because of depression. She said there was no happiness at all in her life; her husband had been threatening to leave because she had been so low and moody. She related that she felt she should be happy because she had just quit her job as church organist, was now staying at home, and had more free time for herself and her children; yet, she was feeling worse than ever. Melanie kept saying that she felt she had let everyone down; however, when pressed for more explanation, she was unable to say anything other than, "I'm just so low that I'm no good to anybody. I feel like such a failure."

As the therapist got more information about Melanie's background, some invisible loyalties became evident. The therapist discovered that Melanie's mother was an avid music lover and was a choir director in a church. However, she had never been able to pursue her love of music in a formal way because of inadequate finances, and she had made a resolve that if she had children, she would give them every opportunity in this area. She had two daughters, one of whom had little talent for music; therefore, Melanie, who seemed adept, received her mother's focus. Her mother had made numerous sacrifices for Melanie to take piano and organ lessons and had been very strict about practice and performances. She had saved money for Melanie to go to college and study music. Instead, Melanie had met someone and married right after finishing high school. To make her mother happy, she had at first volunteered to play the piano at church, and later had taken a position as church organist, but Melanie had never really enjoyed the practice and being tied down.

After Melanie's mother died, she decided to quit the organist job. She had talked it over with her husband who gave his approval. After quitting, she became very depressed but she could not figure out why. Through therapy, she began to see how she felt she had let her mother down by not pursuing music, even after all the opportunities she had been given, and how those loyalties were affecting her relationship with her husband.

It should be noted that in this case, family loyalty created stress for Melanie. However, family loyalty also allows family members to make sacrifices for each other and to care for each other. Spouses who received fair and equitable behavior as children are more aware that they need to repay what they "owe" to their parents by being good parents to their children. Conversely, however, children who did not receive fair and equitable behavior (such as being born to abusive parents) tend, without intervention, to continue the pattern by becoming abusive to their children.

Object Relations   From birth, a person attempts to establish relationships with external objects that can satisfy needs. Object relations theory grew out of the work of Freud, but is based more on early mother–infant relationships and the long-lasting impact of early experiences on later adult functioning. Object relations can be further described as the emotional attachment between one person and another, or a person's capacity for relating and loving others. The theory suggests that an infant's primary need is for attachment to a caring person, such as the mother. The child develops mental images or subjective experiences (introjects) that are carried into adult life. Therefore, adults relate to people in the present at least partly on the basis of perceptions and expectations they developed in formative years.

Each object relation has a self-representation, an object representation, and an affective component (Sperry & Carlson, 1991). The first object relationship—mother and infant—shapes the kind of interpersonal relationships a person will have later. In troubled marriages, one or both partners may have introjects (memories of the parents or other figures) that are negative, which tend to create conflict within the marriage. For instance, a spouse who has a critical introject (a critical relationship that has been internalized) tends to see relationships in that light. Therefore, any comment made to that spouse will be viewed as critical and will bring on defensiveness or an inappropriate response.

One example of an object relations therapeutic approach is seen in the work of Framo. Framo (1981) theorized that intrapsychic conflicts gained from the family of origin continue to be acted out in current relationships, such as those with a spouse or children. He argues that many of a couple's conflicts are related to a spouse trying to resolve inner conflicts through the marital relationship. Framo's theory is based on work by Fairbairn (1954) and Dicks (1967). He also says that people try to influence or change relationships so that they are closer to what they are used to—internalized models. Therefore, couples come into a marriage with preconceived notions about how a wife or husband acts, as well as how a mother or father acts, and they are uncomfortable when those behaviors do not occur.

A second object relations therapeutic approach is offered by Dicks (1967) who expanded Fairbairn's ideas to include interactions between spouses. He said that marital relations are inevitably influenced by experiences in each spouse's family of origin. In disturbed marriages, each partner relates to the other in terms of unconscious needs, and each tries to complete himself through the other.

Some of the major tenets of object relations theory according to Framo (1981, p. 137–138) are:

1. People need a satisfactory object relationship.
2. Since infants can't give up or change the maternal object, they incorporate it into their world as "introjects" or representatives of the objects.
3. The introjects change over the years as people develop new relationships.
4. When conflicts arise in the family, the person tries to repair these by making them fit their internal role models.
5. A person's choice of mate and treatment of children is based on a projective process by which spouses and children become stand-ins for past primary object relationships.
6. Therapy is a process of working through and removing introjects.

Framo (1981) discusses three treatment stages. In the first, he works with the couple to establish a trusting relationship with each spouse. Communication skills are emphasized at this time. He educates the couple about object relations theory, and shows them how unresolved issues in their family of origin may have contributed to their present difficulties. In the second stage, he uses a couples group format, usually with three couples, and the group helps spouses understand their relationships and how to improve them. In the third stage, Framo shifts to family of origin issues. These are individual sessions, and each spouse is encouraged to contact his or her family of origin and work toward resolving some old issues. Framo states that this approach is not appropriate for couples with minor conflicts, but can be effective with couples who have serious conflicts relating back to family of origin issues.

Therapeutic Skills

Transgenerational therapists place much emphasis on understanding and insight. It is the therapist's role to remain objective to reduce the emotional reactivity in the couple. That is, the therapist is an observer who thinks in terms of systems and not in terms of the emotional processes of the couple. Some specific skills that are used in the therapy process follow.

Coaching Bowen (1978) uses the term "coaching" to describe his role in supervising patients in the process of differentiation of self. He described his role as similar to that of a coach–athlete relationship. He motivates and helps get the client started, at which point the client must do the actual work. The real learning occurs when the client is working toward his or her goals outside the therapy session.

Bowen indicated that it is imperative for the therapist to remain impartial and objective and not get caught up in the emotional process of the couple. To do so requires that the therapist have a high level of differentiation from his or her own family of origin and not be "hooked" by the emotionality of the marital system. That is, the therapist must remain calm and objective and become a model for the spouses to remain calm and rational. To maintain such objectivity, the therapist should ask "thinking" questions instead of "feeling" questions and should avoid becoming triangulated.

If the therapist becomes a part of the emotional system, he or she will know that triangulation has occurred. To avoid triangulation, two techniques have been used. Bowen (1978) does not allow spouses to talk to each other; rather, the conversation is directed through him. Boszormenyi-Nagy (1965) and Framo (1965) suggest that the therapist alternate the partner with whom he or she aligns. When the therapist remains unreactive and the couple addresses their concerns through him, the couple then interacts more calmly and learns to communicate emotional concerns without becoming reactive. This helps the spouses to differentiate and detriangulate.

The goal of therapy is self-differentiation, but therapists cannot make this happen unless the client is motivated. Therefore, the therapist serves as consultant, or coach, and helps the client move from a pure feeling level to a rational, intellectual processing level. Therapists can remain neutral better when they fully understand the family projection process and triangulation and remember that the focus is on fact—not feeling.

The transgenerationalist takes the view that for lasting change to occur, spouses must learn not to react emotionally to each other. By interacting calmly with the therapist, each spouse learns to tolerate emotional discussions without reacting to the other. By remaining an objective third party to whom the couple addresses their feelings, the therapist is able to help the couple become less emotionally reactive.

Taking the "I" Position One way to help increase objectivity on the part of the therapist, as well as to help spouses reach differentiation, is through "I" statements. When spouses tell their mates that "I wish you would be more helpful," rather than "You are really lazy," there is less emotional reactivity and a greater probability that the spouse will respond. The therapist may find these statements useful as well.

Work With Genograms The genogram is a tool that allows the therapist and couple to examine their family in its intergenerational context. In his earliest work, Bowen used what he called a "family diagram" to collect and organize data concerning the multigenerational family system (Nichols & Schwartz, 2001). Guerin (1972) renamed the family diagram the "genogram" and that is the name that has been used ever since.

The genogram provides a three-generational map of the family. It is a structured way to receive information about the family. Some information typically collected includes ethnic origins, religious affiliations, economic status, locations of family members, types of contacts, and by whom contacts are made. Significant events such as dates of marriages, deaths, and divorce are listed.

Genograms can provide a great deal of information by visually mapping patterns and relationships. It is helpful to see the family in context. The genogram helps the couple see its roots in its multigenerational history. As details of past family happenings and personalities are brought out, myths, rules, secrets, and skeletons are also brought to light and examined in terms of their impact on the couple. Understanding and mapping some of this history leads to the next technique—dealing with family of origin, or "going home again."

Family of Origin Work According to Bowen, differentiation starts as an individual process, and progresses into the changing of relationships in the marital system. One technique in the process of differentiation is for spouses to be instructed to "go home again." Because spouses may be "stuck" in some patterns and emotions that they brought from their family of origin, Bowen says it is crucial that they return and renew old relationships in an effort to gain insight. He encourages clients to develop specific strategies for visiting their family of origin, and then meets with them when they return.

Bowen's family of origin work involves three prominent strategies (Brown & Christensen, 1999). The first is encouragement of "person-to-person" relationships. This means, practically, that a spouse is able to have a relationship with wife or husband that is not the same as the relationship with mother or father. The wife would see her husband as separate from her father, and would not expect him to behave (either positively or negatively) in the same way her father did.

A second strategy for dealing with family of origin is for a client to observe his or her emotional reactiveness. Bowen stated that to be aware of one's emotional reactiveness is an effective way to control it. Therefore, when a spouse went "home again," it would be in an attitude of observing and learning, and with the resolve not to become emotionally reactive.

The third strategy is for the client to avoid triangulation or taking sides (either emotionally or verbally) during emotional situations. The spouse may be encouraged to go home during times of emotional stress or crisis when triangling is most likely to occur, but he or she goes with the instruction of staying emotionally neutral in issues that involve two other family members. That means that the spouse will not take sides with anyone, will not become defensive, and will not feel himself or herself becoming emotionally aroused. Avoiding triangulation is difficult and requires conscious effort.

Detriangling Detriangling is the process of a person's keeping himself outside the emotional field of two others. Two persons who are in a conflict automatically try to involve a third person in order to decrease anxiety. If that third person gets involved in the emotional system, the anxiety is relieved, but the problem is not solved, and patterns tend to be repeated. The goal of therapy, according to Bowen (1978) is the differentiation of one's self from one's spouse as a cooperative effort. Bowen states that the "magic" of therapy occurs when two people are working on self-differentiation in the presence of a potential "triangle" (the therapist), who remains emotionally detached. The couple must care enough about each other to endure the stress of "differentiation," and anxious enough about their situation to motivate them to work. Because the couple will want to reduce anxiety by attempting to get the therapist to take sides, it is essential that the therapist stay rational and not respond to these attempts. In this way, the spouses can begin to deal directly with each other and change some of their dysfunctional patterns.

Bowen gives an example of two small differentiation steps with a couple. A wife, after much discussion and thought, told her husband, "I've decided to take all the energy I've been spending on making you happy and put it into making myself a more responsible woman and mother. What I've been doing hasn't worked anyway." The husband's response was anger, but within a week, he was happy with his "new" wife. Some weeks later, after much thinking on his part, he related that if he spent time with the family, he felt guilty about neglecting work, and if he worked overtime, he felt guilty about neglecting his family and that he had a plan for dealing with that. These small steps occurred because the therapist remained neutral and allowed them to talk with each other, without becoming a part of their emotional system.

Relationship Experiments Relationship experiments are designed to help family members become aware of systems process and see how they are involved in these processes. Fogarty (1976) has used such experiments with distancers and pursuers. Distancers are encouraged by the therapist to move toward the other person and communicate feelings and emotions, whereas pursuers are encouraged to stop the pursuit and stop expecting closeness from the other. The idea is to see what happens and see what changes occur in each person and in the relationship as a result.

Exoneration In contextual therapy (Boszormenyi-Nagy & Ulrich, 1981), the therapist uses exoneration to help spouses see the positive intent and inter-generational loyalty issues that may help explain behavior of members of pre-vious generations. The family legacy may slate one son to be successful ("You can do anything"), while it slates another to be a failure ("You mess up every-thing you try"). The children seem bound to accommodate their lives to these legacies, messages, or life scripts. Even though some of these legacies are very destructive, the therapist helps the client see them in human context, exoner-ate those past generations, and rebuild responsible, trustworthy behavior. The work of therapy, then, is to uncover and resolve family "obligations" and "debts" incurred over time.

Interpretation Interpretation is the form of communication the therapist uses to bring out unconscious meaning in situations. When it occurs, it typi-cally helps the person become calmer, because it shifts the focus from feelings to thought. It is also reassuring to clients at times to have someone explain behavior that the person cannot understand and may not like about him or herself. Furthermore, this approach models a thinking versus an emotional reactive stance to emotional situations, and helps the couple see an alternative way to respond to situations. Finally, interpretations help take away some "blame" for current situations, in the sense that they reframe difficulties now as unresolved difficulties or relationships in the past, allowing the couple to remove themselves from a very emotionally charged situation. When they can put aside the emotional reactiveness, they are better able to resolve some of the conflict.

The purpose of interpretation is to make the unconscious conscious, in other words, to provide insight to the couple. Interpretations may be made of a couple's resistance, which often operates by avoiding painful and anxiety-provoking unconscious thoughts. By interpreting and working through the resistances, spouses can gain insight and increase marital satisfaction.

Interpretations of transference are also important. When negative images and thoughts are projected onto one spouse, that spouse is likely to respond in a negative manner that may be related to his or her internalized objects. This results in the maintenance of marital discord, which can sometimes be redi-rected when the couple is aware of their distortions. Interpretation gives the couple a way to understand its irrational behavior, and understanding helps spouses feel less guilt, confusion, and self-blame.

Transference Transference refers to a person's earlier experiences, and suggests that the person's current relationships are modeled on past relationships. That is, the model from the past is often transferred to the new situation. Greenberg and Michael (1983, p. 10) state that people react to and interact not just with the actual person but with "internal others"—those models they have brought from earlier situations. Sometimes, those feelings are transferred to the therapist (she or he becomes the critical parent or critical spouse). In the context of treatment, transference refers to the individual's misperceptions of the therapist's feelings and motives. The client may also have similar misperceptions that he or she attributed to parental figures and misperceptions that he or she attributes to the spouse.

Transference analysis is important in transgenerational family therapy because it permits the couple to experience the past in the present. Through the interpretation of the therapeutic relationship as something similar to a past relationship, spouses become aware of how the past relationship was incomplete and how they continue to work on past relationships through present ones. Interpretation of the transference relationship also enables the couple to gain control by shifting the conflict from the unconscious emotional system to the conscious rational system.

Therapeutic Process

When Tim and Patty become emotional during the discussion, the therapist models differentiated (calm) behavior that is empathic, but not emotionally reactive to the couple's level of emotion. When they express anger toward each other over current conflicts, the therapist does not take sides but seeks understanding of each point of view, allowing each to confirm or correct the therapist's understanding. As each side of the conflict is clarified, the therapist begins to ask questions intended to diffuse emotional reactivity and to help Tim and Patty listen to each other. Throughout the session, the therapist monitors himself to avoid triangulation. When Patty complains that Tim is "never there" for her or the baby, the therapist is interested primarily in Patty's thoughts and feelings. Tim is given the opportunity to listen to Patty with some distance instead of having to respond to her in direct interaction. Thus, the process provides an opportunity for the therapist to help Tim and Patty to differentiate, while the content of their interactions is of less importance.

At the end of the session, the therapist gets a brief history of Tim and Patty's families of origin and their emotional evolution with each other. He learns that Patty was never able to speak up in her family of origin, and her behavior was motivated either by feelings of gratitude for all the things her mother did for her, or guilt for being unappreciative or less than perfect. She felt anger toward her mother but could not express it openly; rather, she expressed it in more subtle ways, such as getting pregnant. She established a similar relationship with Tim in that she felt appreciative that he married her, yet guilty that she wanted more from him than he was willing to give. In most instances, she did whatever Tim expected. However, her growing anger that

Tim did not help with the baby was not expressed openly but was dealt with by spending more time with the baby or with her mother who agreed that Tim should be more attentive to her and to the baby.

Tim grew up in a disengaged family where emotions were infrequently expressed but where his mother was very attentive to his needs and to the needs of his father. She did what she was asked to do, rarely asked anything for herself, and never complained. Tim was not expected to help around the house and was given a great deal of freedom. He expected this as a part of his marriage; when his wife seemed unhappy, he spent more and more time at work.

Through therapy, it became clear to both members of the couple that Patty tended to triangulate with her mother or the baby when she experienced anxiety and Tim tended to triangulate work. Tim did not know how to deal with crying and particularly wanted to escape when Patty cried. He felt that if he worked hard, there should be no expectations, for him around the house.

The therapist talked with the two individuals about their background experiences and expectations and since the other person was not allowed to speak—only to listen—that person gained more understanding of the other spouse. This allowed them to respond from a reasoning mode versus an emotionally reactive stance.

Both Patty and Tim were given assignments to gather more family history and write letters to the family members and review these with the therapist. The therapist also asked Tim and Patty to spend more time with each other without interference from friends and work. Each was asked to take turns getting a babysitter so that time with each other would be possible. In subsequent sessions, reviews of the assignment provided useful information to help the couple discuss their unresolved issues. The therapist coached each spouse with assignments to decrease emotional reactivity.

SOLUTION-FOCUSED
MARITAL THERAPY MODEL

Solution-focused therapy represents a departure from earlier models that were heavily influenced by the disease or dysfunction model. In the disease model, the therapist and couple search for underlying family pathology to explain why symptoms occur in a couple, family, or individual. Therapy is aimed at helping the couple achieve insight into reasons for the problem, and provide a way to restructure the family or couple and help them return to health. Solution-focused brief therapy, on the other hand, discourages such speculating about why symptoms arose, and instead encourages the couple and therapist to talk about the solution they want to construct together. Instead of "problem talk," the therapist urges "solution talk." In fact, discussion of "the problem" is avoided.

This approach was based on the work of social worker Steve deShazer, Insoo Berg, and other associates at the Brief Family Therapy Center in Milwaukee. One associate, Michelle Weiner-Davis (1992), has used the solution-focused brief therapy model extensively with couples, and Bill O'Hanlon has helped interpret the model to therapists through his writing and training programs. According to deShazer (1985), dysfunction essentially arises from faulty attempts at problem solution; the couple is simply unable to think of other ways to deal with the problem. Two hallmarks of this approach, both of which come from the work of Milton Erickson, are a future orientation and a focus on solutions rather than problems.

Solution-focused therapists do not have an ideal image of a couple or family and therefore rely on the couple to determine the goals they want to reach in treatment. They assume that clients have the skills and resources to solve their own problems but have lost sight of alternative ways to approach the situation. In some cases, they have practiced the "more of the same" kinds of solutions that did not work the first time and still do not with more practice. The therapist's role, then, is to help them use the skills they already have to find solutions not previously tried or to remind them what they have tried in the past that has been successful.

Solution-focused brief therapy has become a very popular model because of its "pragmatic minimalism, cognitive emphasis, and easily teachable techniques" (Nichols & Schwartz, 2001, p. 371). It deemphasizes history and underlying pathology, is brief, and focuses on solutions that have worked.

Therapeutic Assumptions and Concepts

Focusing on the Past Is Unnecessary   The focus should be on the future, where problems can be solved. In contrast to therapists who think people must understand how the past contributed to their present problems, solution-based therapists see past information as irrelevant and actually ineffective in changing situations. Insight gained from the past may offer no ideas about what to change. Because the solution to a problem may be totally unrelated to how it developed, it is unnecessary and time consuming to go into it. The emphasis, instead, should be on what the couple hopes for the future and how to achieve this.

The Focus Is on Solutions—Not Problems   Solution-focused therapists emphasize exceptions to the problem (when the problem did not occur) and develop new solutions that work.

The Couple Knows What Needs to Be Done to Solve the Problem   Solution-based therapists believe that people know themselves best, and that they know best what needs to change in their relationships. Therapy begins, therefore, with the question, "What would you like to change?" If couples complain about how money is spent, this becomes the area of focus. If they complain about too much time away from each other, they search for solutions to have more time together. The therapist does not assume that there is some underlying problem and does not attribute motive or meaning to how money is spent.

It Is More Effective to Build on Strengths Than on Weaknesses In traditional therapy, clients often talk about their shortcomings and weaknesses. In the solution-based model, the therapist looks instead for strengths of clients to help them feel more capable and creative.

Clients Who Come Asking for Change Do Not Resist Change Clients want to be cooperative and change, but they sometimes are not sure how to go about doing it. If they are resistive, it is to interpretations or interventions that do not seem to fit. Solution-focused therapists have discovered that the less resistance expected from clients, the less is observed.

A Rapid Resolution of Problems Is Possible Solution-focused therapists say that the average length of treatment varies, but it generally falls under ten sessions, and is usually about four to six. Most clients report improvement or goal attainment quickly and follow-up research indicates that the changes are lasting (Kiser, 1990).

Small Changes Lead to Bigger Changes Solution-focused therapists assert that small changes in a troubled marriage can turn things around. Weiner-Davis (1992) gives an example of an unhappy couple that began to see big changes because of a small change. The husband surprised the wife with a kiss one morning. The kiss led to her making coffee, which led to the two of them talking as they shared coffee, which led to a more pleasant work day, greater relaxation in the evening, and more positive feelings about each other. Wiener-Davis goes on to say that one conciliatory gesture can create a positive snowball effect that is in contrast to long-term debating over which person is right.

Understanding Follows Behavior Change The solution-focused therapist believes that behavior should change first and that perceptions and awareness change afterward, in contrast to psychodynamic theorists who contend that real change is not possible without insight. Rather than waiting and striving to get negative thoughts and feelings to go away so the spouse feels like doing something nice for his or her partner, taking action may be the best first step, and changes in feelings will follow.

Therapy Is Action Focused—Not Feeling Focused The solution-focused therapist is not likely to ask, "How do you feel?" Rather, the question is, "What needs to happen for you to be happy?" The focus, then, is on changes that need to occur, and not on the feelings that are maintaining the problems.

Therapeutic Skills

The solution-focused therapist uses a set of very specific skills that are used to work with couples and families. Some of these are discussed in this section.

Focus on What Works No matter how severe a couple's problems may be when they enter therapy, they most likely have experienced some times that are peaceful, smooth, and even enjoyable. When a person is in crisis, however, he or she is not likely to recall those times and may consider them oddities or unusual occurrences. One skill that solution-focused therapists use is to help couples recall some of their trouble-free times, and assess just what was different about those times versus the times of much conflict. As Weiner-Davis (1992, p. 118) expresses it, "people need to do more of what works until the positive times crowd out the negative ones." Suppose that a couple comes to therapy and the wife says, "He is never affectionate." The therapist may ask if there has ever been a time that he was affectionate. When was he affectionate? What was going on at that time? These kinds of questions highlight the false perception of "never" and help the wife think of what she did differently that helped create the affectionate moments. Weiner-Davis (1992, pp. 124, 125) says that exceptions are helpful for four reasons:

1. *"Exceptions shrink problems."* If there is even one exception, words such as "can't," "always," or "never" are no longer correct. The complaint, "He is never affectionate," may become "He is affectionate when we are not arguing," or "He is affectionate when we have a nice evening together."

2. *"Exceptions show that people can change."* A husband who says, "My wife is very critical of my friends. She just can't help herself because that's just the way she is," may realize when he looks for exceptions that she does not always criticize, and that there is some hope for her to have more time that she is not critical.

3. *"Exceptions supply solutions."* When couples talk about exceptions, they actually begin to think of what they did at other times to keep the problem behavior from occurring, and when they leave therapy, they have a plan for how to create more positive times.

4. *"The focus on exceptions empowers people."* Through looking at times when conditions were good or pleasant, the couple realizes that they have been doing some things right. Even though they thought they had tried everything, they realize that they have some resources.

In order for exceptions to exert positive change, a couple must know how to identify them. Some questions that may be helpful in this regard include the following:

▪ What is different about times when your relationship is positive or free of conflict?

▪ Think about earlier years in your marriage when your relationship was satisfying. What was going on then?

▪ How do your conflicts end? (By determining what happens just before the partners call a truce, they can then make choices to cut fights short by meeting the needs of the partner.)

- If you cannot think of any exceptions, when is the problem less intense, less frequent, or shorter in duration?
- What is different about the times when the problem situation occurs, but something good comes out of it?
- What is different about the times the problem situation occurs, but you were not bothered by it?

In addition to questions about exceptions, the solution-focused therapist also asks what deShazer (1991, p. 113) refers to as the "miracle question." This question essentially asks the client to suppose that a miracle occurs some night while he or she is sleeping and that the problem is solved. He asks how the person would know, what would be different, what would tell them the next morning that the miracle occurred, and what the spouse would notice. This allows spouses to talk about what their lives will be like when the problem is solved.

Anticipate Change and Recognize the Power of Small Changes The solution-focused therapist uses questions that provide hope and encouragement to clients. For instance, instead of asking, "What problems brought you here?", the therapist might ask, "How can we work together to help you change your situation?". Through talking about exceptions (or times when the problem behavior has not occurred), the couple creates new, empowering stories about themselves. The therapist also creates expectations for change by virtue of the short number of sessions. Another way the expectation for change is addressed is through the language of the questions. A case is reported by deShazer (1985) of a woman trying to be a perfect mother and expressing frustration about yelling at her children. The therapist asked her, "What sort of thing do you think will happen when you start to take a more calm . . . approach to your children?" Asking a question that uses the "when" versus "if" implies that the mother *will* become calmer, and that there will be some change in children's behavior when this happens.

As mentioned earlier, small changes lead to big changes. This is what Weiner-Davis refers to as the "butterfly effect." Questions that can be answered on a scale of 1 to 10, with 1 being the worst and 10 being the best, can also identify small changes. The therapist might ask, "Rate yourself on how well you showed appreciation for your wife last week—this week." Such ratings might show that there has been some improvement over the week. This also provides a way to discuss what is different about the ratings. What was different on the day your rating was a 9 versus the day your rating was a 4?

Let Client Goals Be the Focus In solution-focused therapy, the therapist listens as the couple describe their situations and the resolution they hope to achieve. The therapist is the leader, but he or she is directed by client goals, and together the therapist and couple develop possible solutions to reach these goals.

Normalize the Couple's Problems Solution-focused therapists devote little time to discussions of problems. In fact, the therapist has little interest in all the details and instead is more interested in what has worked for the clients. By not focusing on problems, couples are likely to be less defensive and to display more hope that their conflict or problem situation can be resolved.

Therapeutic Process

A solution-focused therapist asked Tim and Patty to describe times when things went well (exceptions), even though they were few and far between. When Patty and Tim failed to recognize anything positive about the exceptions, the therapist used his own observations of Patty and Tim to create a picture of competence and cooperation. He then got them to identify times when Tim complied with Patty's request for help, and times when Tim was attentive to her. Subsequent sessions were used to report successes. When the couple got discouraged, the therapist normalized their struggle (caring for an infant) and compared their current progress in working together to their old behavior. The therapist remarked how they were able to stop the old patterns of arguing and focus on what they needed to do for each other and the child. The therapist also addressed the future, "What does this say about you if you continue to work as a team?"

CONCLUSION

In this chapter, five theoretical orientations are discussed. The therapeutic assumptions, concepts, skills, and therapeutic process were presented for each of these orientations. Differences and similarities in content and process between models are highlighted to provide the beginning practitioner a foundation for theory integration. The therapeutic process as it relates to a specific case example was described as well.

KEY POINTS

- While models of marital therapy appear dissimilar, they also share many similarities in practice.
- The structural model of therapy focuses on the interactions of the family to determine the organization or structure of the marital relationship.
- The strategic model of therapy focuses on a specific strategy for each goal.
- Brief family therapy recognizes the therapist's role in helping the couple build on what is working in the relationship to manage problems.

- Behavioral marital therapy examines how rewards and punishments influence the marital relationship.

- Transgenerational therapists are concerned with how the past operates in current marital relationships, and how current marital relationships have evolved over the generations.

- The solution-focused model of therapy shifts the focus from the dysfunctional side of the marital relationship to what is working with the couple.

MARITAL SKILLS INVENTORY

Please check when you have completed these procedures.

_____   Assess the organization of the marital relationship.

_____   Assess interactions around the problem.

_____   Assess exchange of desirable and undesirable behaviors in the relationship.

_____   Assess how past transgenerational issues trigger current problems.

_____   Assess positive changes or exceptions in the relationship.

REFERENCES

Ables, B. S., & Brandsma, J. M. (1977). *Therapy for couples.* San Francisco: Jossey Bass.

Aponte, H. & Van Deusen, J. (1981). Structural family therapy. In A.S. Gurman & D. Kniskern (Eds.), *Handbook of family therapy* (pp. 310–360). New York: Brunner/Mazel.

Becvar, D. S., and Becvar, R. J. (2000). *Family therapy: A systemic intergration.* Boston: Allyn & Bacon.

Boszormenyi-Nagy, I. (1965). A theory of relationships: Experience and transaction. In I. Boszormenyi-Nagy & J. Framo (Eds.), *Intensive family therapy: Theoretical and practical aspects.* New York: Harper & Row.

Boszormenyi-Nagy, I., & Ulrich, D. N. (1981). Contextual family therapy. In A. S. Gurman & D. P. Kniskern (Eds.), *Handbook of family therapy.* New York: Brunner/Mazel.

Bowen, M. (1976). Theory in the practice of psychotherapy. In P. J. Guerin, Jr.

(Ed.), *Family therapy: Theory and practice* (pp. 42–90). New York: Gardner Press.

Bowen, M. (1978). *Family therapy in clinical practice.* New York: Aronson.

Bross, A., & Benjamin, M. (1983). Family therapy: A recursive model of strategic practice. In A. Bross (Ed.), *Family therapy: Principles of strategic practice.* New York: Guilford.

Brown, J. H., & Christensen, D. (1999). *Family therapy: Theory and practice* (2nd ed.). Pacific Grove, CA: Brooks/Cole.

deShazer, S. (1985). *Keys to solution in brief therapy.* New York: Norton.

deShazer, S. (1991) *Putting differences to work.* New York: Norton.

Dicks, H. (1967). *Marital tensions.* New York: Basic Books.

D'Zurilla, T. J., & Goldfried, M. R. (1971). Problem solving and behavior modification. *Journal of American Psychology, 78,* 107–126.

Fairbairn, W. (1954). *An object-relations theory of personality.* New York: Basic Books.

Fogarty, T. F. (1976). Marital crisis. In P. J. Guerin, Jr. (Ed.), *Family therapy: Theory and practice.* New York: Gardner Press

Framo, J. (1965). Rationale and technique of intensive family therapy. In I. Boszormenyi-Nagy & J. Framo (Eds.), *Intensive family therapy: Theoretical and practical aspects.* New York: Harper & Row.

Framo, J. (1981). The integration of marital therapy with sessions with family of origin. In A. S. Gurman & D. P. Kniskern (Eds.), *Handbook of family therapy* (pp. 133–158). New York: Brunner/Mazel.

Gelfland, D. M., & Hartmann, D. P. (1975). *Child behavior: Analysis and therapy.* Elmsford, NJ: Pergamon Press.

Goldfried, M. R., & Davison, G. C. (1976). *Clinical behavior therapy.* New York: Holt, Rinehart & Winston.

Goldfried, M. R., & Sprafkin, J. (1974). *Behavioral personality assessment.* Morristown, NJ: General Learning Press.

Greenberg, J. R. & Mitchell, S. (1983). *Object relations and psychoanalytic theory.* Cambridge, MA: Harvard University Press.

Guerin, P. J. (1972). We became family therapists. In A. Ferber, M. Mendelsohn, and A. Napier (Eds.), *The book of family therapy.* New York: Science House.

Gurman, A. S., & Kniskern, D. P. (1978). Research on marital and family therapy: Progress, perspective and prospect. In S. L. Garfield & A. E. Bergin (Eds.). *Handbook of psychotherapy and behavior change: An empirical analysis* (2nd ed.). New York: Wiley.

Haley, J. (1963). *Strategies of psychotherapy.* New York: Grune & Stratton.

Haley, J. (Ed.). (1976). *Problem-solving therapy.* San Francisco: Jossey Bass.

Hansen, J., Pound, R., & Warner, R. (1976). Use of modeling procedures.

Personnel and Guidance Journal, 54, 242–245.

Harrell, J., & Guerney, B. (1976). Training married couples in conflict negotiation skills. In D. H. L. Olson (Ed.), *Treating relationships.* Lake Mills, IA: Graphic.

Hoffman, L. (1981). *Foundations of family therapy.* New York: Basic Books.

Hosford, R., & de Visser, C. (1974). *Behavioral counseling: An introduction.* Washington, DC: American Personnel and Guidance Press.

Jacob, T. (1976). Assessment of marital dysfunction. In M. Hensen & A. S. Bellack (Eds.), *Behavioral assessment: A practical handbook.* New York: Pergamon Press.

Jacobson, N. S. (1981). Behavioral marital therapy. In A. S. Gurman & D. P. Kniskern (Eds.), *Handbook of family therapy.* New York: Brunner/Mazel.

Jacobson, N. S., & Margolin, G. (1979. *Marital therapy: Strategies based on social learning and behavioral exchange principles.* New York: Brunner/Mazel.

Kerr, M. (1981). Family systems theory and therapy. In A. S. Gurman & D. P. Kniskern (Eds.), *Handbook of family therapy* (pp. 226–266). New York: Brunner/Mazel.

Kiser, D. (1990). Brief therapy on the couch. *Family Therapy Networker.* March–April.

Krumboltz, J., Varenhorst, B., & Thoresen, C. (1967). Nonverbal factors in effectiveness of models in counseling. *Journal of Counseling Psychology, 14,* 412–418.

Mace, D. R. (1979). Marriage and family enrichment—A new field. *Family Coordinator, 28,* 408–419.

Minuchin, S. (1974). *Families and family therapy.* Cambridge, MA: Harvard University Press.

Minuchin, S., & Fishman, H. C. (1981). *Family therapy techniques.* Cambridge, MA: Harvard University Press.

Nichols, M. (1984). *Family therapy: Concepts and methods.* New York: Gardner Press.

Nichols, M., & Schwartz, R. (1991). *Family therapy: Concepts and methods* (2nd ed.), Needham Heights, MA: Allyn & Bacon.

Nichols, M., & Schwartz, R. (2001). *Family therapy: Concepts and methods* (5th ed.). Boston: Allyn & Bacon.

Osborn, A. F. (1963). *Applied imagination* (3rd ed.). New York: Scribner's.

Paolino, T., & McGrady, B. (1978). *Marriage and marital therapy.* New York: Brunner/Mazel.

Papp, P. (1980). The Greek chorus and other techniques of paradoxical therapy. *Family Process, 19,* 45–57.

Patterson, G. R., & Reid, J. B. (1970). Reciprocity and coersion: Two facets of social systems. In Neuringer & J. L. Michael (Eds.), *Behavior modification in clinical psychology.* New York: Appleton.

Rogers, C. (1951). *Client-centered therapy.* Boston: Houghton Mifflin.

Rogers, C. (1961). *On becoming a person.* Boston: Houghton Mifflin.

Rohrbaugh, M., Tennen, H., Press, S., White, L., Raskin, P., & Pickering, M. (1977). *Paradoxical strategies in psychotherapy.* Paper presented at the meeting of the American Psychological Association, San Francisco, CA.

Satir, V. (1967). *Conjoint family therapy.* Palo Alto, CA: Science and Behavior Books.

Speck, R., & Attneave, C. (1973). *Family networks.* New York: Vintage.

Sperry, L., & Carlson, J. (1991). *Marital therapy: Integrating theory and technique.* Denver, CO: Love Publishing.

Stanton, M. D. (1981). Strategic approaches to family therapy. In A. S. Gurman & D. P. Kniskern (Eds.), *Handbook of family therapy* (pp. 361–402). New York: Brunner/Mazel.

Stuart, R. B. (1975). Behavioral remedies for marital ills: A guide to the use of operant-interpersonal techniques. In A. S. Gurman & D. G. Rice (Eds.), *Couples in conflict: New directions in marital therapy.* New York: Aronson.

Stuart, R. B. (1980). *Helping couples change: A social learning approach to marital therapy.* Champaign, IL: Research Press.

Thiabut, J. W., & Kelly, H. H. (1959). *The social psychology of groups.* New York: Wiley.

Warner, R., & Hansen, J. (1970). Verbal-reinforcement and model-reinforcement group counseling with alienated students. *Journal of Counseling Psychology, 14,* 168–172.

Warner, R., Swisher, J., & Horan, J. (1973). Drug abuse prevention: A behavioral approach. *NAASP Bulletin, 372,* 49–54.

Watzlawick, P., Weakland, J. H., & Fisch, R. (1974). *Change: Principles of problem formation and problem resolution.* New York: Norton.

Weeks, G. R., & L'Abate, L. (1982). *Paradoxical psychotherapy: Theory and technique.* New York: Brunner/Mazel.

Weiner-Davis, Michele. (1992). *Divorce busting.* New York: Summit Books.

Weiss, R. L. (1978). The conceptualization of marriage and marriage disorders from a behavioral perspective. In T. J. Paolino, Jr. & B. S. McCrady (Eds.), *Marriage and marital therapy: Psycho-analytic, behavioral and systems theory perspectives.* New York: Brunner/Mazel.

Weiss, R. L., & Perry, B. A. (1979). *Assessment and treatment of marital dysfunction.* Eugene, OR: Marital Studies Program.

PART II

✳

Assessment,
Concepts, and Skills

3

✳

Processing the Referral and Structuring the Initial Interview

CHAPTER OBJECTIVES

Upon completion of this chapter, the reader will be able to:

1. Conduct an initial assessment of the family via telephone (or Internet, if available);

2. Formulate initial hypotheses about the family structure/functioning;

3. Conduct an initial interview, gaining information about the couple, their perception of the problem, prior interventions, and scheduling information;

4. Describe the referral process.

INTRODUCTION

The assessment process begins, even before the initial interview, with information gathered from the initial telephone call, the intake sheet, or the Internet intake form. This initial contact provides an opportunity for the therapist to get a sense of the presenting problem and to gather information for formulating hypotheses. For marital partners, the initial call helps them to get to know the therapist and to learn about the process. Questions about the therapist's trustworthiness, and whether the therapist will be able to understand each partner's position, will be answered by the way the therapist interacts with the couple. The therapist should be careful not to take a position on an issue until the initial interview.

The intake interview may be conducted by telephone, in person or via Internet and includes demographic information about the couple, the referral problem, prior interventions, other pertinent information, and appointment information. Hanna and Brown (1999) suggest that after the information is gathered, the marital therapist may begin to develop initial hypotheses regarding the problem, following the steps described that follow. (See also Figure 3.1.)

COUPLE INFORMATION

At time of intake, the therapist should get full names, addresses, and phone numbers for each partner. This is particularly important in separated and remarried families, whose members are not living together. If the partner does not have a phone, it is important to obtain a phone number of a relative or neighbor who is in regular contact with the partner. This information will help identify other people who are supportive of the marriage (Hanna & Brown, 1999). The spouse who made the call should also be specified, as this may be the person who is most motivated to improve the marriage or change current conditions.

During the initial telephone call, the therapist may begin to trace the referral route that has led the couple to the therapist. It is important to understand why these individuals are seeking treatment *now,* how they have come to contact this particular therapist, and what all of this means to them. This information, if mishandled, may create barriers for assessment, and it may affect the recommendations for treatment. Some of the information (such as couple information) may be obtained during the initial telephone call, and additional information (such as a statement of the problem or prior interventions) may become accessible during the initial couple session (Karpel, 1986).

The couple's initial reaction to therapy depends both on who referred them and on their experience in therapy. The couple's feelings about therapy also influence the initial assessment. For example, if the couple has been referred by a close friend or relative who felt that therapy in the past was helpful, the couple is more likely to believe that the therapist can help them. On the other hand, if the couple is uncertain about the referral source, they may be less hopeful. Regardless, the therapist should assess the influence of the referral source on the therapy.

Often, the partner who calls is more upset with the relationship. In some cases, however, the caller has been unwilling to participate in therapy, but when the other partner threatens to leave, agrees to come to therapy to prevent a separation or divorce. The therapist receives a biased picture of the couple's problems; if only seeing one partner. Therefore, while it is important

---

Couple Informtion
1. Specify names, addresses, and phone numbers.
2. Identify referral source and the relationship between couple and referral source.

Statement of the Problem
3. Get a brief description of the problem.
4. Ask how the problem is affecting other family members.

Prior Interventions
5. Ask if the couple has had previous therapy, either conjointly or individually.
6. Ask what the couple has tried to remedy the problem.

Other Pertinent Information
7. Identify information about partners' ages, occupations, and places of employment.
8. Determine number of children and ages, other people living in the home, etc.

Setting Up Appointments
9. Determine best times for therapy.
10. Encourage both spouses to attend.
11. Schedule a time.

FIGURE 3.1 Steps of the Intake Interview

to pay attention to the referral information on the phone, this information is incomplete until both partners share their viewpoints of the problem (Karpel, 1994).

An initial interview with one partner should not affect the initial intake assessment. Indeed, the major complaints that occur in couple sessions are typically not noted in the initial phone call. If the caller wishes to be treated individually, the therapist should initially respect the partner's wishes. If the caller is in a committed marital relationship, however, it is important for the therapist to suggest meeting with the other partner after the initial individual session (Karpel, 1994). This allows the therapist to connect with the partner's initial request, but makes it easier to ask to meet with the partner later if this seems warranted, either to help the therapist understand the partner or to assess the couple's pattern of interaction around the problem.

Sometimes it is unclear to the therapist whether individual or marital therapy would be most appropriate because the partner may reveal both individual as well as relationship issues. At times, the partner may be unwilling or reluctant to be involved. If the partner is ambivalent, the therapist may want to see the couple in order to assess the level of commitment in their relationship. This allows both the therapist and the couple to examine personal issues within the relationship, and it provides the couple with feedback from an outside professional before decisions regarding treatment are made (Karpel, 1994).

STATEMENT OF THE PROBLEM

It is important to get the partner's perception of the problem in a concise statement. When one partner calls, he or she gives only one view of the problem. Often, the complaints are expressed through vague statements such as "poor communication" or "growing apart from each other." While these labels can inform the therapist about the problem, they have different meanings for different people and have a different connotation for each partner. Therefore, it is critical to obtain specific cognitions and behaviors for each label. For example, "poor communication" may mean either that the partners are not talking at all, have intense arguments, or that one or both person's needs are not being met.

The intake person should also find out how the "problem" is influencing other family members and friends. For example, if a wife calls and reports that her husband is "depressed," it is important to determine how his behavior is influencing her and her relationship with him. Finally, it is important to summarize the referring spouse's view of the problem; for example, in the instance above: "So you think your husband's depression is affecting your relationship?"

A brief illustration of how initial information can be gathered from the partner follows:

Therapist: What made you decide to come to therapy?

Wife: I'm feeling really depressed recently and I'm unhappy with our relationship.

Therapist: What are you unhappy about?

Wife: We never have fun anymore. He watches games on TV and I do my thing. We never do anything together.

An ongoing part of the intake is getting operational definitions of terms, such as, "unhappy," as the partner gives this information. Therefore, by the end of the interview, the therapist will have some idea of the specific behaviors that are problematic for the couple.

Additional information that should be gathered includes previous marriages, separations, divorce dates, recent deaths, illnesses, and any other significant changes that have occurred in the family system. This information may be useful in formulating hypotheses, particularly if a marriage has followed soon after a divorce, a death, or other immediate changes (Hanna & Brown, 1999).

PRIOR INTERVENTIONS

It is important for the therapist to determine if the couple has had previous therapy, either as individuals or as a couple. It gives the therapist information about what methods seem to work, or not work, and also helps the therapist determine the couple's expectations and willingness to follow through on what is discussed. If the couple left therapy because they were unwilling to follow through on "homework," the current therapist has information that may be useful in planning interventions. Similarly, if one person felt misunderstood, or the couple felt that the therapy did not focus specifically enough on their problems, this information helps the current therapist to know what the couple expects and to provide interventions that are more acceptable to them.

It is also helpful for the therapist to know what has been tried in the past to deal with the problem. What has the couple tried? What have friends suggested? Have clergy members or physicians given suggestions or advice? Was this advice followed by the couple? Why or why not?

OTHER PERTINENT INFORMATION

Marital information includes names of the client or clients, birthdates, children, ages, level of education, and place of employment. A line can also be included for each child. It is critical to determine whether both partners, as well as those who are connected to the problem, are living in the home. If one partner is living outside the home, it is important to get the address and phone number. This information will help to determine whether one or both spouses will attend the initial session. Ideally, both spouses should attend the initial session. However, if the contact person is unwilling to bring the spouse to the initial session, treatment options may vary. For example, the therapist may inform the contact person that he or she wants to include or consult with the other partner. If the partner is excluded, the marital therapist must ask questions during the assessment process to bring to light information about the missing party's point of view, for example, "What do you think your husband would say if he were here?" or "Does your wife have a different view?" The therapist should look for opportunities to address the exclusion of the spouse, and negotiate a subsequent inclusion of both partners as therapy progresses. This allows the therapist the opportunity to connect with, and understand the position of, each spouse.

SETTING UP APPOINTMENTS

Therapists should obtain information about the best times for couples to meet, as well as to determine who will be involved. It is beneficial to include both spouses at the first session. Once this information is gathered, an appointment date should be set. The date, time, and location of therapy should be provided. Couples should be instructed when to arrive, and should be given all relevant information about the intake procedure and fees. The couple should also be made aware of the cancellation policy (if there is one) and any other information needed by the therapist or agency.

In the event that the person making the appointment is reluctant to invite the spouse to the first session—for example, giving excuses such as the spouse's work schedule—the therapist should encourage the other person's involvement. A sample follows:

Therapist: Who will be attending the session with you?

Wife: Well . . . I guess I'll be coming alone.

Therapist: Would your husband consider coming?

Wife: I don't think he wants to. He sees this as my problem.

Therapist: Do you agree with him?

Wife: I know I'm more concerned than he is. He thinks counseling is kind of silly.

Therapist: What would happen if you asked him to come?

Wife: He'd probably say no. Anyway, if he comes, I'd probably be uncomfortable because he thinks my concerns are stupid.

Therapist: When you tell him your concerns and he "thinks they're stupid," what does he do?

Wife: He says things like, "I can't believe you let things like that get to you." Then I feel silly—like my concerns don't matter.

Therapist: It sounds like you're afraid you'd just end up feeling bad again. How do your discussions end after your husband says you're being silly?

Wife: He says the situation isn't worth talking about, and I just stop talking.

Therapist: I understand that you're worried about repeating the same old patterns. However, in order to be of most help, it is important for the therapist to hear both sides of the situation. Even if your husband thinks the problem is yours, it is important to hear his point of view as well as yours.

Wife: I know he won't want to come. What should I say to him?

Therapist: Just tell him what I've told you. Tell him the therapist said his opinion is important in helping you. Even though he isn't really concerned about the situation right now, it would be helpful to get his idea about what is going on. Tell him I said I usually ask the spouse to come to a session and ask him if he will come.

Wife: What if he says no?

Therapist: Call me back and we'll talk about some other things to try.

In this example, the therapist discusses both the reluctance of the wife to include her husband as well as her husband's resistance to be involved. By stating that it is customary for the other spouse to be included, the therapist normalizes the process and gives a rationale that will enhance the likelihood of involvement by both spouses. If the wife gives any indication that the relationship is violent (for example, seeming scared, mentioning physical threats, and so on), the initial interview should be conducted individually.

SETTING THE STAGE FOR THERAPY

The information gathered from the initial telephone contact helps provide a starting point for the therapist. The therapist will be able to assess where the couple is developmentally, and to determine whether the couple has completed the appropriate tasks for that stage. For example, if a couple comes to therapy soon after the birth of their first child stating that their relationship is distant and dissatisfying, the therapist will have some ideas and hypotheses about the difficulties the couple is experiencing:

1. The couple has much less freedom than they have had before to spend time with each other, and go places with each other.
2. The wife's attention is placed more on the baby than on the husband or on the relationship itself.
3. As is common, the wife's marital satisfaction seems to drop with the birth of the first child.
4. The wife feels that the husband is not being helpful. The husband does not feel appreciated.

Some additional information the therapist needs to obtain includes:

1. Is this a problem that has just started that may be related to the transition or developmental stage (an addition to the family), or has it been ongoing?
2. Are both partners concerned about this problem?
3. Is this a situation which is likely to change as the couple adjusts to a child? Will it help the couple to know that this is common? Or, do they need to learn some problem-solving skills to deal with the conflicts incurred by the new situation?
4. Has the wife not shown appreciation for the husband trying to help?

By approaching the initial session with an array of questions to be answered, the marital therapist can be directive in providing a structure for the interview, while remaining tentative enough to allow the uniqueness of the couple to emerge.

CONDUCTING THE INITIAL INTERVIEW

The task of the first session is twofold: to connect with both partners and to begin to gather information to assess the couple and make treatment recommendations. Unfortunately, the questions the therapist asks to get information about the couple's interactions may sometimes spark resistance or negative feelings on the part of one spouse or the other. At this stage, the therapist is unaware of the topics which trigger negative feelings, so he or she must balance the interview between joining techniques (making the couple comfortable, and assuring them that their concerns are valid) and getting information on which to build an intervention plan. In addition, the therapist has the challenge of integrating and balancing the sometimes converging and sometimes differing viewpoints between therapist and couple (Karpel, 1994).

JOINING

Joining with a couple is an ongoing process, beginning with the initial contact, and continuing throughout the treatment process. Joining is a process of showing couples that the therapist is interested in their welfare, respectful of their differences, and empathic with their feelings. It leads to an understanding of, and process for, building alliances with each marital partner. While positions of the spouses may vary, an understanding of each spouse is often necessary if marital therapy is to be successful.

Methods of Joining

Various methods are used by therapists to join with a couple. Some are fairly contrived, such as using the same body language as the identified spouse or using similar language patterns (such as slang, profanity, or slow or quick speech). The most effective joining techniques, however, appear to be those which are used to develop positive relationships in everyday life. Specifically, these include respect for the couple, attentiveness, responsiveness, and communication that suggests that the therapist takes the couple's concerns seriously and considers them valid. Phrases such as, "We really hit it off," or "I felt very comfortable with the therapist" suggest that joining was successful.

If therapists are to be effective with the couple, they must connect with both parties. This can sometimes be tricky because the spouses are saying contradictory things. Even so, the therapist must convey acceptance and respect for each spouse and acknowledge the reality of that spouse's experience. Couples must be encouraged to express their feelings and views and to understand that their feelings are normal. Following are some ways the therapist can join with a couple:

1. Greet each spouse by name and ask each spouse specific, friendly questions about work, hobbies, and interests.
2. Acknowledge each spouse's experience, position, and actions.
3. Normalize experiences, views, and actions ("This is a common feeling/ reaction.")
4. Validate spouses when possible ("I know you've tried to meet your wife's needs. It shows your concern about her.")
5. Connect specifically with one spouse, a process referred to as selective joining (Colapinto, 1991). The therapist may choose to affiliate with the more distant spouse, or make special efforts (mimesis of language and

tone of voice) to get closer to the spouse who will most likely keep the couple coming to therapy (Hanna & Brown, 1999, p. 141).

Joining is sometimes difficult because the therapist may disagree with the values, biases, or behaviors of the couple he or she is seeing. In fact, some of the couple's behaviors or personality traits may be off-putting to the therapist. While these feelings may be understandable, the therapist must find some way to engage the couple if they are to be effective in altering the situation. Reframing is one way to deal with these behaviors and beliefs without sounding judgmental. For instance, the behavior of a very domineering husband may be reframed as "caring," and then discussed as to how the behavior could be useful. (This assumes, however, that his domineering is not related to social control and violence.) Part of the therapy might involve the husband allowing his wife more independence, resulting in her needing less "caring" from him. Such reframing helps spouses feel that the therapist is supportive and understanding, a necessary prerequisite for the therapist to be effective in working with the couple.

The therapist should understand what the spouses are experiencing, how they think, and how they feel about each other. This attitude of sympathetic understanding should be conveyed to the couple. While this is quite easy in individual work, it becomes more complicated when one spouse is critical of the other. An approach derived from contextual therapy (Boszormenyi-Nagy & Krasner, 1986; Boszormenyi-Nagy & Spark, 1973) provides a useful frame for alliance building. This approach encourages the therapist to take both sides, by extending sympathy to each partner in turn. The therapist makes clear his or her understanding of one spouse's feelings, as well as making clear his or her understanding of how the other spouse feels.

IDENTIFYING WHAT IS "RIGHT"
IN THE RELATIONSHIP

In a good relationship with a couple, the therapist focuses not only on their deficits but also on their assets. Knowledge of these assets will help the therapist understand how couples cope with problems, allowing the therapist to focus on those aspects of the relationship that are healthy, rather than adopting a deficit (problem) model. This gives the couple hope that they can solve their own problems. While this may seem obvious to most clinicians, it is frequently overlooked when marital therapists become more intent on solving the couple's marital problem, rather than developing a good relationship with them.

The therapist must help the couple to identify its strengths and resources (internally and externally), identify what is working in the family, and organize themselves to keep the problems manageable (Brown & Christensen, 1999). These strengths and resources often lie dormant, and must be probed by the therapist.

The following guidelines (adapted from Hanna & Brown, 1999, pp. 142–143) will help beginning clinicians to join with the couple by identifying their strengths and resources:

- *Emphasize positive statements reported by the couple.* ("My husband listens to me when I have a problem.") It is also important to observe behaviors that reflect sensitivity, appreciation, or cooperation between family members.

- *Encourage both spouses to share their story about themselves.* Pay particular attention to those aspects of their story that reveal how the couple has coped successfully with problems.

- *Note family interactions that reflect strength and competency.* ("I like the way you give your husband space to decide for himself.")

- *Emphasize those times that the couple enjoys together.* Focus on what they are doing at those times and why it is enjoyable.

- *Reframe problems or negative statements in a more positive way.* ("Your anger shows that you really care about him.") Reframing consists of changing the conceptual or emotional viewpoint so as to change the client's perception of the problem without changing the facts. The situation does not change, but the interpretation does.

- *Emphasize what couples do well.* All couples have areas of strength. By asking questions, the therapist can learn how couples utilize these strengths to solve problems (for example, "How do you influence your wife?").

Depathologizing the actions of both spouses and focusing on strengths will greatly increase the couple's receptivity to trying new things. Time is often wasted unnecessarily and therapeutic relationships are weakened, with endless discussions of problems and deficits. This is particularly true for couples that have had a history of negative experiences with previous therapists. It does not take much for the therapist to trigger more defensiveness and resistance during the initial interview. Anticipating this, the marital therapist can work toward minimizing defensiveness by normalizing the couple's problems as part of the developmental process that all couples face. This does not assume that the therapist normalizes violence in the relationship; rather, it recognizes both what the couple views as the problem, and what the marital therapist views as an unsuccessful solution (Brown & Christensen, 1999).

As the interview progresses, the therapist tries to develop a relationship with the couple in the following ways:

1. The therapist adjusts to the couple's style and pace.
2. The therapist asks open-ended questions, and reflects the content and feelings of the couple.
3. The therapist tries to identify strengths and resources to establish a relationship.

BEGINNING THERAPY

One of the first questions the therapist needs to answer is how the couple came to seek therapy. Part of this exploration includes determining who recommended it, why they are going through with it, what other people in the immediate environment are saying, and so on. The reason for finding answers to these questions is to determine what the motivation for therapy is and who is most motivated to change the current situation.

These questions may be answered through conversation with the couple. In cases where spouses are being interviewed alone, however, the therapist should assess the partner's motivation for being there and determine who thought the couple needed help.

When it is discovered that an outside party (such as a spouse or relative) has suggested counseling, it is likely that the definition of the problem will have to focus initially on the relationship between those being interviewed and the referral source. Hanna and Brown (1999, p. 144) state:

> For instance, if a husband has come alone for counseling because his wife has given him an ultimatum, the therapist must determine who has defined the problem and whether the husband agrees or disagrees with this point of view. He may want to save his marriage, but he may be unable to fully present his wife's point of view. The intricate politics that have led to her exclusion from the session must also be investigated: Does she have her own therapist and feel that he should take his turn? Has she already privately decided on divorce and identified the therapist as someone her husband can turn to when she "lowers the boom"? Does she think he is totally to blame for the marriage problems? Has he been violent so that she has had to separate in order to capture some degree of control over her life? Detailed questions about the referral process will often help the therapist to expand the definition of the problem. When it is not feasible for the referring person to be included in sessions (as in the case of abused or abusing spouses, for example) the problem can still be defined as an issue between the client(s) and the outside party.

If the couple has previously been in therapy, the therapist should ask the couple about their experience and whether it is related to their current problem. In any case, the therapist should gain information about previous experiences in therapy, how the partners related to the therapist, what they found to be helpful or not helpful, why they did not return to that therapist, and how they decided to seek therapy again with another therapist.

These questions often facilitate the joining process with couples by revealing how other types of help have influenced them (Hanna & Brown, 1999). The therapist may ask not only about other professional help but also about help from friends, family, or coworkers.

By focusing on the referral process, the therapist gets a view of diverse relationships that may have some bearing on the problem. The larger context helps the therapist pursue more specific questions which in turn help determine goals for subsequent therapy sessions. The therapist then needs to use this information to determine what will be most effective and provide the best fit in the current therapy.

DEVELOPING AN OPERATIONAL DEFINITION OF "THE PROBLEM"

The couple typically arrives at the therapist's office armed with a wide array of global complaints. It is not unusual for a spouse to report dissatisfaction without knowing the reason or even to be unable to give any immediate examples of his or her partner's displeasing behavior. Instead, the therapist hears general complaints such as, "He doesn't respect me enough," or "I just don't feel as much love as I used to," or even "I don't know. Maybe it is just me." The marital therapist is interested in narrowing down such statements of dissatisfaction into more specific and objectively verifiable problems. As questions are asked and answered, the partners move closer to adopting an interactional perspective.

ASSESSING WHO OWNS THE PROBLEM

The definition of the problem must include both spouses' views of the problem. Hanna and Brown (1999, pp. 147–148) suggest that to begin a dialogue about a problem with a couple or spouse, the therapist might ask the following (adapted) questions:

1. What brings you here?
2. What would be helpful for us to discuss?
3. Who first noticed the problem and how long ago?
4. What led you (or your spouse) to conclude that this was a problem?
5. Who else (inside or outside the family) has had an opinion about the problem?
6. Have you or anyone else thought of any other possibilities regarding what the problem might be?
7. Are there times when the problem does not occur? What was going on at those times?
8. What are the differences between times when the problem does and does not occur?
9. What will happen if things do not change?

It is important to accept the couple's description of the problem without criticism or premature advice. It is also essential to validate the importance of each member's contribution ("That's a very good point. You seem to have thought a lot about this issue"). If spouses interrupt each other, remind them that each will have an opportunity to express their views (pp. 147–148).

Couples will feel more comfortable and involved in therapy if they do not feel attacked. One way to join with both partners, and avoid the criticisms that often occur, is to redefine the problem as an interactive situation versus an individual problem. When couples come to therapy, the presenting problem is typically related to individual behavior. For example, Jill reports that Harvey expects her to take care of housework such as cooking and cleaning and he never helps. Furthermore, he does not talk with her or express appreciation that she manages the house well. Harvey reports that Jill tends to get angry for no reason and then "nags." Therefore, he decides that ignoring her is the best solution. The therapist's task in such situations is to help partners develop an interactive definition of the problem, so that they can both view the situation as one where both are involved and neither is solely to blame. Using some of the information gleaned from the interview (family interactions, family or origins, and so on), the therapist may help the couple view the problem as, "We haven't negotiated spousal roles." In the case of Harvey and Jill, Harvey came from a home where his father was the primary "breadwinner" and had reached an agreement with his wife that she would handle all the household activities while he would bring in a regular paycheck. Jill grew up in a home where both spouses worked and where each shared in the household tasks. Because they had never discussed expectations, each was resentful that the other didn't operate in the same way as their parents had. As they came to perceive the problem as an interactive one ("We haven't negotiated how we will handle roles"), they developed shared expectations of each other.

Marital therapists must be prepared to ask questions that help the couple describe the problem in concrete terms. Clients will often express global concerns through the use of labels (being "depressed," "angry," "unhappy," and so on). While labels offer a general indication of the problem area, they often mean different things to different people. For example, a spouse may say she is "unhappy," which really means, "I don't want to be married." Hanna and Brown (1999) suggest that a therapist might use these questions to help clarify the problem:

1. What do you mean by _____?
2. Give me some examples of _____.
3. Describe a situation when you _____.
4. How does this affect you now?
5. How does _____ affect you?
6. Tell me the last time _____ happened. (148–149)

If a spouse presents several problems, the clinician needs to ask questions that address the most pressing concerns—what needs to be changed most, and what would happen if the situation goes unchanged.

1. What needs to be changed now?
2. The first change we need to make, then, is _____.

The therapist will also want to focus on times when the problem is not occurring. Questions such as those used in brief therapy are helpful in identifying exceptions to the problem, such as:

1. When have you handled the problem well?
2. What were you doing differently then?

There are also questions that pertain specifically to the developmental history of the marriage:

1. How did you meet?
2. Describe your courtship.
3. What was your relationship with your father? mother?
4. Were they supportive of your relationship with your partner? If not, how did you deal with this?
5. What were the similarities and differences of cultures and how did this impact your relationship?
6. How did you handle conflict in the early years of the marriage?
7. How do you handle conflict now?
8. Who do you go to when you are unable to handle conflict?
9. Is each of you working on the marriage?
10. How have past separations and losses affected your relationship?
11. What rules have you developed to handle closeness and distance?
12. How do you support each other?
13. How has your relationship changed over time?

Couples who are able to manage their problems are often aware of their strengths and resources. When gathering information, the therapist should focus on interactional patterns around the problem.

CONCLUSION

The assessment process begins even before the initial interview. When a spouse or couple makes an appointment, selected information should be gathered to create a "picture" of the couple's functioning. It is significant to know who referred the client and why, whether the couple or individuals have received previous therapy and their experiences there, and who will be coming to the therapy sessions. From such information, the therapist can begin to make hypotheses about the couple. During the initial interview, it is crucial that the therapist connect emotionally to the couple and understand the couple's definition of the problem before the goal-setting phase.

KEY POINTS

- Assessment of the family begins with information about the referral—who made the referral, and the relationship between the couple and the referral source.

- The intake worker should:
    1. Ask questions that encourage a precise definition of the problem.
    2. Gather data about previous therapy (if any).
    3. Get information about family and encourage attendance by both spouses at the initial session.
    4. Schedule the first appointment.

- The marital therapist can form hypotheses about a couple from the referral and intake information.

- One of the major tasks of the initial interview is to join with both spouses and focus on strengths and resources of the couple.

- The marital therapist must explore who should be included in the therapy sessions.

MARITAL SKILLS INVENTORY

Please check when you have completed these procedures.

Referral Information

_____   Specify names, addresses, phone numbers.

_____   Identify referral source.

Clinical Information

_____   Get a description of the problem and recent change.

_____   Ask how the problem is affecting other family members.

Previous Therapy

_____   Ask if any family members have been involved in previous therapy.

_____   Determine if there are any informal helpers.

Family Information

_____   Identify family members and others who are related to the problem.

_____   Determine whether there are additional extended family members.

Scheduling Information

_____   Ask for other relevant parties related to the problem.

_____   Specify date, time of appointment, and location of the facility.

Conduct Initial Interview

_____   Join with the family.

_____   Explore the referral process.

_____   Define the problem.

_____   Assess client's definition of the problem.

_____   Identify family strengths.

REFERENCES

Boszormenyi-Nagy, I., & Krasner, B. (1986). *Between give and take: A clinical guide to contextual therapy.* New York: Brunner/Mazel.

Boszormenyi-Nagy, I., & Spark, G. M. (1973) *Invisible loyalties: Reciprocity in intergenerational family therapy.* New York: Harper & Row.

Brown, J. H., & Christensen, D. N. (1999). *Family therapy: Theory and practice.* Pacific Grove, CA: Brooks/Cole.

Calapinto, J. (1991). Structural family therapy. In A. S. Gurman & D. P. Kniskern (Eds.), *Handbook of family therapy* (Vol. 2, pp. 417–433). New York: Brunner/Mazel.

Hanna, S. M., & Brown, J. H. (1999). *The practice of family therapy: Key elements across models.* Belmont, CA: Wadsworth.

Karpel, M. (1986). Questions, obstacles, and contributions. In M. A. Karpel (Ed.), *Family resources: The hidden partner in family therapy* (pp. 3–64). New York: Guilford Press.

Karpel, M. (1994). *Evaluating couples.* New York: Norton.

4

✳

Assessing the Problem
for Treatment Planning

CHAPTER OBJECTIVES

Upon completion of this chapter, the reader will be able to:

1. Assess the relationship history of the family;

2. Assess interactions;

3. Describe interactional patterns;

4. Set up an enactment of an interactional sequence;

5. Establish therapeutic goals;

6. Determine comorbidity;

7. Determine whether the couple would benefit from couple or individual therapy;

8. Create an atmosphere of change;

9. Obtain the couple's commitment;

10. Formulate a contract with the couple.

INTRODUCTION

It takes considerable courage for a couple to come to treatment; therefore, the therapist should capitalize on the fact that they have made the first step toward change, and then create an atmosphere conducive to change. The therapist should also ascertain the couple's commitment to change. Then the therapist must assess the couple to understand dysfunctional patterns in order to determine the most effective intervention. Assessment may be conducted through various methods. These include assessment of the relationship history (through interview or genograms), and assessment of typical interactions (through interview and/or objective assessment). Interactional patterns may be better understood by focusing on specific patterns that seem central to the problem, and then having couples enact these in the therapy setting.

In conducting an assessment, the marital therapist must move from theory to practice, and from concepts to actual dialogue with couples or spouses. The assessment process includes an identification of "the problem" from the perspective of each spouse, an analysis of the validity of each spouse's concerns, and the development of an interactional definition of "the problem." In this chapter, we will review specific techniques to create a positive atmosphere, as well as techniques to assess the couple's interactional patterns and show how these techniques can be incorporated into the initial stages of marital therapy.

ASSESSING RELATIONSHIP HISTORY

After partners relate their concerns and reasons for coming to marital therapy, the therapist can add to his or her understanding of the problem through assessing the relationship history of the couple. The genogram is a useful tool in this regard. The genogram provides a graphic depiction of a family's changes over generations and provides important information about partners' families of origin for a three- or four-generation period. It shows the family history, structure, and relationships during this time, and gives an indication of partners' past experiences, as well as likely expectations in a relationship. The genogram includes family members (and their relationships to one another), ages, dates of marriage, death, divorce, adoption, and places of residence. Women are symbolized by circles and men by squares. Vertical lines connect parents and children, and horizontal lines are used for marriage and dates. For detailed instructions on the conventions of genograms, consult McGoldrick and Gerson (1985), or Carter and McGoldrick (1989).

Genograms may be constructed as the therapist talks with the couple about their families of origin. Such a graphic helps the couple begin to see the relationships of their parents and make some connection with their own current way of relating to each other. This helps to expand the information available about the presenting problem. As the marital therapist becomes aware of certain relationships that are important to the client of record, these relationships can be explored in greater detail. This is also a way to determine support systems for couples. In marital sessions, the genogram helps the couple consider where the presenting problem fits into the larger context of their heritage. In individual sessions, the marital therapist learns to understand each spouse through knowledge and understanding of their families. Hanna and Brown (1999) suggest a list of questions for clients and directions for therapists which are helpful in constructing a genogram (See Figure 4.1).

It should be noted that the genogram is merely a useful way to visualize relationships across generations; to understand the interpersonal patterns that influenced current behaviors; and to recognize thoughts, behaviors, and values that were internalized and transferred to significant relationships. Similarities and differences in relationships can readily be noted, and the patterns can help target attitudes or behaviors that currently may be perpetuating the identified problem. In short, the genogram helps the couple consider

---

Roman numeral entries are questions to clients. Alphabet entries are directions to the therapist.

I. How is your marriage different from other marriages you know?
   A. Begin writing brief words on the genogram that represent the responses to this question.
   B. Use public note-taking as a form of acknowledging each spouse's comments.

II. How are husband and wife different from each other?
   A. List adjectives near the corresponding person on the genogram.
   B. When negative labels are given, try to reframe in a neutral, positive, or emphatic way.
   C. Use these questions as an opportunity to tease, joke, and set people at ease.
   D. Many people will privately fear judgment, criticism, and psychological analysis. Therefore, the less "therapeutic" the environment, the better.

III. How do you express affection?
   A. What do they do to communicate positive feelings to one another?
   B. How do they know when a given family member is feeling positive toward them?

IV. Who gets the angriest? How do you know when _____ is mad?
   A. Reframe anger as pain or feeling overwhelmed.
   B. Where did you learn to express anger in this way?
   C. How does this _____ affect others?

V. Who runs the family? Who gets the last word?
   A. Give each member a chance to respond.

Adapted from Hanna, S. M., & Brown, J. H. (1999). *The practice of family therapy: Key elements across models* (2nd ed.). Belmont, CA: Wadsworth, p. 172.

FIGURE 4.1 Questions and Guidelines for Genograms

where the presenting problems fit into the larger context of their families of origin, and in turn the marital therapist gains a better understanding of each spouse through greater knowledge and understanding of the families of origin.

While the genogram is typically used for biological patterns of behavior, it can readily be adapted for various situations. For example, in cases where clients were adopted or transferred through many foster placements, the genogram can depict the multiple settings and relationships that have become the norm for their development.

ASSESSING INTERACTIONS
THROUGH THE INTERVIEW

The marital interview is important for tracking interactional sequences that both trigger and maintain the problem. Certain types of information can be more easily obtained through the free exchange that is offered in an interview format. The important subtleties of time and setting in which the problem occurs (for example, the husband asks for attention while his wife is trying to sleep) may be more easily obtained through the interview than by other means. Likewise, the marital therapist may be aided in determining what is maintaining the problem by knowing when the problem is both most severe and least severe, and how those situations differ. See Figure 4.2 for an example outline of a marital interview (From Brown and Christensen, pp. 172–173).

OBJECTIVE ASSESSMENT
OF MARITAL INTERACTION

At times, assessment may be aided by instruments which have been developed to record interactional data. One such instrument has been developed by the Oregon Marital Studies Program (Weiss & Perry, 1979). Its ten-session assessment/intervention package begins with a two-session assessment phase in which spouses are phoned each night for observational data (Gurman & Knudson, 1978). Weiss and Perry have developed another mechanism called the Spouse Observation Checklist (SOC) to aid couples in their collection of observational data in the home. The Spouse Observation Checklist contains a checklist of "pleases" (p's) and "displeases" (d's)—behaviors of the spouse that the respondent finds pleasing or displeasing. Both instrumental and affectional p's and d's are recorded from twelve categories: affection, companionship, consideration, sex, communication process, coupling activities, child care and parenting, household responsibilities, financial management, work, personal habits, and self and spouse independence. The SOC can also be useful in monitoring changes during therapy. Several research investigations support the validity of the instrument (Weiss, Hops, & Patterson, 1973; Wills, Weiss, & Patterson, 1974).

  I. Relationship in time and place
      A. Trajectory: moving toward past, future, nowhere
      B. Degree of dyadic involvement: more, less, no change
      C. Other viable relationship alternatives, such as separation
 II. Lifestyle and tempo
      A. In space: home
      B. With others as individuals: animals, children, etc.
      C. With others as collectives: community, etc.
      D. Role of pleasure: work-to-pleasure ratio
      E. Responsibilities: kinfolk, legal, etc.
III. Factors impeding attainment of relationship goals
      A. Structural
          1. Limitations of individual resources
          2. Limitations of joint resources
          3. Individual vs. dyadic energy imbalance
      B. Functional
          1. Communication skills deficits (specify)
          2. Deficient rewards (amount vs. contingency)
          3. Failures of stimulus control (specify)
 IV. The couple's aptitudes for intervention
      A. Background factors
          1. Seeking relationship goals defined as reciprocity or otherwise
              consistent with behavioral exchange model
          2. Physical gratification important to both
          3. Common investment, such as children, social status, business
          4. Clear statment of objectives
      B. Process factors
          1. Clients' in-session behaviors
              a. Follow therapist
              b. Adopt therapist's model for viewing problems
              c. Progress in focusing issues
              d. Relevant questioning of program
          2. Therapist's estimate of movement
              a. Aversive behaviors brought under control
              b. On average, problem solving greater than name calling
              c. Ability to understand clients' complaints
              d. The therapist can define three goals of intervention for these
                  clients
  V. Obstacles to intervention progress
      A. Client expectations
          1. Attachment to previous therapist
          2. Model of behavior antagonistic to therapist's
          3. Extra therapeutic agents

(continues)

FIGURE 4.2 Outline for Marital Interview From Brown, J. H. &
Christensen, D. N.

(continued)

    B. Intellectual/educational limitations
       1. Verbal skills (including reading and writing)
       2. Underdeveloped work habits
    C. Resource limitations
       1. Time, money for intervention
       2. Medical and health-related conditions, such as addictions
VI. Treatment planning
    A. Alternative treatment options
    B. Therapist-client match
    C. Menus of treatment options within system

FIGURE 4.2 Continued

The Oregon group has also developed the Marital Interaction Coding System (MICS) (Hops, Wills, Patterson, & Weiss, 1972) The MICS is a behavioral coding system used for describing the content and process of a couple's interactions, usually while attempting to negotiate a marital conflict. The videotaped (or audiotaped) interaction is coded by trained coders, and the stream of ongoing, coded behaviors is then subjected to a computer analysis, the results of which include rate-per-minute of problem solving, positive behaviors, negative behaviors, frequency and content of interruptions, and successful and unsuccessful interruptions. For example, how do spouses agree, disagree, talk, and turn each other off?

The MICS differs from other forms of laboratory observations in that observational codes are designed to examine the couple's interactional patterns as they actually occur (Ciminero, Calhoun, & Adams, 1977). The MICS can be used to assess the couple's problem-solving and communication abilities. It consists of 30 codes, some of which include: AG (Agree), DG (Disagree), AP (Approve), AR (Accept responsibility), PP (Positive Physical contact), NO (No response), HM (Humor), CR (Criticize), and CP (Complain). The codes account for most responses in a problem-solving situation (Patterson, Hops, & Weiss, 1974). These codes were derived from videotapes of marital interactions. The thirty codes are often condensed into three summary scores: positive social reinforcement, negative social reinforcement, and problem solving. One major disadvantage of the MICS, however, is that it requires trained observers to score the data.

Marital satisfaction can be measured in a number of ways. In some cases, the therapist may want to design his or her own categories of observation, depending on the goals of therapy. For example, if the therapeutic goal is to increase marital satisfaction, the therapist may want to count the number of positive and negative statements each spouse makes to the other. The important thing here is for the therapist to operationalize (in other words, define the desired behavior in concrete terms) the goal and then develop appropriate categories to measure progress. For example, if the couple wishes to improve communication, the therapist may want to develop specific categories (empathy, validation, compromise) to measure improved communication.

For selected cases, the therapist may want the couple to observe their own behavior. Spouses may be taught how to observe and record positive and negative thoughts about each other. The therapist might provide a form that includes the dates of observation, the operational definition of the behavior to be observed, times of the observation, and the location (such as home or work). The therapist can graph the data by recording the time on the horizontal axis and the frequency of behavior on the vertical axis. The therapist should be cautious, since self-observation is open to bias and may not be an accurate measure of the couple's behavior.

If the therapist wishes to use standardized self-report instruments, he or she might consider the Locke-Wallace Marital Status Inventory (L-W), the Dyadic Adjustment Scale (DAS), or the Marital Pre-Counseling Inventory (MPI).

The Locke-Wallace Marital Status Inventory contains a set of true/false items to assess steps toward the dissolution of the marriage. According to Weiss and Perry (1979), the test was designed to provide "an intensity scale (e.g., Guttman scale) such that any given step would necessarily include all preceding steps. Thus, before one sought legal aid for a divorce, it would be reasonable to assume that one had thoughts about divorce and engaged in behaviors preparatory to that of seeking legal advice"(p. 17).

The **Dyadic Adjustment Scale** (Spanier, 1976) includes many items from the Locke-Wallace Inventory (Locke & Wallace, 1959). Weiss and Perry (1979) altered the items omitted by Spanier so that both measures are incorporated into one questionnaire. The DAS is somewhat more modern in its wording than the Locke-Wallace Marital Status Inventory and provides four factor scales: dyadic consensus (problem solving), dyadic satisfaction (good feelings and sentiment in the relationship), dyadic cohesion (outside interests, exchange of ideas, cooperation), and affectional expression (sexual and emotional expression). The DAS is easy to score and can be very useful to the marital therapist.

The **Marital Precounseling Inventory (MPI)** (Stuart & Stuart, 1972) is administered before treatment to aid in treatment planning. The eleven-page inventory provides assessment information in the following areas: daily activities of both spouses, general goals and resources for change, spouse satisfaction and targets for change in twelve areas of marital and family functioning, rationale for decision making, and level of commitment to the marriage (Stuart, 1976).

The data from the MPI serves several purposes. It provides the therapist with data for planning a treatment program. It also helps to orient the couple to treatment. Each spouse can often anticipate those issues that will be discussed. When treatment ends, the inventory can be completed to evaluate therapy.

These self-report instruments serve a variety of assessment functions. First, they provide objective measures of behaviors critical to the satisfaction of both spouses. Second, these instruments often reveal information that spouses might be resistant to provide in an interview. For example, the spouse may find it embarrassing to discuss sexual issues in the interview. The therapist can often use this information to help spouses focus on critical issues that otherwise might be avoided. Finally, instruments often provide an ongoing measure of subjective satisfaction that cannot be obtained through observation.

Focusing on Interactional Patterns

As the marital therapist gathers information from the genogram, interview, and selected marital assessment instruments, he or she begins to focus on specific interactional patterns that appear to be central to the problem. For example, the therapist might note "low affectional expression" on the Dyadic Adjustment Scale. Further examination of the couple's relationship history might reveal patterns of pursuit and withdrawal in both spouses' families of origin. The interview may provide additional data as the therapist tracks interactional patterns gleaned from each partner's description of "the problem."

When the therapist asks each spouse to describe the problem, the couple's interactional patterns begin to emerge. For example, a wife's attempts to involve her husband in the relationship may result in the husband's withdrawal. The more she pursues, the more he distances himself.

A typical sequence of communication in a pursuer–distancer relationship is given in the example following:

1. The wife tries to initiate a conversation with her husband.
2. The husband, seated at the table, does not respond.
3. The wife repeats her attempt to get her husband to respond.
4. The husband gets up and walks into another room.
5. The wife follows him.
6. The husband says, "What do you want?"
7. The wife says, "I want to talk with you about our plans for Saturday night."
8. The husband says, "Not now. I've had a hard day."

Some questions the therapist may ask to assess patterns of interaction are:

1. When did you first notice the problem? What is going on? Who notices first?
2. Where does the problem take place? Where is he or she when this happens?
3. What next? What does he or she do then? What does he or she say then?
4. How do others get involved in the problem?
5. What happens after he or she leaves? How long is he or she gone? What happens when he or she returns?

6. Who agrees or disagrees with you that this is a problem?

7. Has it always been this way? When was it different? What else was different then?

   Questions which help the couple develop an interactional description of the problem take the focus away from one person who is to blame, and rather address who should be talking to whom and when. A good way to do this is by tracking interactional sequences that have occurred in the couple's relationships. Note the example below. The couple has initiated therapy because of increasing hostility on the part of the wife and communication that has been shut off.

> **Therapist:** Tell me about your relationship with your parents.
>
> **Susan:** I get along well with my mother, but I sometimes try to avoid my father because I'm always afraid he'll be upset with me.
>
> **Therapist:** (Draws a line from Susan to her father and writes "avoids father" next to Susan's name.) Why are you afraid your father will be upset with you?
>
> **Susan:** My father can be very intimidating. If I express a thought to him and he disagrees, he tends to get loud and say something like, "Oh, no, you know better than that."
>
> **Therapist:** (Writes "intimidating" on the genogram next to father.) When he says that you "know better," how do you respond?
>
> **Susan:** A couple of times I've spoken up and repeated how I feel. But the way he looks at me just makes me feel so stupid that I just cave in.
>
> **Therapist:** (Writes "caves in" next to client's name.) What do you do when you cave in?
>
> **Susan:** Sometimes I say, "I guess you're right." At other times, I just stop talking.
>
> **Therapist:** So when your father intimidates you or questions your thoughts, you just stop expressing them or agree with your father that the thoughts are invalid?
>
> **Susan:** Yes.
>
> **Therapist:** From what you've told me, you do the same with your husband. You express your feelings or thoughts. He disagrees and tells you he can't believe you think that. Then you back down.
>
> **Susan:** Yes.

In this interaction, the wife expresses a tendency to be easily intimidated by her father. The therapist listens to this without challenging and then makes a connection to similar behavior with her husband. As the client describes ways of interacting with family members, the therapist listens for patterns of thinking or behaving that may serve as obstacles to more appropriate behaviors. The client believes that her father disagrees with everything she says, and that if he disagrees, she must be wrong. Therefore, she does not express her feelings and wants to avoid her father. The therapist needs to challenge her belief that her father always thinks she is wrong and consider that his motivation may not be to get her to back off, but rather to think the situation through more thoroughly. This kind of discussion may then allow the wife to consider that the husband's motivation is not to get her to stop communicating, but rather to think situations through and to communicate more persuasively.

ENACTING THE
INTERACTIONAL PATTERNS

Still another way to assess the problem is to stop talking about "the problem" and instead have the couple *show* how they respond to situations, as well as what happens before and after the problem. This can be done through the use of enactments.

Enactment occurs when the therapist decentralizes his or her participation and directs the couple to enact, rather than describe, the situation. The therapist may ask the couple to "talk to each other about the problem," or "continue last night's argument." The therapist's directives must be specific: "Tell your husband what you would like him to do" (Brown & Christensen, 1999). Hanna and Brown (1999) suggest that after giving the directive, the therapist may use the following guidelines (adapted, p. 153) to assess the couple's interactional patterns:

- How is the message delivered?
- Does the spouse talk firmly?
- Is eye contact made?
- How does the other spouse respond?
- Does he or she get angry?
- Does he or she acknowledge the other spouse's point of view? How?
- Do any of the children get pulled into the discussion?
- When do the children get involved?
- How do the children get involved?
- Does the therapist get involved in the interaction?
- When does each spouse change the subject?
- How does the interactional pattern end?

These guidelines help the therapist move the problem from an individual to an interactional perspective. When couples talk about "the problem," it often sounds as though it resides in the other person. When the therapist directs them to talk *to* each other, rather than *about* each other—for example, to "continue last night's argument"—the therapist can observe interactions such as intimidation by one spouse and withdrawal by the other, negative statements by one spouse which escalates when the other replies with put-downs, and so on. The therapist can then show how the problem is interactional, and explain how the common patterns of interaction hinder problem resolution. This helps the couple gain a broader perspective on the problem, leading to creating an atmosphere for change, formulating goals for treatment, and getting a commitment from the couple to work toward those goals.

ASSESSING SUPPORT SYSTEMS

The need for support is critical to the well being of the marriage. Friends, family, and coworkers can be sources of support to the relationship. On the other hand, they can act in ways to undermine the health and stability of the relationship. Karpel (1994) notes the following:

> The couple relationship is embedded in a wider relational context of family, friends, neighbors, co-workers and others. These outside relationships constitute potential resources as well as potential threats to their relationship. Family, friends and others can provide safety and stability, a sense of belonging, and concrete and emotional support in times of stress. They can dilute the pressure to have all needs met within the couple relationship. However, they may also impinge on the couple's privacy, limit their ability to take control over their lives, foster conflict, and damage trust within the relationship. In contextual terms, it involves the effort to balance multiple legacies and loyalties. The most problematic relationships are usually those that are most intimate and intense. These typically involve children—either from the current or previous relationships—and members of the partners' families of origin. (p. 44)

The degree to which couples can renegotiate their relationships with friends, family, and coworkers determines the level of satisfaction in the marriage.

ASSESSING FOR COMORBIDITY

It is essential for the therapist to consider other issues that may be affecting the marital relationship. Of special importance are conditions such as suicidal ideation (thoughts, wishes, or plans to kill oneself), actual suicidal attempts, substance abuse, mental illness, and domestic violence. Many therapists can give examples of client couples who seem to make no progress, no matter what intervention is used, about whom they find out later that one of the partners has a serious problem, such as addiction or depression, that has never been mentioned.

Marital therapy conducted when one (or both) partners is addicted may be ineffective, and it may actually be harmful to one party in cases of domestic violence. When couples are seen together, it may be more difficult for these issues to be discussed. There is benefit in seeing partners individually as a part of the assessment process.

Domestic Violence Assessment

Domestic violence has become fairly common in the United States. Some estimates suggest that about a third of newlyweds have had an argument containing a physical confrontation, and that in clinic samples, this estimate goes up to 50 percent. Furthermore, the research on battering (a pattern of behavior in which one person establishes power and control over another person through fear and intimidation, often including the threat or use of violence) suggests that there are no antecedents that elicit violence and that there is nothing the partner can do to stop it once it has begun. Therefore, there is an ethical issue in seeing a couple together if one or the other tends to be violent. Gottman (2000) says it is unethical because marital therapy, with its conjoint format, may implicitly suggest that the problem is mutual, that the perpetrator is not entirely responsible, and may place the partner at increased risk. Gottman assesses the risk of violence through the Straus-Gelles Conflict Tactics Scale, a 19-item scale describing various ways to handle conflict, ranging from discussing issues to using a gun or knife. The Waltz-Rushe-Gottman Emotional Abuse Questionnaire (EAQ) (Gottman, 2000) is also used to assess less tangible signs of abuse, such as social isolation, degradation, sexual coercion, and property damage. If there is evidence of battering or violence, marital therapy may be contraindicated.

Suicidal Risk

Clinical depression is a very common psychiatric disorder which results in suicidal ideation and suicidal attempts by approximately 15 percent of those afflicted (Hirschfeld & Goodwin, 1988). There is a relationship between marital distress and depression, even though causation is not clear. Marital discord may result in a depressive episode, or depression in one spouse may lead to marital distress. Whatever the reason, the therapist should assess whether or not there is a safety risk for one of the partners. If so, the depression must be addressed prior to marital therapy.

Assessment of suicidal risk may take the following form. In the individual session, the therapist should ask if the partner has had suicidal thoughts or thoughts of inflicting self-hurt. If so, the therapist must assess lethality; in other words, the likelihood of the person's acting on those thoughts. Questions such as, "When would you do it?" or "How would you do it?" help the therapist determine whether or not the partner has already developed a plan. If a plan has been developed, the risk level is high and warrants a suicide watch or hospitalization.

Alcohol/Drug Use

It is not uncommon for clients to request marital therapy because of problems such as poor communication and conflicts, and never mention that one spouse or the other is addicted to drugs or alcohol. In fact, some marital conflict is so closely related to problems resulting from substance use that attention only to communication skills would be of no benefit. Therefore, the therapist must learn to routinely ask about substance abuse. Lukas (1993) says that this question should be asked in every intake session.

The therapist should also be aware that clients frequently discount their alcohol/drug use as less significant than it is. They may report drinking, but not be totally honest about the extent of it or say that it "poses no problems." By meeting with partners individually, the therapist may get more accurate information about the extent of the problem and how it relates to the marital discord. Also, screening instruments which ask questions about alcohol/drug use as a matter of course may produce less anxiety for clients because this same procedure is followed for everyone.

Addressing the alcohol/drug issue too strongly may result in driving couples away from therapy. Therefore, the therapist should be aware of signs and ask general questions about use but do so in a non-judgmental way and in a way related to the presenting problem. (See more about this in Chapter 12, in the case study on addiction.)

DECIDING ON COUPLE THERAPY
VERSUS INDIVIDUAL THERAPY

There are three reasons for recommending couple therapy. First, the couple must view the problem as relational. Second, when couples see the problem as a problem between them, they are more likely to be committed to solving the problem together. The third and final reason focuses on the need to be in agreement about the problem and goals of therapy. Each spouse is not likely to agree on all aspects of the problem; however, it is critical that each spouse sees some validity in the other spouse's complaint. When these conditions are met, the couple is more likely to benefit from couple therapy.

A summary of Karpel's (1994) list of contraindications for couple therapy follows:

- *Poor Alliances With One or Both Partners.* When the therapist has a poor alliance with one or both partners the couple is not likely to benefit from conjoint treatment.

- *The Partners' Inability to Agree on Goals for Treatment.* When spouses are opposed to each other's goals and focus only on their own personal needs, couple therapy is not likely to be beneficial.

- *Unmanageable Conflict Between Partners.* When conflict is so intense and cannot be managed by the therapist, separate sessions with each spouse are recommended.

- *Characteristics of One Individual Makes Couple Therapy Impossible.* When one spouse's symptoms (for example, depression, alcohol consumption, or anxiety) make it impossible to focus on the other spouse's complaints, couple therapy should be delayed until there is improvement in the spouse's symptomatology.

■ *Domestic Violence.* Because of the potential danger, couple therapy should not be conducted where there is evidence of domestic violence.

■ *A History of Unsuccessful Couple Therapy.* When couples have experienced many unsuccessful attempts at therapy, couple therapy is not recommended unless some new information is reported (for example, disclosure of family secrets that would indicate the possibility that couple therapy would be beneficial).

Moreover, couple therapy is unlikely to work where one or both partners have little commitment to the relationship. It is not at all unusual for couples to come to therapy, even though at least one of them has determined that he or she no longer wants to be in the relationship. The "last ditch effort" helps that spouse overcome guilt about ending the relationship; however, there will be minimal commitment and effort to change. The therapist can assess commitment by whether one or both partners respond to treatment; the failure of one or both spouses to respond to treatment suggests that couple therapy is unlikely to work. In such cases, therapists should recommend to the couple that couple therapy likely would not be productive. In some cases, the feedback may facilitate the couple's decision to end the relationship or possibly move them beyond a "stuck position" in their relationship. When confronted with the possibility that the relationship may end, a couple may decide they want to work to keep it intact.

In cases where couple therapy is not the preferred mode of treatment, Karpel (1994, p. 193) recommends treatment for one partner when the following conditions occur:

■ *When an Individualized Symptom Requires Specialized Treatment.* When a spouse experiences symptoms such as anxiety disorder, depression, alcoholism or other illness, he/she should be referred to a physician to determine the appropriate treatment. Such symptoms are a risk to the spouse and other family members and should be alleviated before couple treatment is considered.

■ *When the Client's Level of Anguish Calls for Specialized Treatment.* When a spouse feels that (s)he requires specialized treatment his/her request should be honored even in cases where the therapist believes the treatment is unwarranted. When a spouse's requests are not met, the therapeutic relationship may be damaged.

■ *When a Particular Problem Blocks Productive Couple Therapy.* When a spouse's symptoms (e.g., depression, alcohol, substance abuse) hinder his/her ability to address the other spouse's concerns, individual treatment is recommended. In such cases, the symptomatic spouse is unable to commit to the relationship.

■ *When One Partner Is Unmotivated for Couple Therapy and the Other Is Distressed and Requests Help.* When one spouse is reluctant to participate in marital therapy, the therapist should attempt to help the cooperating spouse to decide how to respond to the reluctant spouse.

- *When the Couple Is "Too Much" for One Therapist.* Some couples can overwhelm a therapist. This often occurs with "difficult" people who are experiencing many problems. Couples who are constantly under stress will likely place great demands on the therapist and warrant individual treatment.

In some cases, individual treatment may be offered concurrently with couple therapy. For example, one spouse may be treated for anxiety, while at the same time participating in couple therapy. This may occur with the same therapist or with different therapists. Concurrent and individual therapy with one spouse works best when both spouses agree to it. The progress of the spouse in individual therapy can be shared with the other spouse in couple therapy to help both cope with the problem. The therapist should discuss in advance the extra time and money that will be required for both individual and couple therapy.

CREATING AN ATMOSPHERE FOR CHANGE

Seldom, if ever, does a couple come for marital therapy in a positive, optimistic, confident, and eager manner to hear what the therapist has to say and to rush home and put it into practice. Even when the couple is able to establish goals, there are still feelings of mistrust, envy, grief, fear, and vulnerability. Moreover, one or both spouses may not feel aligned with the therapist, and fear that the therapist is an ally of the other spouse. Such conditions do not create an atmosphere for change. If therapy is to be successful, an initial strategy that will facilitate positive change is necessary.

The marital therapist handles this threatening climate by defining it as one in which positive changes are necessary to increase satisfaction in the marriage with as few costs as possible. Rather than focusing on change immediately, the therapist discusses the history of the couple's relationship as part of the ongoing process of assessment (Jacobson & Margolin, 1979). By viewing the period of the couple's early courtship, the therapist evokes cognitive images of pleasant interactions between them, which momentarily replace the bitter, conflicted images of the present relationship. This effect gives the therapist an opportunity to reinforce those images socially and to be presented as sensitive to the complexity of the relationship. The couple who had entered the office expecting all the negatives in their relationship to be displayed in full view to a total stranger has a different experience. Instead, they find themselves reminiscing about better times with someone who appreciates the fact that they did not set out to create a marriage full of pain and dissatisfaction. By focusing on the positive behaviors, each spouse can view the couple's current problems with greater perspective, and move closer to accepting responsibility in and for the relationship. At this point, goals for therapy should be established.

ESTABLISHING GOALS

Goal setting evolves from behaviors that the couple wishes to change in order to eliminate "the problem." The therapist must help the couple select goals which are achievable and which address the couple's definition of the problem. Goals should be stated in positive terms ("I want to spend more time with you"), replacing the problem behavior ("You don't care about me.")

The therapist must often negotiate with the couple to set reasonable goals. Couples will often set goals that are vague ("We want to be happy") and unreasonable ("We want to feel better about our relationship"). In this case, the therapist must shift the focus from large goals to smaller process goals. For example, the therapist might say, "What are some things that you will be doing when you feel better about your relationship?" If the couple is able to describe specific behaviors that are connected to their feelings, the therapist can break the larger goal into smaller goals, such as "We will be spending more time together," or "We will be doing kinder things for each other." Couples are more likely to change their behavior when they also change their perceptions (O'Hanlon, 1991).

The most difficult challenge for the therapist is to develop an interactional statement of the goal. Because each spouse often blames the other and does not see his or her part in the problem, he or she must be convinced that the problem is relational. Take the example of Clyde and Jeri:

Jeri: He never picks up his clothes when I ask him to.

Therapist: What about it, Clyde? Does she have a point?

Clyde: I get tired of being yelled at.

Therapist: Jeri, do you often use a "yelling" tone of voice when you ask him?

Jeri: I have to gripe at him to get him to do anything.

Therapist: But it sounds like it isn't working.

Jeri: That's because he doesn't care. I don't think it makes any difference what kind of tone I use.

In this example, Jeri resists the therapist's attempts to convince her that she played a role (changing her tone of voice) in helping her husband change his behavior (picking up his clothes). In order to develop an interactive goal, the therapist must convince Jeri that a positive change in her behavior might result in a positive change in her husband. For example:

Therapist: I don't know, but I'm wondering if you tried a different way of asking whether he might pick his things up.

Jeri: What if he doesn't? What then?

Therapist: Then we will try something else.

Jeri: I'll try, but I think it will take more than that.

Therapist: Good.

At this point, the couple is willing to work on an interactional change (that the wife will ask in a softer tone for her husband to pick up his clothes and see if he would comply). In this case, the changes are reciprocal with each person influencing the other. Gottman (1994) suggests that spouses who are able to influence each other are more satisfied with their marriage. While the above example may not lead to complete satisfaction or happiness in the marriage, it is an initial step, which might make other goals more achievable.

In working on interactional change, it is also helpful to describe the problem situation as outside the couple. For instance, the problem may be referred to as the "noncooperation" problem—that is, the wife does not address the husband the way he likes and therefore he does not help with what she wants. By discussing the "noncooperation" problem, it becomes a situation that both spouses must work on, and neither is wholly to blame. By describing the problem situation as outside the couple, the therapist has a greater likelihood of getting the couple to commit to change.

OBTAINING THE COUPLE'S COMMITMENT

The therapist may get couples to work together by obtaining from them an agreement that they will follow the therapist's advice and counsel. In short, the couple expresses its commitment to do what the therapist instructs. The agreement then establishes the framework within which the therapist instructs the couple to collaborate (Jacobson, 1981). Rather than doing something nice in response to the partner's request, each does something because he or she has told the therapist he or she would, and it just happens to please the other spouse. This experience allows them both to save face, an experience necessary to every embittered adversary.

The therapist should obtain the couple's commitment to follow his or her instructions, because without it, the therapist would see little likelihood for success. However, simply demanding this commitment is ineffective; rather, the commitment should instead be gradually built through the pretreatment assessment process. This is done through verbal and nonverbal cues that the therapist has something to offer the couple, sees their problems as manageable, and is a reasonable and sensitive professional who can be trusted. After summarizing the results of pretreatment assessment and after outlining the goals, procedure, and rationale of treatment, the therapist then asks for the couple's commitment to follow his or her instructions.

After the marital therapist has worked to create an atmosphere for change in the couple and has focused on the more salient treatment goals that emerged in the assessment process, he or she must develop a contract with the couple.

FORMULATING THE CONTRACT

The contract is the spouses' formal commitment to change. Contracting is a structure that specifies clearly what is expected. The therapist is a mediator who facilitates mutual agreements between the spouses about the reciprocal exchanges of mutual behaviors. In addition, Hanna and Brown (1999) provide the following checklist (adapted, p. 159) to achieve a satisfactory understanding with couples about what should happen in therapy:

1. Who will attend? (One spouse, both spouses, others)
2. What will each spouse's role be? (Client, provider of information)
3. What are the goals? (Assessment, then treatment, specific behavioral change)
4. When will sessions be held? (Frequency, pace)
5. How will sessions be conducted? (Homework assignments, in-session tasks, psychoeducation)
6. When will the terms of the contract be negotiated?
7. What resources, space, time, and help are needed?
8. Who else needs to be made aware of the contract?
9. Are there any barriers or costs to the contract?
10. Have fees or releases of information been discussed?

Contracts should be evaluated and renegotiated when one or more of the following occurs:

- Spouses fail to reach their goals in a reasonable period of time.
- Spouses make excuses for not fulfilling the contract.
- Spouses frequently complain about the conditions of the contract.

In many cases, the therapist and couple may have misjudged what could be achieved in a given period of time. It is not evidence of failure to revisit the goal, and in fact, it is empowering to the couple to know that they are able to change the conditions of the contract if they so desire.

CONCLUSION

Beginning therapists will need to allow sufficient time to complete the assessment process, because an inadequate assessment may result in unsuccessful therapy. The assessment includes information about the relationship history of the couple, as well as their families of origin. Of special value is the assessment of interactions and interactional sequences observed in sessions as couples discuss their marital issues. Interactional patterns observed within the sessions are good indicators of the kinds of patterns enacted at home and help the therapist determine where couples routinely "get stuck." After the assessment is completed, measurable goals should be established. In order for these goals to be realized, however, the therapist must create an atmosphere conducive to change, elicit the couple's commitment to change, and work with the couple on formulating a contract. The beginning therapist should be very aware of the assessment process's impact in helping couples fully understand each other.

KEY POINTS

- The assessment process includes an identification of "the problem" from the perspective of each spouse, an analysis of the validity of each spouse's concerns, and an interactional definition of "the problem."
- The genogram is a useful tool for assessing the history of the relationship across generations.
- The marital interview is important for tracking interactional sequences that both trigger and maintain the problem.
- If the therapist wishes to use standardized self-report instruments, he or she might consider the Locke-Wallace Marital Status Inventory (L-W), the Dyadic Adjustment Scale (DAS), or the Marital Pre-Counseling Inventory (MPI).
- When the therapist asks each spouse to describe the problem, the couple's interactional patterns begin to emerge.
- Enactment occurs when the therapist decentralizes his or her participation, and directs the couple to enact, rather than describe, the situation.
- The need for support is critical to the well-being of the marriage.
- Marital therapy is contraindicated in cases of marital violence.
- Couple therapy is unlikely to work where one or both partners have little commitment to the relationship.
- Concurrent and individual therapy with one spouse works best when both spouses agree to it.
- The contract is the spouse's formal commitment to change.

MARITAL SKILLS INVENTORY

Please check when you have completed these procedures.

_____ Assess the relationship history of the client(s).

_____ Assess interactions:

    _____ Observation

    _____ Self-observation

    _____ Self-report

_____ Focus on interactional patterns.

_____ Establish therapeutic goals.

_____ Create an atmosphere of change.

_____ Obtain the couple's commitment.

_____ Formulate the contract.

REFERENCES

Brown, J. H. & Christensen, D. N. (1999). *Family Therapy: Theory and practice* (2nd Ed.) Pacific Grove, CA: Brooks/Cole.

Carter, B., & McGoldrick, M. (1989). *The changing family life cycle: Framework for family therapy* (2nd ed.). Needham Heights, MA: Allyn & Bacon.

Gottman, J. (1994). *Why marriages succeed or fail.* New York: Simon & Schuster.

Gottman, J. (2000). *Clinical manual for marital therapy: A research-based approach.* Seattle: The Gottman Institute.

Gurman, A. S., & Knudson, R. M. (1978). Behavioral marriage therapy: A psychodynamic systems analysis and critique. *Family Process, 17,* 121–138.

Hanna, S. M., & Brown, J. H. (1999). *The practice of family therapy: Key elements across models* (2nd ed.). Belmont, CA: Wadsworth.

Hirschfeld, R. A., & Goodwin, F. K. (1988). Mood disorders. In J. A. Talbott, R. E. Hales, & S. C. Yudofsky (Ed.), *Textbook of psychiatry* (pp. 403–441). Washington, DC: American Psychiatric Press.

Hops, H., Wills, T. A., Patterson, G. R., & Weiss, R. L. (1972). *Marital interaction coding system.* Eugene: University of Oregon & Oregon Research.

Jacobson, N. S. (1981). Marital problems. In J. L. Shelton & R. L. Levy (Eds.), *Behavioral assignments & treatment* (pp. 147–166). Champaign, IL: Research Press.

Karpel, M. A. (1994). *Evaluating couples: A handbook for practitioners.* New York: Norton.

Locke, H., & Wallace, K. (1959). Short marital-adjustment and prediction tests: The reliability and validity. *Marrriage & Family Living, 21,* 251–255.

Lukas, S. (1993). *Where to start and what to ask.* New York: Norton.

McGoldrick, M., & Gerson, R. (1985). *Genograms in family assessment.* New York: Norton.

O'Hanlon, W. H. (1991). Acknowledgement and possibility. Paper presented at the Family and Children's Agency, Louisville, KY.

Patterson, G. R., Hops, H., & Weiss, R. L. (1974). A social learning approach to reducing rates of marital conflict. In R. Stuart, R. Liberman, & S. Wilder (Eds.). *Advances in behavior therapy.* New York: Academic Press.

Spanier, G. B. (1976). Measuring dyadic adjustment: New scales for addressing the quality of marriage and similar dyads. *Journal of Marriage and the Family, 38,* 15–28.

Weiss, R. L., & Perry, B. A. (1979). *Assessment and treatment of marital dysfunction.* Eugene: Oregon Marital Studies Program.

Weiss, R. L., Hops, H., & Patterson, G. R. (1973). A framework for conceptualizing marital conflict, technology for altering it, some data for evaluating it. In L. A. Hamerlynch, L. C. Handy, & E. J. Mash (Eds.). *Behavior change: Methodology, concepts and practice.* Champaign, IL: Research Press.

5

✳

Developing Treatment Recommendations

CHAPTER OBJECTIVES

Upon completion of this chapter, the reader will be able to develop a treatment plan by:

1. Identifying problem areas and goals;

2. Prioritizing areas of change;

3. Identifying problem-solving strengths;

4. Describing ways to overcome initial resistance;

5. Selecting an intervention that fits with the goals and identified problems.

INTRODUCTION

Treatment plans should be tailored and should fit the unique personality of the couple. For example, in one couple where there is conflict, the treatment plan might call for conflict management skills. In another couple with a similar problem, but more hostility, the plan might call for separate sessions with each spouse, to establish trust. Sometimes a treatment plan can be presented in the initial contract for service. In those cases, couples already have their problem defined in concrete, behavioral terms, and the process of problem resolution is straightforward. For example, if a couple is seeking help with a health problem, the goal may be to decide who will be responsible for which tasks, after some psychoeducational sessions regarding the impact of the illness on couples. In another case, a couple may be seeking help for problems related to alcohol abuse. The goal may be to reduce alcohol consumption and improve problem solving and communication. A common treatment plan for such a presenting problem would be to assess the effects of alcohol use on the relationship and to utilize outside resources such as Alcoholics Anonymous. The couple also may benefit from training in problem solving and communications skills.

In developing goals for treatment plans, the therapist must consider the following. First, goals should be developed from assessment data to fit the characteristics of the couple. Second, the couple and extended family are considered as potential participants and they, with the therapist, determine who should be involved in therapy and how. Then, interventions that fit the couple's developmental level and the clinician's skill level should be selected, either spontaneously or deliberately. This chapter will review each of these elements of treatment planning.

CONSTRUCTING GOALS

Spouses or couples often begin with vague hopes: "I want help dealing with my low self-esteem," or "We want to communicate better." The marital therapist helps the couple go beyond such generalizations and describe their hopes in concrete terms, for example, "When we discuss finances, we'll avoid impasses and be able to develop a budget which will meet the needs/concerns of both partners." The treatment plan should include assessment data, which specifies the nature of the problem and outlines a course of action, or it may address the couple's goals and hypotheses generated during the assessment process. A good treatment plan requires the therapist to analyze hypotheses in order to establish operational definitions of goals and to identify strengths of the partners.

Consider the following case:

> Judy and Gene have come for marital therapy because Judy has threatened to leave Gene. She related that she feels totally overwhelmed with the responsibilities of two children, her own work as a secretary, and housework. In addition, she reported that she feels very lonely and that she has to deal with all situations by herself. Arguments have escalated recently, and the couple has difficulty talking with each other.

> **Judy:** I don't know where to start.

> **Therapist:** What do you mean?

> **Judy:** He is never around. He never tells me when he will be home. The other day he was supposed to meet me at the insurance office, and he didn't show up. He never spends time with our children. They hardly know him.

> **Therapist:** Okay. You mentioned several things. Which of these is most important?

Judy: I don't know . . . It's that . . . I can't count on him.

Therapist: Is that it? You want to be able to count on him?

Judy: Yes, I think that's the main concern.

STARTING TREATMENT

One of the greatest challenges a marital therapist faces is knowing where to start treatment. Where the intervention begins is often determined by the therapist's own theoretical framework. The structural marital therapist might intervene by developing an interactional relationship with the couple. The therapist probes both to elicit information about the problem and to alter the boundaries of the couple. The strategic marital therapist, on the other hand, might intervene through messages or directives. Directives require the couple to respond or behave in a specific way. Likewise, the intergenerational therapist attempts to maintain objectivity from the outset by (1) asking "thinking" questions rather than "feeling" questions, and (2) avoiding triangulation by asking each spouse to speak to the therapist rather than to each other. When developing a treatment plan, we suggest that beginning practitioners avoid interventions that are model-specific until after the couple's goals have been prioritized and clarified.

If the couple presents several problem areas, the marital therapist must begin to set priorities for treatment. Four criteria are critical in making this determination. The **first criterion** is determining *which problem is of most immediate importance to the couple.* The couple must be asked to select the problem of greatest concern to them. For example, a couple may want to improve their marital relationship. The therapist then must ask, "Which problem is most pressing to you" or, "Which problem must you solve now?" Alternatively, the therapist might say, "So, the first issue we need to resolve is _____." Unless the therapist has reasons for choosing another area to change, the couple is told that the one selected will be addressed initially.

In many cases, additional criteria must be considered in prioritizing areas of change. The **second criterion** is determining *which problem has the greatest negative consequence if not handled immediately.* Although a spouse may feel that one problem has the most pressing importance (for example, loss of friends), another problem may have greater negative consequence (for example, break-up of the marriage.)

By examining what has happened in the past with the couple under similar conditions, the therapist can better predict the consequences of the problem and weigh it accordingly. The therapist may ask, "What might happen if this problem is not resolved?" or, "What would likely happen to your marriage if _____ occurred?" Once this is determined, the **third criterion** comes into play: determining *which problem can be corrected most easily, considering the resources and constraints.* What forces (people as well as situations) stand in the way of problem resolution? What resources exist that could help solve the problem? For example, a wife who feels trapped may list going to school to complete an advanced degree as a goal. If her husband's resistance is an obstacle, however, the therapist might ask, "What are some things that might prevent this problem from being solved?" and, "What are some things that will help you resolve the problem?"

Finally, the **fourth criterion** for prioritizing change is determining *which problems require handling before other problems can be solved*. For example, it makes little sense to work on improving the marriage if both spouses are abusing alcohol. Likewise, before a couple can control their children, they must learn to work cooperatively. The therapist might ask what would happen if the problem were solved. Would the couple be more satisfied with their marriage? Would they do a better job parenting their children?

OPERATIONALIZING GOALS

The process of operationalizing goals not only specifies, "Where are we going?", but also provides standards by which the therapist can demonstrate his or her effectiveness in getting there. Subgoals and objectives, which are specifically defined, can be used to measure the couple's progress from week to week. Operationalizing goals provides direction in the therapy and prevents the therapist from claiming effectiveness without demonstrating it.

Goals in marital therapy, having evolved directly from the assessment, refer to the specific behaviors each spouse desires in the other, and how to increase the frequency of those behaviors. There are two basic reasons underlying the specification of reciprocal goals:

- Because the feelings one spouse has toward the other is a direct function of the other's behavior, a change in one spouse's behavior may result in changing the other;
- Marital problems arise from interaction, not intrapsychic problems (Gurman & Knudson, 1978).

On the basis of these assumptions, spouses are encouraged to communicate their desires in terms of what they would like their mate to do differently. That is, the therapist must ask each partner what behaviors the other will be performing to demonstrate that he or she has reached the goal.

In therapy, goals describe what each spouse will be doing as a result of treatment. Vague goal descriptions such as, "I want you to care about me," and "You have to think about someone besides yourself," are not acceptable, because there is no way to measure them reliably. Instead, a spouse might be asked to communicate his or her desires or complaints in specific terms: for example, "I want you to ask me about my job at least once each day." Regardless, goals should be stated clearly so that all parties know when the goal has been reached.

The following guidelines will help the therapist to operationalize goals:

- Ask each spouse to describe three specific changes he or she would like the other spouse to make. (What would you like Mary to do differently?")

- Ask each spouse to describe these changes in positive terms. ("How would you like for your husband to show you that you are appreciated?")
- Ask each spouse to describe any validity in the other's request. ("Can you understand how your wife might feel when you don't listen to her?", or "Can you see any part of her request that might be valid?")

By asking each spouse to make three requests, the therapist makes sure the changes are manageable and do not overwhelm each spouse. Moreover, the therapist is able to maintain balance without scapegoating either spouse. Finally, each spouse must validate the other spouse's request, thereby giving the therapist a platform for change.

Case of Gene and Judy:

Therapist: So . . . give me some examples. What would he be doing . . . what are some things he could do that would tell you that you could count on him?

Judy: Well, he could start by coming home on time.

Gene: You know that I can't always predict that. You know my schedule.

Judy: You could at least call.

Therapist: So—Judy, if Gene couldn't make it on time, he should call.
Judy: Yes.

Therapist: Gene, what is your usual time to get home?

Gene: I try to leave the office by 5:45 and arrive home at 6:00. Sometimes, though, I have to stay for a late appointment. Or I sometimes have work that I just need to complete before leaving.

Judy: I understand that, and I would be happy if you were home by 6:00. But it just seems that you often don't make it. Maybe I have dinner ready and you're not there. Or one of the children has a problem and you're not there. I never know if you'll be there or not. It would help if you just let me know.

Therapist: Is there a problem with that?

Gene: No.

Therapist: What else? What is it that you want him to do?

Judy: There are times I need him for things, and he's just never there.

Therapist: How would he know that you need him?

Judy: He's just never around.

Therapist: You may be talking about two different things. How do you let him know that you need him for something?

Judy: I don't. What's the use?

Gene: You know that if you need something, I'll be there.

Therapist: If Judy needs you for something—like helping one of your children with homework, helping with the housework, cooking, or even to discuss something, can she count on you?

Gene: Yes, if I'm not working. I don't mind to help when I'm off. And I enjoy our talks together.

Judy: They're very few and far between.

UTILIZING PARTNER STRENGTHS
IN DEVELOPING GOALS

Every couple will evidence various strengths or positive characteristics, and these provide a good starting place for therapy. When the therapist focuses on strengths, it affirms that the couple has assets, helps increase their motivation (or at least decrease anxiety) for change, and provides a base on which to build. It also helps establish rapport with the therapist and increase the couple's hope that they can resolve some of their differences.

Building on a couple's strengths is also important for other reasons. Couples have various untapped resources and strengths to resolve problems. They are often aware of alternative ways to change a situation; even though they may not have tried these, they are more likely to implement a solution if they suggest it or it makes sense to them.

Many couples present a therapist with multiple problems and may feel overwhelmed by the sheer magnitude of their differences. As stated earlier in this chapter, goals must be prioritized according to immediate importance, negative consequences for ignoring, ease in resolving, and desired sequence (which has to be resolved first in order for others to be resolved). After determining a beginning goal, establishing strengths of the couple, and identifying previous times they have resolved a difficult situation, the therapist creates a positive, hopeful environment.

One way a therapist uses a couple's strengths is helping them interpret or define their problem in a different way. That is, the behavior that is sometimes referred to as a "problem" is reframed in a way that describes it as more of an asset than a liability. For instance, when a wife says, "He is so nosy, always asking me one hundred questions about where I've been, who I've seen, and what I've done," the therapist may reframe that as the husband's concern and caring about her. The couple may then discuss other ways he can express that concern and caring. Similarly, a wife's statement of ineffectiveness, "I can't get him to pay any attention to me," may be reframed as "protectiveness" that makes it difficult for her to make a firm request. When she perceives herself not as "weak" or "ineffective" but as "protective," she has a new way of thinking about the problem so that it can be resolved. Furthermore, the therapist then can help her to expand her sense of protectiveness to include additional behaviors.

Still another way to emphasize strengths is to utilize the problem situation—such as being ignored by her husband—and identify times that the desired behavior (attention) has actually occurred. For instance, the therapist may ask, "Can you think of a time when your husband paid attention to you?" It seems a fact of human nature that people focus more on times when nega-

tive behavior occurs (being ignored) than on positive times (times of attention). By shifting the focus to times when the desired behavior occurs, the wife
is likely to be less disturbed about the times she is ignored. She is also likely to
gain some insight into what was going on at the different times her husband
paid attention or did not pay attention. This information may help the wife
make some small changes that will result in getting more attention, and it may
help the husband be more aware of times he ignored his wife.

By searching for strengths in each partner, the therapist can help the partners to view each other and the situation more positively. The therapist will
want to start by looking for exceptions to the problem. In some cases, the therapist can get the couple to focus on joint assets, or the strengths they share as
a couple (Young & Long, 1998). In other cases, the therapist might ask the
couple to talk about their courtship or a time when they felt close, in order to
evoke more positive feelings and strengths in the relationship.

The following points are helpful in identifying strengths:

- *Emphasize positive statements that spouses report about each other.* (For example, "My wife listens to me when I have a problem.") Also, make note of
  any comments spouses make that suggest positive affect.

- *Encourage couples to describe their courtship.* The therapist should pay particular attention to those aspects of their courtship that reveal strengths in
  their relationship.

- *Ask each spouse to identify strengths and competencies in the other.* For example, "What are some things that you admire most about your husband?"
  or "During your courtship, what attracted you to your wife?"

- *Emphasize activities the couple enjoys.* How is this activity better when the
  couple is together? How does this activity strengthen their marriage?

- *Attribute positive motives to negative behavior.* For example, "Your jealousy
  shows how much you care about him," or "Your anger may show you
  want more attention from him." (It should be noted, however, that it is
  important *not* to attribute positive motives to destructive behavior, such
  as emotional or physical abuse.)

- *Emphasize positive interactions.* Underscore positive marital interactions that
  illustrate how the couple copes with problems, or handles differences in
  their relationship. This will help the therapist to identify other strengths
  and skills in their relationship.

Eliciting marital strengths will help the marital therapist to understand how
couples cope with problems, and will provide information on how to promote
growth and development in the marriage.

Case of Gene and Judy

Therapist: Judy, does Gene do anything that is supportive or helpful?

Judy: I don't know. Sometimes he makes breakfast for the children and me.

Therapist: That's nice. How often does he do that?

Gene: One or two times a week—when I don't go in early.

Judy: Yeah, about that.

Therapist: That's pretty nice. Do you let him know you appreciate that?

Judy: Probably not as much as I should. I'm pretty tired . . . but I do appreciate it.

Therapist: So there are times that Gene is supportive and attentive. How can we build on this?

Judy: What I resent, though, is that when he helps me, I'm supposed to be really grateful. But . . . he feels no obligation to help just because he's part of the household. I want him to just get in there and help, even when he's not asked.

Therapist: Is there ever a time he does that?

Judy: When I'm sick, he always comes through.

Therapist: It sounds like he recognizes some times when you need his support. What do you do so that he cares for you at those times?

Judy: I'm not sure.

Gene: You let me know when you're not feeling well. And you always thank me.

Judy: I don't remember.

Therapist: Do you feel closer to Gene at those times?

Judy: Sure. I just wish he would do it more often.

Therapist: I guess you'll have to get sick more often (laughs). Seriously, it sounds like he is there for you when he recognizes that you need him. What does that say about your ability to get him to support you in the future?

Judy: Why do I have to be tired or sick for him to notice I need help?

Therapist: I think you may be underestimating his concern. It sounds like he is there for you when you need him. It's just that he doesn't notice.

Judy: I just wish I didn't have to ask him.

Therapist: What makes that so difficult for you? Does Gene do anything that makes it difficult for you to ask him? It might be helpful if he heard what you really need.

Judy: He is easy to talk with. But there are times that I just get down and don't feel like asking for things or even discussing my feelings.

Gene: Yes, Judy, I've noticed that you sometimes seem depressed or stressed about things in general. When I ask you what's going on, you don't seem to want to talk.

Judy: I know, but this week when I need help, I will work at asking you specifically to help me with the children or other tasks around the house. I also want you to sometimes ask me if there's anything you can do to help. Or just look around and see if there is anything that needs to be done.

Gene: I will try that for a while. I'll ask how I can help. And I'll also look around.

Therapist: Let's try this for a week and see what happens. Judy, you will ask for help as you need it. Gene, you will look around, as well as asking how you can help. And you will let Judy know when you'll be home. If you're to be late, you'll call. Okay?

In this case, the therapist helped Judy identify exactly what the presenting concern was, helped the couple set specific goals, and used the strengths Judy had identified (Gene notices when she's ill, and is attentive and helpful) to develop new behaviors. The therapist will also need to follow up on Judy's feelings of depression if these trends continue, and determine whether this is an individual issue that needs to be dealt with.

The case of Gene and Judy is not an atypical one, and indicates couples' tendencies to assume the other's intentions without asking. Gene assumes that if he helps when asked, he is being a supportive and helpful husband. Judy thinks Gene is being negligent when he does not offer to help because she assumes that it is obvious to everyone that certain chores need to be done. Her initial complaint was that she could not "count on Gene." For Gene, this was a surprise because he viewed himself as a hard worker who did whatever he could to take care of his family. The therapist first helped Judy operationalize "can't count on Gene" to specific behaviors:

1. He comes home late sometimes and does not call.
2. He does not see what needs to be done and pitch in without being asked.

The therapist also helped the couple verbalize positive behavior that was occurring:

1. Gene prepares breakfast sometimes without being asked.
2. He is helpful in times of Judy's illness.
3. Judy expresses appreciation.

The therapist framed the situation in a way that required change on the part of both spouses, without placing blame or judgment solely on one of them:

1. Judy should ask for help when she needs it.
2. Gene should look around and help with chores that need to be done to keep the household going.
3. Judy should express appreciation when Gene helps.

The therapist might also have pointed out the importance of Gene showing appreciation for the daily responsibilities Judy assumes, such as taking care of the house and meals, caring for the children, and helping with homework.

Even more critical is Gene's awareness of Judy's feelings and activities. According to Gottman (2000), such lack of awareness is a strong predictor of marital instability. Gottman states that couples, particularly husbands, who have a "map" of their spouses' psychological world are less likely to experience a drop in marital satisfaction, which could ultimately lead to divorce. A spouse with a strong love map would possess information such as the partner's best friends, stresses, dreams, favorite music, favorite relatives, and religious beliefs.

In short, when the therapist and couple prioritize the areas for change, make goals specific and concrete, and develop goals from the couple's strengths, it becomes more likely that marital therapy will be effective.

OVERCOMING RELUCTANCE
TO ATTEND THERAPY

It is not unusual for one spouse to suggest therapy and for the other spouse to be somewhat reluctant to participate. Husbands characteristically have been more reluctant than wives to become involved in therapy, perhaps for several reasons. They may feel that private matters should stay within the family, they may not "believe" in therapy, or they may fear losing control.

Other reasons for resistance include:

- Spouses have differential levels of commitment to the marriage. In fact, it is frequently the case that one person wants to keep the marriage intact, and therefore is very amenable to therapy, while the other wants the marriage to end.
- Spouses have differential expectations for therapy. One may think it can be helpful while the other thinks it is "silly" to talk about their problems.
- Affairs and betrayals may be difficult to discuss. The person who has had the affair may be concerned about an affair being brought up. If it is ongoing, there may be ambivalence about stopping it.
- Marital violence may create resistance. The person who is violent may be uncomfortable in a setting where his or her "bad" behavior is discussed. The other person may be fearful of bringing it up because of later retribution.
- Some spouses may not want to talk about marital problems, because they fear behaviors such as alcohol or other substance abuse will be brought up, and they would not want to stop that behavior.
- Blame is likely to be assessed by both partners. It is uncomfortable to have private issues discussed in front of someone who may be "judgmental."

Beginning therapists must be aware of all of these natural feelings and understand the difficulties they pose. They must also be aware of techniques that can be used to reduce the resistance and get the reluctant spouse involved. Since some therapists refuse to work with marital issues unless both members are present, one spouse has to figure out how to get the other involved.

In many cases, a spouse may have the untested belief or feeling that the other spouse would never consider therapy. Therefore, he or she is hesitant to ask; however, the therapist may challenge this belief by saying things such as, "Why do you think he/she wouldn't talk?", or "Maybe he/she would also like to express concerns." This might allow the spouse to consider that his or her assumption is wrong, and to consider that therapy may be beneficial for both.

The beginning marital therapist needs to assess resistance to therapy. In cases where the reluctance is related to safety issues, the therapist may not want to see the couple together. In other situations where it appears that the most effective treatment would be conjoint therapy, the therapist must help allay the fears and concerns behind the resistance. This begins with investigating the motivational level of the spouse who makes the initial contact, and assessing whether this person wants the other spouse to be involved. If the partner does not want his or her spouse to be involved, this should be discussed, and the information gained may be quite significant in the therapy.

If the spouse wants his or her partner to attend, and has exhausted all ideas to persuade the partner to do so, the therapist may agree to help by making a call. Sometimes the spouse is fearful that the therapist and the spouse who makes the initial call will "gang up" on the other partner. If the therapist can begin to join with the partner on the phone and help allay the fears of that person, he or she is more likely to get involved in treatment.

Sometimes one partner will refuse to attend, leaving the therapist to work with only the concerned spouse. It should be noted that while change may be more rapid with both spouses involved, a spouse system can be changed by working with only one member (O'Hanlon and Weiner-Davis, 1989). The therapist may work with the motivated partner, while keeping in touch with the other. David Treadway (1989) indicated that this is frequently the case with substance-abusing partners, and described a technique he uses where he calls the nonparticipating partner and asks for support and cooperation in treating the participating partner. The drinker will be motivated not to be personally involved, so will likely agree to help the spouse.

In the event that both spouses attend, there must be a connection on the therapist's part with both partners, which will help ensure that they both feel hopeful that the process can produce positive changes.

CHOOSING THE BEST INTERVENTION

At this point in therapy, a couple or individual has outlined concerns and problems, that have been prioritized and agreed upon by the therapist and couple. The therapist has also analyzed the context in which the problem occurs. Hanna and Brown (1999) suggest that the therapist should then ask and get answers to the following questions (adapted):

- What is the problem, how often does it occur, and how intense is it?
- What are the consequences of the problem behavior to the couple?
- What resources can the couple use for changing the problem?
- How would a change in the problem behavior affect the couple and others?

The next step is to choose a therapeutic intervention. There is no "one size fits all" intervention, and in fact, the critical questions in choosing an effective, efficient intervention are, "What intervention, by whom, is most effective for the couple, with what specific problem, and under which set of circumstances?" (Paul, 1967, p. 111).

The beginning marital therapist should have a valid rationale for working with a particular problem situation—one that is grounded in research. Although various approaches may work with any given problem, certain interventions have proven more effective than others in ameliorating certain types of problems. For instance, couples who are in conflict often respond better to a communication and problem-solving approach (Jacobson, 1984). There are some combinations of interventions, however, that are often most effective in changing behavior problems. Although each strategy is discussed separately in Chapter Two, more than one intervention will likely be used with any particular couple in actual practice. For example, a couple lacking the skills to interact appropriately with each other may need a conflict management and communication skills program. After learning how to communicate with each other, they may be given the in-session task of managing a more conflictual issue (such as a husband's neglect of his wife).

Gottman (1999) talks of forming a mental image of each spouse and their relationship as he works with them. He relates that his image of the couple helps him understand what healing needs to take place. He then designs an individualized intervention for each couple, based on the clinician's checklist for marital assessment. This begins with his assessment of where each of the spouses is in the marriage, followed by the marital friendship assessment and whether the couple needs to rebuild positive aspects of their life together. Other parts of the checklist include sentiment override, partners' physiological arousal to conflict, how the couple regulates conflict, and how the partners help each other fulfill their life dreams. He has a "menu" of intervention choices, and the couple is involved in determining which interventions are used. Treatment formats vary by methods and time. Some examples include more traditional marital sessions, weekend workshops followed by individual sessions, psychoeducational courses (course modules followed by individualized sessions), and bibliotherapy.

Wright and Leahey (1984) discuss common marital and family interventions along a continuum of *direct* and *indirect* interventions. The authors note that direct interventions are compliance-based, straightforward attempts at change with cooperative spouses, such as psychoeducation, task assignments, and directives. Indirect interventions, on the other hand, are not based on compliance; they are less threatening attempts at change with spouses who are less comfortable with the course of therapy. These attempts include the use of questions, strategic tasks, positive connotations, and paradoxes. Indirect approaches are often used when there has been a history of failure with direct interventions, or when the therapist is discouraged about the progress of treatment. It is recommended that the therapist begin with direct interventions, and move to indirect interventions when direct interventions do not work.

CONCLUSION

The therapist must use assessment data to: formulate hypotheses regarding the problem, establish goals, prioritize concerns, operationalize goals, determine how to deal with resistance, and then develop interventions appropriate to these goals and concerns. In order to maximize effectiveness, the therapist should build on identified strengths and assets of the couple. The therapist should be ready to alter the treatment plan if the couple presents new information or rejects the initial proposal, and the couple should have input into the interventions chosen.

KEY POINTS

- Treatment plans should be tailored to fit the unique personality of the couple.

- The treatment plan should include assessment data, which specifies the nature of the problem and outlines a course of action to meet the couple's goals.

- In the problem definition stage, the therapist helps the couple to identify what they want changed.

- Goals should be stated clearly so that everyone can agree when the goal has been reached.

- Goals should specify conditions that will ensure that the goal behavior will occur, as well as acceptable levels of performance.

- Every couple exhibits various strengths or positive characteristics, which provide a good starting place for therapy.

- Starting treatment based on strengths helps the therapist focus on those areas in the relationship that are working.

- Eliciting marital strengths will help the marital therapist to understand how couples cope with problems and provide information on how to promote growth and development in the marriage.

- Husbands characteristically have been more reluctant than wives to become involved in therapy.

- The beginning marital therapist needs to assess resistance to therapy.

- Therapeutic interventions should be geared to a couple's specific circumstances and concerns.

MARITAL SKILLS INVENTORY

Please check when you have completed these procedures.

_____ Prioritize areas of change.

_____ Make goals concrete and specific.

_____ Develop goals from couple and/or family strengths.

_____ Build on existing strengths.

_____ Overcome initial resistance.

_____ Select interventions.

REFERENCES

Gottman, J. M. (1999). The marriage clinic: *A scientifically based marital therapy.* New York: Norton.

Gottman, J. M. (2000) *Clinical manual for marital therapy: A research-based approach.* Seattle, WA: The Gottman Institute.

Gurman, A. S., & Knudson, R. M. (1978). Behavioral marriage therapy: A psychodynamic systems analysis and critique. *Family Process, 17,* 121–138.

Hanna, S. M., & Brown, J. H. (1999). *The practice of family therapy: Key elements across models* (2nd ed.). Belmont, CA: Wadsworth.

Jacobson, N. S. (1984). A component analysis of behavioral marital therapy: The relative effectiveness of behavior exchange and communication 6060 problem-solving training. *Journal*

of Consulting and Clinical Psychology, 52, 295–305.

O'Hanlon, W. H. & Weiner-Davis, M. (1989). *In search of solutions: A new direction in psychotherapy.* New York: Norton.

Paul, G. C. (1967). Insight vs. desensitization in psychotherapy two years after termination. *Journal of Consulting Psychology, 31,* 333–348.

Treadway, D. (1989). *Before it's too late: Working with substance abuse in the family.* New York: Norton.

Wright, L., & Leahey, M. (1984). *Nurses and families: A guide to family assessment and intervention.* Philadelphia: Davis.

Young, M. E. & Long, L. L. (1998). *Counseling and therapy for couples.* Pacific Grove, CA: Brooks/Cole.

PART III

Treatment Concepts and Skills

6

✳

Developing Rules
for Negotiating Conflict

CHAPTER OBJECTIVES

Upon completion of this chapter, the reader will be able to:

1. Describe four patterns of conflictual interaction;
2. Describe gender differences in handling conflict;
3. Describe three styles for handling marital conflict;
4. Describe the "four horsemen of the apocalypse";
5. Identify the characteristics of battering;
6. Identify warning signs that indicate violence;
7. Utilize a "decision tree" to assess the level of violence in a marital relationship;
8. Specify steps for negotiating conflict;
9. Ask questions to determine whether the problem is resolvable.

INTRODUCTION

Skills in conflict resolution and problem solving comprise a set of well-developed strategies for dealing with disagreements (Stuart, 1980), and problem solving and conflict resolution have proven effective in treating marital conflict (Jacobson & Margolin, 1979). The process has two distinct phases—problem definition and problem resolution. In the problem-definition phase, the critical issue or problem ("You don't care about me") is defined in operational or measurable terms. An operational definition of the problem is much more likely to lead to an effective response.

The problem-resolution phase emphasizes behavior change rather than insight. It is best to choose a solution that can be implemented by the family with a minimum of help. Solutions should be kept simple, because complex plans often fail due to the costs (time and energy spent) which often outweigh the benefits (the relationship itself).

COMMON CONFLICTED INTERACTIONS

Markman, Stanley, and Blumberg (1994) list four patterns of conflictual interactions that often lead to marital distress:

1. *Escalation.* Escalation occurs when arguments become out of control. It is likely to occur when spouses try to "one-up" each other through personal attacks and verbal abuse. The spouse who is attacked attempts to defend himself or herself by attacking the other. Intimate knowledge that erodes the emotional health of the relationship is often present when arguments escalate. John Gottman (1994) reports that escalating cycles of negative interaction over time often lead to divorce.

2. *Invalidation.* Invalidation occurs when one spouse puts down thoughts, feelings, and behaviors of the other spouse. Such a pattern often reduces self-esteem and self-respect, leaving the other spouse feeling discounted. Invalidation often leads to spouses withholding thoughts and feelings to protect themselves against put-downs. Markman et al. (1994) indicate that invalidation is a good predictor for future problems in the marriage and ultimately divorce.

3. *Withdrawal and Avoidance.* Withdrawal and avoidance occur when one spouse is unwilling to participate in an interaction. A spouse may withdraw from a conversation by not talking, rolling his or her eyes, or by withdrawing more obviously by leaving the room. Avoidance occurs when a spouse attempts to avoid a conversation. Avoidance and withdrawal of one spouse often leads to pursuit by the other spouse ("Why don't you ever want to talk?"). The more one spouse withdraws, the more the other spouse will pursue. Like other patterns of conflict, avoidance and withdrawal often leads to marital distress and divorce.

4. *Negative Interpretations.* Negative interpretations occur when a spouse believes that the beliefs and intentions of the other spouse are more negative than warranted. This often occurs when there has been a history of negative interactions, and spouses begin to question each other's motives. Under these conditions, it is very difficult for the couple to manage conflict in a constructive manner. Negative interpretations often

lead to conditions of hopelessness and despair. Since negative interpretations are hard to identify, they are likely to become embedded into destructive cycles of interaction. Negative interpretations are often maintained through self-fulfilling prophecy. If we expect to see a negative behavior such as uncaring, then we are likely to find it. Even when a spouse exhibits positive behavior ~~maybe to please us~~ it is viewed negatively—for example, as manipulation—by the other spouse.

In each of these conflictual patterns, spouses feel unheard. This often leads to disappointment, bitterness, and mistrust, thus blocking intimacy, which in turn leads to further conflict. Couples who are unable to resolve conflict often "fall out of love." One or both partners begin to distance themselves from the other and often seek the affections of a third party. The result is often alternating cycles of intense arguing or distance that bring couples to treatment.

GENDER DIFFERENCES

Men and women appear to handle conflict differently, and the marital therapist should be attuned to these differences. Each spouse's experience should be heard. In cases of marital conflict, gender differences are often the core issue and should be identified. For example, Jacobson, Holtzworth-Monroe, and Schmaling (1989) have found that women often complain more than men about their current relationship. Indeed, women often desire greater involvement and closeness from their husbands, while husbands desire to maintain the status quo and create greater autonomy and separateness for themselves. Moreover, women are more likely to seek therapy and push for an egalitarian relationship, whereas men are less likely to seek therapy and are inclined to maintain traditional gender roles.

Take the case of Paul and Lauren who have been married for twelve years. Paul was an insurance agent and Lauren was a physical therapist. Paul often had appointments at night and Lauren often worked weekends. Lauren felt that they were drifting apart but did not know how to express her feelings to Paul, who often seemed preoccupied. At times Lauren felt that Paul cared little for her. The following dialogue illustrates their dilemma:

Lauren: I wish we had more time together.

Paul: We've got weekends. We could do something today.

Lauren: We only have Sundays. Maybe I shouldn't work Saturdays.

Paul: It won't always be this way.

Lauren: When is it going to be better?

Paul: I don't know. Look, I have to work these hours to build my client base.

Lauren: When we discussed this earlier, you told me you were only going to work one night a week.

Paul: I don't remember saying that.

Lauren: Things aren't going to change. Just admit it.

Paul: We're together now but you want to argue.

In this case, Lauren wants Paul to talk about the problem and Paul wishes to maintain the status quo. Markman et al. (1994) suggest that research shows that women prefer to get close through verbal communication, while men express closeness through physical activity. Lauren would prefer to get close by discussing the problem, while Paul would prefer doing something. Attitudes about intimacy are often based on childrearing habits, where girls are socialized through words, while boys are nurtured through activities and sports.

Gottman (1994) reports that men avoid conflict because it is tougher physiologically on them as opposed to women. Gottman notes that during periods of intense conflict, a man's pulse and blood pressure will be more likely to rise. Thus, a husband may withdraw from conflict instinctively if nothing more than to protect his health. Likewise, he is more likely to become overwhelmed and disorganized by his wife's negativity, and often avoids or leaves a situation that produces conflict. These differences are important for couples to understand.

MARITAL CONFLICT STYLES

John Gottman (1994) in his book *Why Marriages Succeed or Fail* reports that based on twenty years of research with 2,179 couples, similar marital styles for dealing—or not dealing—with conflict predicts a healthy marriage. Gottman found three styles of a healthy stable marriage:

1. *Conflict Avoider.* According to Gottman, this is perhaps the most unexpectedly stable style of marriage. These couples conspire to avoid discussion that will end in gridlock. They, in effect, agree to disagree. This style of marriage is characterized by two strong individuals with traditional beliefs. Each spouse often takes the lead in a particular domain of the marriage (for example, she may be responsible for scheduling activities with friends, and he may be responsible for house repairs). Rather than try to resolve conflict, they focus on what is positive in the marriage. They have strong support systems—religious, social, community, and recreational—outside the marriage. They tend to be active and to utilize their core values as a guide to resolving conflict. The cost, however, for avoiding conflict is loss of intimacy. When conflict does arise, both feel unskilled in resolving the problem. This often leads to avoidance, isolation, loneliness, and a general uneasiness about the relationship.

2. *Volatile Marriage.* Most marital therapists believe that volatility is unhealthy. On the contrary, Gottman found that for some couples, volcanic arguments are just a small part of a loving marriage. The energy and passion that they put into fighting often fuels their positive

interactions more. The men never stay disengaged from the women in this style of marriage.

In these marriages, the couple expresses more anger, but at the same time, they balance it by sharing more affection. These couples have no difficulty making up and moving on to resolve their differences. The cost to the volatile couple is endless bickering and potential for violence when there is too much negativity.

3. *Validating Marriage.* In the validating marriage, couples negotiate problems to their mutual satisfaction. Each spouse hears the opinions of the other. Even in the midst of disagreement, each still considers the other spouse's opinions important. With these types of couples, you often hear the use of "I see," or "I understand." This, however, does not mean that the spouses understand each other. Instead, it means "I have a different view but I want to hear your view." The mutual respect shown by each tends to limit the number of disagreements. These couples value "we"-ness, and unlike the conflict-avoiding couple, do not have a need for individual privacy. Validating couples are often good friends who value communication, honesty, affection, and shared time. In some cases individual pursuits may be sacrificed for friendship and togetherness.

Gottman's research suggests that successful marriages generally evolve into one of these styles. In truly stable marriages both spouses use the same style, and only in unstable styles are there mismatches. These mismatches help explain why some marriages do not last when they appear to be stable. Gottman (1999, p. 95) elaborates:

> The mismatches—mixing types in a couple—may explain why it is that some people get divorced who have a lot of everything else going for them, but they just don't have what feels like a "right" or a "natural" or a "deep and meaningful" connection in the marriage. They may even be able to manage many of the practical aspects of being married and appear to be an ideal couple. Yet they experience their marriage as hollow, as "just not working." The passion is either "off" or simply not there. Appearances to the contrary, they are unsuited for one another. Often those feelings of an ill fit are due to a fundamental mismatch in typology.

For example, if a validator (one who usually stays calm and rationally works out problems) or a conflict-minimizer marries a volatile type (who loves a good fight), serious problems in the marriage are predictable. The volatile spouse feels frustrated when the conflict-minimizing or validating spouse refuses to participate in the fight. The more reasonable the conflict-minimizer becomes, the more angry and loud the volatile mate becomes. For that type of marriage to last, one or the other spouse must change his or her way of fighting.

Gottman's research suggests that it is not the conflict itself, or the lack of conflict, that leads to divorce, but rather the way couples handle their inevitable conflict. Whether couples fight all the time or never fight is not the primary issue; rather, it is the way they resolve conflict, as well as the quality of emotional interaction that determines satisfaction in the marriage. There must be a balance between positive (mutual pleasure, humor, and support) and negative (criticism, anger, and disgust) interactions for the marriage to maintain a satisfactory relationship. According to Gottman, satisfied couples maintain a five to one ratio of positive to negative interactions, regardless of their style for handling conflict. Some conflict is necessary to keep the couple engaged. However, couples that are unable to negotiate a style for managing conflict are at risk for "the four horsemen of the apocalypse" in their marriage (Gottman, 1994).

FOUR HORSEMEN OF THE APOCALYPSE

Couples who are unable to resolve the way they manage conflict and who experience an absence of positive interactions often face a downward spiral of escalating conflict that often leads to separation or divorce. Gottman (1994) has identified four behaviors, "the four horsemen of the apocalypse," that are characteristic of these marriages. They are from least to most threatening: criticism, contempt, defensiveness, and stonewalling.

- *Criticism*. Criticism occurs when spouses attack each other's character, rather than a specific behavior. For example, when a husband says to his wife, "You only think about yourself," he is criticizing her. This is different than complaining, which is an expression of anger or distress. For example, a wife might complain by saying "You spend all your free time with your friends." However, if her complaints go unheard, she may criticize by saying, "You never want to do anything with me." In this case, the complaint about a specific behavior turned to criticism about the person. Criticism becomes a problem over time, or when it leads to contempt.

- *Contempt*. Contempt differs from criticism because it is designed to emotionally abuse the partner. Name calling or personal attacks such as "You're stupid," or "You're dumb," corrode the relationship and prevent the expression of positive interactions. Obscene words, such as "bitch," and "bastard," and ridicule, such as "You are worthless" are forms of emotional abuse that lead to arguments and potential physical violence in the relationship.

- *Defensiveness*. Contemptuous interaction often leads to the third horseman—defensiveness. Defensiveness occurs when both partners blame each other and fail to take ownership of the problem. Defensiveness is a common response to contempt when one or both spouses feel blamed. Excuses, "yes-but's," whining, and other forms of defensive behavior prevent couples from resolving problems and lead to the fourth horseman.

- *Stonewalling*. Stonewalling often occurs when one or both spouses remove themselves from the conversation, either emotionally or physically. Because men are easier to arouse, they are more likely to withdraw as tension increases. This often explains the circular interaction patterns where wives emotionally pursue their husbands with complaints, criticism, and demands, resulting in the husband's use of rationalizations or withdrawal, followed by the wife's increased pursuit. These men are more likely to withdraw to avoid the pain because they are more physiologically aroused by the conflict than their wives.

Case Study: Janice and Jerry

Janice and Jerry have been married five years and recently came to marital therapy because of conflict that has become unmanageable. In fact, Jerry has moved out of the house. The couple reports that much of their conflict centered around Jerry's gambling. Jerry reports that he never loses more money than he can afford and he finds that the activity helps him deal with the increasing stress of running a business. Janice complains that not only does the gambling take more of Jerry's time (on top of the number of hours in his job), but he is using money they could use for joint recreation. Janice has decided to open a cleaning business and needs some help. Recently, they are unable to be together without loud conflict, and the interactions have become extremely critical and hurtful. For example, Janice has called Jerry an "obsessive gambler, just like your no-good father," and Jerry has responded with hurtful statements such as, "Who are you to talk? If you hadn't married me, you'd be living in the projects right now." Both Janice and Jerry say they love each other, but they are unable to be together without fighting. This has led to Jerry's moving out and Janice's tendency to avoid getting together with Jerry.

Analysis: The therapist determines that Janice and Jerry are employing all four horsemen of the apocalypse, which puts their marriage at great risk. They are very critical of each other, and the criticism has turned to contempt—with each making very hurtful and demeaning statements. This has led to each becoming defensive of his or her position and finally has led to stonewalling—actual physical departure by Jerry, and emotional withdrawal by Janice. The therapist is aware that for Janice and Jerry to avoid a divorce, they need to define the conflict and determine if it is resolvable. If so, they both need to learn effective ways of resolving conflict, as well as to create many more positive interactions to offset the negative ones.

Intervention: The therapist begins by hearing each partner's view of the problem. Jerry says he really enjoys gambling, sometimes wins money, and even in bad circumstances, does not lose more than he can afford. He says he controls himself but is annoyed with Janice's constant nagging and put-downs. He adds that he left because he cannot stand listening to her and has, on occasion, become so frustrated that he has made threats to her. Janice reports that she frequently feels lonely and has started the cleaning business to occupy herself. She said she would like Jerry's help because of his good "business sense," but also adds that she needs some start-up money.

Both Janice and Jerry report that they would like to feel closer. However, both agree that they should be able to pursue individual interests, as well as foster a more positive marital relationship.

With the therapist's help, Janice and Jerry set the following short-term goals: (1) to plan time for talking and being together so they could feel closer, and (2) to negotiate the amount of money available for individual interests and time to be devoted to these.

As Jerry and Janice discuss their families of origin, they gain some insight into their expectations for marriage. Jerry came from a very conflictual family, and his father retreated by gambling. In Janice's family, her father and mother jointly ran a business and she observed them frequently talking together about how to make it more efficient. The therapist helped Jerry and Janice see that they brought some expectations from their own families of origin that may not be appropriate for their relationship. The therapist also externalized the problem by referring to the conflict as their "drifting apart" behavior.

CONFLICT THAT TURNS TO VIOLENCE

Unresolved conflict often leads to violence, and the level of domestic violence is alarming. Approximately 25 percent of couples report incidents of shoving, pushing, or hitting (Markman, Stanley, & Blumberg, 1994). It is estimated that violence occurs on 35 occasions before it is reported (Avis, 1992). Domestic violence includes battering, sexual abuse, psychological abuse, and the physical destruction of property—forms of violence that are often overlooked by therapists. For many violent couples, domestic violence is the result of both poor handling of escalation and withdrawal.

Characteristics of Battering

It is often quite difficult to get accurate information about battering. According to Neil Jacobson and John Gottman (1998), psychological research demonstrates that people are not reliable observers of their own or their spouse's behavior. In a landmark investigation, Jacobson and Gottman wired sixty-three battering couples and a control group that were equally dissatisfied with partners but did not manifest this through violence. Over an eight-year period, the authors identified the following characteristics of batterers. Battering is physical aggression that is designed to control a spouse. It involves physical injury more often to women than men.

- Batterers share a common profile; they are unpredictable, unable to be influenced by their wives, and impossible to prevent from battering once an argument has begun.

- Battered women are neither passive nor submissive. Sometimes they are as angry as the batterers. But women almost never batter men.

- Batterers can be classified into two distinct types—men whose temper slowly simmers until it suddenly erupts into violence and those who strike out immediately. This difference has important implications for women leaving abusive relationships.

- Emotional abuse plays a vital role in battering, undermining a woman's confidence.

- Domestic violence can decrease on its own—but it almost never stops.

- Battered women do leave at high rates, despite the increased danger they face when leaving the relationship. (p. 62)

The research by Gottman and Jacobson cited above suggests that most batterers are men, and this was apparently true in their samples. However, it should be noted that limited research has been conducted on other kinds of couples, such as lesbian couples.

Assessing the Violence
in Marital Conflict

When discussing conflictual issues, the therapist should always ask about violence. There are several warning signs that may indicate violence:

- Frequent use of name-calling and put-downs

- Alcohol/drug use

- Poor problem-solving and communication skills

- Threats by one spouse to the other

- Control of one spouse by the other spouse

- Need to isolate spouse from friends and family

- History of witnessing abuse

- Aggressiveness when other spouse asserts self

When interviewing the couple, the therapist should ask the following questions to assess the level of violence in the family:

- Does the couple have a way to withdraw from the conflict?

- Are spouses able to recognize the other's position?

- Do couples recognize the warning signs of violence?

- Does one spouse blame the other for his actions?

- Are couples aware of volatile situations?

- Are spouses aware of their actions?

- Has either spouse done something during the conflict that he or she regrets?

- Can both spouses state differences of opinions?

- Is there a high level of emotion during times of stress?

- Does either spouse get angry?
- Does either spouse raise his or her voice?
- Is either spouse using alcohol or drugs at the time of the conflict?
- Is it difficult for one or both spouses to calm down?
- Does either spouse come from a family where he or she, or another family member, was a victim of abuse?

Dealing with Couple Violence

Increased awareness of family violence has drawn the attention of family therapists to their responsibilities in this area. O'Leary, Vivian, and Malone (1991) assert that violence, at least in its milder forms, appears to be quite common in couples seeking therapy. However, it is quite easy for therapists to miss this, and, therapists may be treating violence in couples without realizing it. Therefore, it is imperative that the therapist look for warning signs of abuse. Christensen (1992) developed a decision tree for therapists to assess violence in the marital relationship. If the therapist suspects violence, he or she should remain calm and not overreact. Here it is important to assess the amplitude of violence by discussing the worst case scenario ("Was there ever a time when you hit your partner?"). If there is no physical aggression, the therapist can continue to discuss issues the couple wants changed. However, if physical contact is present, the therapist should pursue this area by saying, "Would it be O.K. to talk?", or "Is it too difficult to talk about this?". If the interaction seems volatile (for example, if either partner raises his or her voice) and/or one partner looks scared, the therapist should meet with the perpetrator first and then the victim. The purpose here is to cool things down and get the perpetrator to take responsibility. When meeting with the victim alone, the therapist should discuss whether there is a safety plan. After this, the therapist should meet with both spouses to design a course of action. If the couple is not volatile, the therapist should talk about issues and their relationship history and ask for some individual time with each before plotting a course of action.

Therapists are legally bound to report violence to the appropriate agency (for example, protective services) if they suspect it. It is important, however, to properly inform clients of this legal responsibility early in the interview so that, if abuse or violence becomes apparent, spouses will not feel betrayed by the therapist.

As the issue of reporting is addressed with spouses, marital therapists should explain the procedure as it is carried out in the given community. If clients are already voluntarily seeking therapy, the consequences of reporting may be minimal in some communities, and provide little disruption to the couple or their therapy. However, in other cases, there may be more formal involvement with the legal system. In view of this diversity, beginning therapists should thoroughly investigate local procedures under a variety of circumstances in order to be as accurate as possible in explaining the process to couples. In addition, it is important for marital therapists to understand the legal definition of abuse in their community in order to avoid unnecessary reports. It is also important for the therapist to receive training on how to report incidences of violence.

In all cases, it is best to maintain a position of collaboration with the couple, with special emphasis placed upon maintaining an empathic bond with the abuser. The process of reporting can then be an opportunity to join with the family through highlighting the courage it takes to discuss the violence, and by suggesting that many people are never able to muster the courage to do so (Jenkins, 1991). By emphasizing what courage has already been shown, the therapist can lay a positive foundation for the reporting process and help the couple develop a plan for dealing with the violence.

In some cases, therapists are able to persuade spouses to make the call themselves in the office as a manifestation of their commitment to improving the relationship. By speaking directly with authorities, spouses are able to take greater control over their lives and, correspondingly, they often seem empowered and respected. They may receive information directly from social services, and may not have to be dependent on the therapist for interpreting the process. Couples who remain reluctant to report may be helped by the therapist encouraging them to make an anonymous telephone call for information, followed by an actual report. If danger is not imminent, it may also be possible to delay the report until the therapist and couple can agree upon how the report will be made. In those cases, however, the issue should not be confused. *The questions is not whether a report will be made, but only how a report will be made—who will call, what will be said, and so on.*

MANAGING CONFLICT

The first step in helping a couple to manage conflict is to help them recognize whether the problem is changeable. If both parties agree to the definition of the problem and agree they need to change, conflict negotiation and communication strategies are the preferred mode of treatment. If the couple cannot agree on the problem, and the differences cannot be accepted, the therapist should utilize strategies to help the couple accept those differences and live with the problem. In either case the therapist should emphasize that the constructive management of conflict can help each partner experience more closeness and cooperation.

Changeable Problems

Spouses are better able to manage conflict when they agree on the problem definition and agree on what needs to change. Spouses who have a shared view of the problem become more empowered to resolve it. The following steps will be useful in helping couples negotiate conflict.

1. *Ask each spouse to make (a) request(s) of his or her partner.* It is extremely important to find out what each spouse wants the other spouse to change. It is also important to limit complaining and help each partner focus specifically on what he or she wants changed in the other (for example, "I want you to pay more attention to me," or "I want you to quit putting me down in front of my friends."). It is critical that the request be stated as clearly and concretely as possible.

2. *Help each partner to put his or her complaint in an interactional context.* Questions such as "When do you feel that he doesn't pay attention to you? What is he doing? What are you doing? Then what happens?", will help put the request in an interactional context. It is important not to begin negotiation at this point, however. The therapist should stay with one partner to get a clear understanding of the request before moving to the other partner.

3. *Find out what each thinks about the other's request.* Ask each spouse about the request(s) the other has made. Does the request have merit? Try to phrase questions in a way to get *some* acknowledgment (such as, "Is there a kernel of truth?", or "What part can you accept?") The therapist should avoid discussing areas of disagreement as much as possible. Try to summarize what each can accept in the other's request.

4. *Establish agreement on the problem the couple wants changed.* It is very important that the couple agrees on what needs to be changed. The therapist can assist by helping the couple to select a problem that is meaningful but one than can be resolved most easily, considering resources and constraints. Likewise, there may be a problem that must be resolved before other problems can be resolved. For example, a husband's command that triggers an angry response from his wife may be related to other problems in the relationship.

5. *Examine developmental/individual issues related to the problem.* The therapist may need to explore historical issues related to the problem. For example, a husband who is angry and gets loud when an argument escalates may need to explore developmental issues related to the problem. When did he learn to get loud? Did his parents get loud with him? How did others in his family treat him? Did he need to get loud or angry to get his way? Answers to these questions will help him to better understand his anger and help him get control over it. It will also help his wife to recognize that his anger may not just be directed at her but at other members of his family. Learning about these issues will often help to create a climate where change may occur.

6. *Get the partner who brings up the problem to request a solution while the other partner listens.* Either partner can make a request, but it is helpful to start with the partner who initiated the discussion. Ask the partners to confine themselves to one issue at a time; otherwise, the other partner may not know what is being requested. It is also critical that the therapist

not allow a counter request until the original request is clearly understood. Allow three to five minutes for this step.

7. *Get the other spouse to restate the request.* In this case, you are trying to get the listener to acknowledge the other spouse's request. This does not mean accepting their partner's position. The listener does not have to paraphrase the request, but merely acknowledge his or her understanding of it (for example, "O.K., you want _____.", or "You think it would be a good idea if _____.".

8. *Get the other spouse (listener) to make a counter request.* The counter request should not be a reaction to the sender's message but instead a statement that reflects his or her wishes or desires for a solution. It should also be a request that involves both spouses.

9. *If the conflict escalates, call time-out.* Either spouse should be permitted to call time-out if they feel that they or their partner is getting out of control ("This is getting out of hand—let's talk later.") The person who initiates the time-out should suggest a time to get back together at least within 24 hours. The decision to get back together should be mutual, co-planned, and help to reduce the conflict.

10. *Discuss several solutions until the couple chooses one solution or a combination that is agreeable to both parties.* Here the therapist should help the couple select the most workable solution. This may not be an *ideal* solution, but one that both parties can support. This often will be a solution where both partners have sacrificed something. It should be an agreement that describes how each spouse will behave differently. Otherwise, each spouse may have a different interpretation of the agreement.

11. *Discuss how you will put your agreement into action.* Once the couple has reached an agreement, they must decide how they will carry it out. Who will do what and when? The therapist should request that the agreement be put in writing so there will be no misunderstanding about what should happen. The agreement should be posted in the house (perhaps on the refrigerator or bulletin board) to remind the couple of their agreement. The therapist should ask the couple to review the agreement to make sure that the plan addresses the problem (Karpel, 1994).

12. *Congratulate the couple for their efforts.* The therapist should review the couple's willingness to sacrifice and congratulate them for what each has given up. This is a time when the couple can reaffirm their relationship and celebrate their success in reducing the conflict.

13. *Set up regular times to meet.* The final step requires the couple to establish a time for regular meetings. Regular meetings are a tangible way for couples to make their relationship the top priority (Markman et al., 1994). Meeting times should be approximately 30–45 minutes at a time when there are few distractions—no ringing telephone or children around. Emphasis should be given to meeting even when things are going well. Meetings are useful for discussing differences and making future plans.

14. *Start with an easy issue.* The therapist should encourage the couple to start with a small problem. For example, it is much easier to learn the skills if you start with an issue where you can make progress (household chores) rather than a more difficult problem (husband's neglect of the wife). The therapist should allow enough time to practice the steps (approximately one hour). Once the couple has mastered the skills, the therapist can go on to a more difficult issue. Within time the couple's efforts will seem less awkward and more natural (Weeks & Treat, 1992).

The Case of Jerry & Janice (Continued)

The therapist leads Janice to make a request of Jerry, specifically, "I want more time with you and I want more say in how our money is spent." The therapist suggests that only the first request be handled at this time and asks her to be specific about what they would be doing during that time together. She asks that she and Jerry go out at least once a week and that he give her at least two hours a week to discuss the cleaning business. Jerry is asked what he thought of the request, and he says he is both willing and interested in spending more time with Janice if the time could be pleasant.

The therapist then asks Jerry to make a request of Janice as to how the problem could be resolved. Jerry requests that the time they spend together be absent of any nagging or complaints. This request is discussed and agreed upon. Janice states, however, that while she would work at making their fun-time together free of conflict, there would have to be some time for them to negotiate their differences. Jerry agrees to this. The couple then works out which night they would go out and how they would spend that first night.

Analysis: It should be noted that this first issue was an easier one than the money issue or gambling issue; however, if the couple experiences success with the first task, it will provide a positive base for other interactions. This will help them begin to develop a better ratio of positive to negative interactions.

Unchangeable Problems

John Gottman (1998) suggests that when one chooses a partner, he or she automatically selects a set of unresolvable problems. Likewise if that relationship doesn't work and he or she chooses someone else, he or she has chosen another set of unresolvable problems. Gottman further states:

> . . . This is very much like a set of ailments we develop as we age. Trick knees, bad backs, indigestion. We learn to live with these chronic ailments and to make the best of life in spite of them. The same is true in any marriage. We have discovered in our study of long-term happy marriages that when people stay married for a long time, they learn to become mellower about one another's faults. They become more accept-

ing of one another, and they communicate this acceptance. A big part of marital gridlock is that usually both people feel criticized and unaccepted by their partner. (p. 200)

Specifically, Gottman suggests that marriage is similar to many problems in our lives that we tolerate. There may be little we can do about these problems but we can learn to live with our limitations and avoid situations that make them worse. Likewise, in marriage both partners may have expectations that are unresolvable, in which case both partners need to accept what they cannot change in the other spouse.

Gottman (1998) poses a set of questions that are helpful to couples in determining whether their problem can be resolved:

- What adaptations have each of us already made in our marriage? How have we already adjusted to differences in our two personalities?

- Are there parts of one another's personalities that are not ideal but to which we have already made adjustments?

- Are one person's feelings more important on this issue than the other's? For example, this issue may be more central to one person than to the other.

- Is it possible to have some kind of trade-off, for exampl across issues, with one person "winning" on one issue and the other person "winning" on another issue?

- How can we further adapt to this?

- Can we minimize the importance of this issue, emphasize common ground, laugh about this, and accept one another's foibles?

- Is it okay for this problem to never be fully resolved? (pp. 201–202)

The answers to these questions will help the therapist and couples to determine which problems are unresolvable. One spouse must then learn to accept what they cannot change in the other, and thereby learn to live with the problem. Christensen, Jacobson, and Babcock (1995) utilize four strategies to promote acceptance of unresolvable problems: (1) emotional acceptance through empathic joining around the problem, (2) emotional acceptance through detachment from the problem, (3) emotional acceptance through tolerance building, and (4) emotional acceptance through greater self-care. Each of these strategies is discussed in great detail in Chapter 9, Handling Unresolvable Problems.

CONCLUSION

Conflict is inevitable. How married couples manage it, however, determines the success or failure of the marriage. Assuming that violence is not present in the relationship, couples can learn skills to manage conflict if the problem is changeable. If both partners agree to the problem and that they want to work on it, conflict negotiation and communications skills are preferred. However, if the couple cannot agree on the problem, they need to learn skills to accept those differences.

KEY POINTS

- Ongoing marital conflict often leads to disappointment, bitterness, and mistrust, thus blocking intimacy, and leading to further conflict.
- Men and women appear to handle conflict differently, and the marital therapist should be attuned to these differences.
- Different styles for handling conflict often lead to serious problems in marriage.
- Couples who are unable to resolve the way they manage conflict, and who experience an absence of positive interactions, often experience more frequent and escalating conflict.
- Unresolved conflict often leads to violence.
- Batterers share a common profile. They are unpredictable, unable to be influenced by their wives, and impossible to prevent from battering once an argument has begun.
- If violence is suspected, the therapist should remain calm and discuss the worst-case scenario.
- The first step in helping a couple manage conflict is to help them recognize whether the problem is changeable.
- Spouses are better able to manage conflict when they agree on the problem definition and agree on what needs to change.
- Spouses may have problems that are unresolvable, in which case both partners need to accept what they cannot change in the other spouse.

MARITAL SKILLS INVENTORY

Please check when you have completed these procedures.

_____   Assess patterns of conflictual interaction.
_____   Assess gender differences in handling conflict.
_____   Identify typical style for handling marital conflict.
_____   Identify "four horsemen of the apocalypse" if they are occurring in the couple relationship.
_____   Identify characteristics of battering.
_____   Identify warning signs of violence.

_____ Assess level of violence in a marital relationship.

_____ Specify steps for negotiating conflict.

_____ Ask questions to determine whether or not the problem is resolvable.

REFERENCES

Avis, J. (1992). Where are all the family therapists? Abuse and violence within families and family therapy's response. *Journal of Marital and Family Therapy, 18,* 225–232.

Christensen, D. (1992). Couple violence: Decision tree as intake. Classroom handout from University of Louisville, Louisville, KY.

Christensen, A., Jacobson, N. S., & Babcock, J. C. (1995). Integrative behavior couple therapy, Chapter 3 in Neil Jacobson and Allan Gurman (Eds.), *Clinical Handbook of Couple Therapy,* New York: Guilford Press.

Gottman, J. (1994). *Why marriages succeed or fail.* New York: Simon and Schuster.

Gottman, J. (1998). Clinical manual for marital therapy: A research-based approach. Seattle, WA: The Seattle Marital and Family Institute.

Hanna, S., & Brown, J. (1995). *The practice of family therapy: Key elements across models.* Belmont, CA. Brooks/Cole.

Jacobson, N., & Gurman, A. (1995). *Clinical handbook of couple therapy.* New York: Guilford Press.

Jacobson, N., & Gottman, J. (1998). Anatomy of a violent relationship. *Psychology Today,* March/April, 60–65.

Jacobson, N., & Margolin, G. (1979). *Marital therapy.* New York: Brunner/Mazel.

Jacobson, N., Holtzworth-Monroe, A., and Schmaling, K. (1989). Marital therapy and spouse involvement in the treatment of depression, agoraphobia, and alcoholism. *Journal of Consulting and Clinical Psychology, 57,* 5–10.

Jenkins, A. (1991). *Invitations to responsibility.* Adelaide, South Australia: Dulwich Centre Publications.

Karpel, M. (1994). *Evaluating couples: A handbook for practitioners.* New York: Norton.

Markman, H., Stanley, S., & Blumberg, S. (1994). *Fighting for your marriage.* San Francisco: Jossey-Bass.

O'Leary, K. D., Vivian, D., & Malone, J. (1991). *Assessment of physical aggression in marriage.* Paper presented at the annual meeting of the Association for the Advancement of Behavior Therapy, San Francisco.

Stuart, R. B. (1980). *Helping couples change: A social learning approach to marital therapy.* Champaign, IL: Research Press.

Weeks, G., & Treat, S. (1992). *Couples in treatment: Techniques and approaches for effective practice.* New York: Brunner/Mazel.

7

✳

Enhancing Communication and Problem-Solving

CHAPTER OBJECTIVES

Upon completion of this chapter, the reader will be able to list and discuss:

1. Gender issues that block empathy within a relationship.

2. The procedures for effective modeling.

3. Instructions for practicing new relationship behaviors.

4. Steps for practicing the new behaviors.

5. Steps for providing feedback to the couple.

6. Rules for effective communication between partners.

7. Obstacles to effective communication.

INTRODUCTION

Having good communication skills—the ability to talk, especially about problems—is considered by behaviorists to be *the* most important feature of healthy relationships (Gottman, Markman, & Notarius, 1977; Jacobson, Waldron, & Moore, 1980). It is also the feature of relationships that is most obvious and most easily observed. Good communication increases the rewards and pleasures of relating by leading to effective stimulus control over behavior. Clear communication enables family members to discriminate among and between behavioral events, and enhances their ability to show understanding and to give support. Communication skills also predict later marital satisfaction levels (Markman, 1981).

Communication is of great importance to healthy family and couple functioning. Well-functioning couples speak clearly and congruently, so that both verbal and nonverbal levels match. Partners attend to each other and acknowledge that they have heard messages from the other. Discussions are not chaotic, nor are they characterized by rigid and inflexible positions on issues. Individuals are able to assert themselves, yet they tend to agree more than they disagree. The environment is one of friendliness, good will, and optimism, with evidence of a good sense of humor. Mind-reading and intrusiveness rarely occur, and arguments are followed quickly by friendly interactions. Individual differences are encouraged and respected, and cooperation and collaboration are the norm when working together on a task. The uniqueness of each individual is encouraged and successes are acknowledged appropriately (Becvar 1974; Riskin, 1982; Satir, 1972). Indeed, by practicing effective communication, healthy processes are modeled and thus encouraged.

In a good relationship, the partners are able to speak openly and directly about conflicts. They focus on issues and keep them in perspective, and they discuss specific behaviors that are of concern to them. They describe their own feelings and request changes in the behavior of others, as opposed to just criticizing and complaining. "I've been kind of lonely and I wish you and I could go out and do things more often," is more likely to get a positive response than, "You never care about what I want! All you care about is yourself!" In addition to expressing their concerns as requests rather than attacks, successful partners listen to the other's point of view and attempt to understand what is being said. When problems arise or when circumstances change, couples need communication skills to change behavior.

Many people assume that good marriages will occur naturally if people are well-matched and if they love each other. Behaviorists, on the other hand, consistently emphasize the need to develop relationship skills. Good marriages, they believe, are not made in heaven, but are products of learning effective coping behavior. Jacobson (1981) described a good marriage as one in which the partners maintain a high rate of rewards and a low rate of costs in the relationship.

CULTURAL ISSUES

Almost any marriage will involve some cultural differences. Even if the couple is of the same race and nationality, they will likely differ in some way in their family of origin: different family rituals, ecological settings (rural versus urban), religious backgrounds, social classes, occupations, political leanings,

and so on. Some theories stress the importance of similarities for marital com-
patibility, while others stress the belief that "opposites attract." In fact, some
cultural differences matter little to a couple, while others matter a lot. Take
Jared and Susan, for example. Jared is a black male from a poor family and
Susan is a white female from an upper-middle-class family. Both Jared and
Susan graduated from college (the same one) and both have professional jobs,
similar religious beliefs, and similar political views. They are much more compatible than Jane and Robert. Jane and Robert are both white and both come
from middle-class backgrounds. However, Jane graduated from college, earned
a Master's degree, and is a social worker, while Robert competed only high
school before starting a small business. They tend to have conflicts related to
values, politics, lifestyles, and goals.

According to Gottman (2000), every newlywed couple (family) must create a "new" culture based on a union of cultures that may be very similar or
dissimilar. Gottman argues that in a "sound marital house" (p. 61), the couple
creates shared symbolic meaning—the meshing of individual life dreams,
myths and metaphors. This means that the couple must explore the meanings
of family rituals, roles, goals, and symbols. For instance, because many marital
conflicts occur due to different meanings partners attribute to situations or
communications, the therapist will assess meanings each partner gives to simple everyday things such as "fun," "love," "illness," "home," and "family." One of
the tasks of a couple in marital therapy is to talk with each other about meanings and life goals and learn how to support and honor one another's life
dreams.

GENDER ISSUES

Given the often considerable difference in martial partners' experiences and
expectations within a relationship, increasing the empathic understanding
between them can play a critical role in improving their relationship. A number of gender issues may block the expression of empathy within the relationship, including ignorance of the other's experience, premature problem
solving, negative expectations, and differences in timing between partners.
Each of these obstacles requires therapeutic management.

Although many wives (and some therapists) believe that men are not as
capable of empathic responses as women, research has shown otherwise.
Hare-Mustin and Marecek (1990) suggest, interestingly, that men are as capable of demonstrating empathy as women *when they are motivated to do so.* There
is some difference, however, in women's and men's perceptions of what constitutes an adequate response to a conversational partner (Tannen, 1990).
When women listen to their partners' problems, they assume that their
responses should demonstrate *concern, caring, and understanding* of the other
person (Jordan et al., 1991). Men, on the other hand, tend to listen to problems with an expectation that they should provide *solutions.* These differences

in expectations lead to communication gridlock. That is, the wife feels angry because she wants to solve her own problems, and experiences her husband's suggested solutions as patronizing and unhelpful. He, on the other hand, feels frustrated that his caring and helpfulness are being misconstrued and rejected unreasonably.

An important step in marital therapy is helping a couple define what they want from each other. Men, because they have learned from early childhood that they are valued as problem solvers, frequently believe that simply listening, understanding, and facilitating their partner's efforts to solve a problem is an inadequate response. When reassured that this is exactly what the wife wants, most husbands are able and willing to provide this sort of mirroring for their wives.

A second step in increasing marital empathy is helping spouses to be patient with each other. Often a wife enters marital therapy hoping for greater emotional responsivity from her husband but is discouraged that she has been hitherto unable to evoke the desired response. In conversation, she shares experiences or asks questions, hoping that he will respond to her feelings. If his response is not immediately forthcoming, she may interpret his silence as a lack of interest and give up, either withdrawing from the relationship or becoming angry, whereupon a fight may ensue. Encouraging her to be patient with the silence and to expect that he will be responsive if given enough time can be helpful in interrupting the negative cycle and allowing an empathic bond to be deepened (Bergman, 1991).

Still another facet of increasing marital empathy involves breaking down gender stereotypes. It is difficult to be free of sexist bias, and this bias inevitably creeps into the beliefs we have about our spouses, as well as ourselves. Sometimes this bias gets expressed stereotypically: "You're just like all men!", or "You women are all alike!" More frequently, such bias is perceived subtly as attributions made to the other spouse, based on assumptions about gender. Communication is important between spouses so that unspoken assumptions or stereotypes do not create misunderstandings. In fact, information is an antidote to bias. Encouraging spouses to challenge their own gender biases, and to be curious about their partner's feelings, thoughts, beliefs, and attitudes, can be critical elements in creating empathy. This can be done in a variety of ways, from letter writing to conversation, from communicating their reactions to shared experiences to hearing each other's life story.

Vague communication and unclear role expectations often characterize dysfunctional couples. When a problem arises, the couple often adheres to the same old rules and customs. Satir (1972, p. 115) describes these families as "closed systems" where communication is growth-impeding rather than growth-producing. In these families, honest self-expression is discouraged and considered deviant by the family. Such families often reach an impasse during a life cycle transition. When passing through this transition, interactions become more rigidified and symptomatic behavior may develop.

COACHING COMMUNICATION

Regardless of the therapist's orientation, coaching communication is an important element in therapeutic change strategies. Coaching communication is effective for couples (Rappaport, 1976), and divorced parents (Brown, Brown, & Portes, 1991). Coaching communication contains the following core components: modeling ("show me how"), instruction ("tell me how"), practice ("let me try it"), and feedback ("tell me how I did").

Modeling

The first step in helping a couple to communicate more effectively is to demonstrate, or model, the appropriate communication skill; that is, the therapist shows each spouse what the response looks like or how it sounds. The therapists themselves should model behavior throughout the treatment process. Modeling has been effective in teaching information-seeking behavior (Krumboltz, Varenhorst, & Thoresen, 1967), reducing feelings of alienation (Warner & Hansen, 1970), and improving attitudes toward drug abuse (Warner, Swisher, & Horan, 1973).

Another common practice is to provide live or symbolic models—on audiotapes or videotapes—showing, in sequential steps, the specific behaviors necessary to solve the problem (Hosford & de Visser, 1974). Taped or filmed models have been successfully used (Hansen, Pound, & Warner, 1976). The models only demonstrate the desired behaviors; there is no opportunity for interaction between the models and the spouses. However, the taped models may help to simulate discussion, which is important in preventing rote imitation by the spouses. If new behaviors are to be effective, spouses need to learn a variety of responses for a particular problem situation.

The therapist may also wish to develop models for each of several sessions. For example, the therapist could develop tapes that teach each spouse to: (1) listen, (2) express a compliment, (3) express appreciation, (4) ask for help, (5) give feedback, and (6) express affection (Goldstein, 1973). Each skill could be modeled and practiced during a session, if the spouses' skill levels allows. Each modeling sequence could thus represent a closer approximation of the final behavior.

Effective modeling including the following procedures.

1. *Model a clear delineation of the desired behavior.* The behavior must be identified clearly, so that the couple knows precisely what the therapist is actually modeling. If the modeling sequence is too vague, there is little likelihood that any learning will take place. For example, rather than trying to model "awareness" to a partner, the therapist should operationalize this by identifying and labeling emotions. To teach relationship skills, the therapist might break the relationship down into "expressing" and "responding." These areas might be broken down further into sub-skills—responding to anger, affection, and so on. It is always beneficial to operationalize the skill that is to be learned; that is, the skill should be defined such that it can be seen and heard. After operationalizing the skill,

the therapist explains what the model (in this case, the therapist) will be saying or doing, and tells the couple what they should look for. For example, if a spouse is having difficulty asking for help, the therapist might say, "John, I need you to _____ when I'm feeling down."

2. *Model behaviors that will hold the couple's attention.* Familiar and relevant experiences are more likely to hold attention and facilitate learning. Also, models are generally most effective when they are the same sex as a family member, and similar in appearance, age, and so on. Because of this, the therapist may want the couple to identify personal resources (such as friends) that could serve as models. If a spouse is having difficulty asking for help, a friend who is accepted in that situation and who is similar to the family member might be asked to model or demonstrate how to ask for help. The therapist might say, "I would like you to show Mary what to do when she wants to ask for help." A model who verbalizes his or her own uncertainty (as in, "I'm not sure, but here is one way to try it."), and offers subsequent problem-solving or coping strategies can be helpful in eliciting the couple's attention. Another useful technique is to emphasize those behaviors to be modeled. The therapist might ask the model to speak more loudly during the relevant responses or to repeat a key passage ("Would you repeat that, please?"). Tone of voice and mannerisms can also be used to gain the couple's attention.

3. *Ask couples to discuss what they have observed.* Unless couples are able to understand and retain the essential characteristics of the model's behavior, the intervention will be of no help. In cases where the modeled behavior is particularly abstract, retention may be facilitated if either the model or therapist discusses the important features of the model's performance. For example, a model demonstrating how to express affection could discuss different ways to show affection. The therapist could evaluate the couple's understanding by asking them to summarize the main features or general rules of the model's performance.

4. *Reinforce the modeled behavior.* The therapist must provide incentives so as to encourage couples to perform the modeled behavior. When modeled behavior is not reinforced, initiation will not occur; the likelihood that initiative behavior will occur increases with the probability of receiving reinforcement. To reinforce the modeled behavior, the therapist might respond to the model's statements with positive comments ("That's an interesting point," or "That's a thoughtful idea."). By observing that the model is reinforced for expressing an opinion or solving a problem, the family members learn the most effective response in that situation.

Instruction

Once the couple has attended to and understood the model's behavior, the therapist should provide instructions before the couple begins practicing the new behavior. The therapist can focus attention on the relevant and essential aspects of the model's performance. The instructions may be spoken or written by the therapist. The therapist might say, "Watch how I show appreciation to your husband," and then model the appropriate behavior, adding, "Now I want you to show appreciation for something your husband has done recently." Instructions can be provided in the following ways:

1. *Prompt specific behavior for members to try out.* The therapist is now essentially serving as coach who prompts specific behavior for the couple to try out. Instructions generally may be positive "Do this," or negative "Don't do that." The therapist gives numerous specific examples. Instructing a wife to give feedback to her husband, the therapist might say: "Look directly at your husband and tell him how it makes you feel when he doesn't call to say he won't be home. Don't just accuse him of being inconsiderate."

2. *Help partners decide when to give feedback to each other.* The therapist might discuss when to give feedback—for example, "when you have time to sit down" or "when you are not so angry"—since partners may know what to say but not when to say it. By going over the demonstration, the therapist can pinpoint behaviors of the model, and discuss why such behaviors can serve as a cue to a partner to perform a specific behavior.

Practice

Having received instructions on what to say and do, the couple is ready to practice the behavior: Practice is an essential part of the learning process, since people learn by doing. The couple can role-play new relationships or problem-solving behaviors. If either spouse shows resistance to this idea, the therapist can provide examples of the usefulness of practice. The crucial point is that each partner must feel that he or she is not just learning a role that is artificial and unusable. Consequently, the role-playing situations should be as realistic as possible, and should include verbal responses with which each partner feels comfortable. The following are important guidelines:

1. *Prepare the couple for practice.* The couple must accept the idea that practice would be an appropriate way to develop new coping or problem-solving behaviors. If the couple shows some resistance to this idea, the therapist can provide examples where practice has proven useful. Experience, drill, rehearsal, recitation, homework, and exercise all involve practice. The therapist might say, "Maybe we could practice expressing appreciation to your husband. I'll role-play your husband, and we'll see how it goes. If you have trouble thinking of something to say, I'll help you."

2. *Start with a situation that the couple can perform with little difficulty.* Practice is more successful when the initial situation is familiar to the couple. For example, in a conflictual situation, the therapist might ask both parties

to start by "talking about something that happened at home today." If they are unable to do this, the therapist might ask them to engage in less threatening activities, such as sitting next to each other. Regardless of the activity, the therapist should begin with a nonthreatening situation.

3. *Break the behavior down into small steps.* These steps should range in complexity from simple (such as giving a compliment) to the completely new behavior (such as asking for help). In this case, the social interaction varies according to the level of difficulty.

4. *Prompt partners when they cannot think of what to say or do.* The therapist can provide a sentence that fits within the context of the interaction (for example, "It's important to me to know how you feel"). It is essential that the prompt occur only when the family member pauses or hesitates (generally for about five seconds). In addition, the therapist can use hand signals to raise or lower the partner's voice or to motion for him to come closer. Prompts should be faded as family members become able to practice the behavior unaided. At this point the therapist should praise the partner for expressing the desired behavior in his or her own words.

Feedback

When couples have practiced the skills, each must receive feedback on their performance. Such feedback provides an incentive for improvement. Information received about poor performance potentially can be as helpful as knowledge regarding positive performance. The following guidelines are important in providing feedback:

1. *Solicit the couple's ideas about feedback prior to practice.* The therapist might say, "I'll observe you and try to give you some helpful hints." When a partner denies or disagrees with feedback from the therapist ("That's not the way it sounded to me."), or attempts to justify his response ("The reason I said that was . . ."), then feedback was probably not solicited or agreed upon prior to practice.

2. *Describe rather than evaluate the couple's behaviors.* The therapist might restate what a spouse said and comment, "Here you say 'My wife thinks I should . . .' Do you remember we agreed you would say, 'I think I should . . .'?" The therapist's feedback statements should avoid blame. Statements such as, "That just doesn't sound right," or "I don't know why you can't do that" fail to provide helpful information to the partners.

3. *Reinforce a partner's response and at the same time prompt similar responses.* The therapist might say, "That is a good question to get him to talk to you. Sometimes, however, your husband may not want to talk about his job. Can you think of some other questions you could ask him?" By prompting additional questions, the therapist not only helps to reinforce

the spouse's use of questions in a practice session, but also facilitates its generalization to other situations and people.

The therapist should provide opportunities for the family to practice their skills at home, and should supply guidelines or worksheets to facilitate such practice. Therapy is more effective when couples are able to practice skills successfully in everyday interactions.

RULES FOR EFFECTIVE COMMUNICATION

Several rules for effective communication follow:

1. *Speaking in the first person.* Partners should speak in the first person and express what each thinks or feels. Each partner should take the "I" position. "I statements" indicate that partners are taking responsibility for themselves. Likewise, "I statements" also encourage others to express their feelings and disclose differences of opinion (Miller, Nunnally, & Wackman, 1976). Consider the following dialogue:

Wife: Every time we go to his mother's house, it's trouble.

Therapist: Tell me how you feel when you go to her house.

Wife: Well, it makes me . . .

Therapist: No, "I feel . . .

Wife: I feel helpless. I feel she has an answer for everything.

Only when the wife states "I feel helpless" does she communicate her own feeling and take responsibility for the accuracy of the message.

2. *Level with each other.* Partners must level with each other. "In this response, all parts of the message are going in the same direction—the voice says words that match facial expression, the body position and the voice tone" (Satir, 1972). For example:

Wife: My husband doesn't do anything around the house, but that's O.K., I guess.

Therapist: Let's level with him and be specific. Describe the things you want him to do.

Wife: He needs to put his clothes in the closet and . . .

Satir (1972) notes that when partners level with one another, they are communicating acceptance of each other, thus improving self-esteem.

3. *Listen to each other.* Many couples will complain about not communicating or talking when in fact they really do not feel the other partner is listening. Crucial to understanding another's problem is the ability to listen; specifically, this involves responding in such a way that partners

understand each other's feelings. Tone of voice, rapidity of speech, and nonverbal gestures, as well as verbal content, helps partners to determine each other's feelings. For instance, slow speech may indicate discouragement, whereas rapid speech may indicate either anxiety or excitement. Tone of voice is a good indicator of the client's emotions; blushes and stammers also give clues about feelings. For example:

Husband: I can't take it any more. You are never satisfied . . . I can never please you.

Wife: (sarcastically) *You* can't take it any more!

Therapist: Let him know you heard him.

Wife: It sounds like you are frustrated and don't know what to do.

The ability to listen helps each spouse to feel understood and encourages exploration.

4. *State your complaint concisely.* If your complaint cannot be resolved in 10–15 minutes, then drop it. It is easier to hear a brief complaint than a long lecture. Moreover, conflict is more likely to escalate and destructive patterns emerge with a lengthy complaint. For example:

Wife: I've got several things to say—so you had better listen.

Therapist: Just describe your complaint and keep it brief.

Wife: O.K., I need you to spend more time with me in the evening.

Keeping the complaints brief also avoids bringing up past conflict that undermines efforts to resolve the current problem.

5. *Describe what you need and avoid mind reading.* It is critical for both partners to state their needs clearly and avoid "mind reading." It is important for spouses to be explicit so that each pays attention to the content of the message rather than making assumptions. For example:

Husband: You never want to go out.

Therapist: See if you can be more specific. What is it you want her to do?

Husband: I want her to go to the ball game with me on Saturday.

In some cases, a partner will anticipate what the other person will say. In such cases the other partner should repeat the message and ask for confirmation (Markman et al., 1994).

6. *Show appreciation.* Presenting a request in a positive context is more likely to get attention (Gottman, 2000). Spouses are more likely to hear the complaint if they have first heard the appreciation. For example:

Wife: You don't act like you are interested in what I have to say.

Therapist: Tell him how much you appreciated it the last time he showed interest in what you had to say.

Wife: I liked it when you asked me about my job when we were at your brother's three weeks ago.

It is better to cite specific examples of the past and how much you would appreciate more of that behavior ("interest in what I have to say") now.

7. *Start Softly.* It is important when making a request to start softly. Soft start-ups often predict the course of the interaction. For example:

Husband: Why are you never on time?

Therapist: Let's think of a softer way to say that.

Husband: Why are you late? I was really getting worried.

Soft start-ups are expressed in a lighter tone, which is more likely to elicit a nondefensive response (Gottman, 1998). Therefore, the partner does not feel under personal attack. Gottman further suggests that a spouse express a soft emotion (fear, worry, insecurity) rather than a hard emotion (anger, resentment) to get the other spouse's attention.

These techniques help the therapist raise the couple's self-awareness to a new level. When clients are helped to address issues that they normally observe but do not discuss, they begin to metacommunicate (Watzlawick, Beavin, & Jackson, 1967)—to communicate about their own interpersonal process. As this occurs, each spouse begins to accept the reality that the problem involves more than his or her own singular point of view.

The therapist provides structured interventions and attends to the process as the couple enacts situations. In doing so, he or she helps couples develop a clearer understanding of their communication patterns. Moreover, the couple begins to develop more self-control (for example, refraining from interrupting each other.) Not only does the couple perceive the situation differently, but also they behave differently.

8. *Apologize at the end of an argument.* It is important for the partner to end an argument by apologizing or admitting a wrong. Apologies help keep anger under control and allow the couple's relationship to move forward. Apologizing for a put-down, for forgetting, or for making a destructive comment, allows the couple to stay connected. For example:

Wife: Maybe we should stop. I think we know what happened. I forgot.

Therapist: Maybe you could let him know that you are sorry for what happened.

Wife: I am. I'm sorry that I forgot to call you. I feel really bad—I guess I just had too much on my mind.

Apologizing is a way to restore the relationship by taking responsibility for one's actions. It's a way to repair the relationship so that both partners can feel closer to each other.

OBSTACLES TO EFFECTIVE COMMUNICATION

Karpel (1994) suggests that there are several obstacles to effective communication:

1. *One or both partners fail to listen to each other.* When both partners fail to listen to each other, communication is likely to break down. Most couples are able to express their views, but have difficulty listening to each other (Karpel, 1994). Consequently, each comes to therapy feeling that the other "doesn't understand," or that they "aren't heard." Markman et al. (1994) suggest that both external distractions (child crying, loud noise) or internal ones (fatigue, boredom) are factors which contribute to the problem.

Suggestions for Overcoming the Obstacle:

- Pick a time and place to talk where it is quiet.
- Make sure there are no distractions.
- Make sure the couple is relaxed and is ready to listen to each other.

2. *Men and women have different expectations for intimacy independence.* Many communication problems are related to the different expectations men and women hold concerning intimacy and independence. Weiner-Davis (1992) provides the following illustration:

A wife gets a request for a social engagement and responds by saying she will have to check with her husband regarding his plans since she assumes that partners behave interdependently. Conversely, the husband gets asked to do something after work, calls his wife to announce his plans and she gets insulted. "Why don't you first ask me if we have plans," she complains. He cannot believe that she expects him to ask her permission to do something. Her expectation that he should check with her first feels like an intrusion on his independence, and he tells her, "You are such a nag. All you do is bitch, bitch, bitch" (pp. 53–54).

In this case, the husband felt the wife was trying to control him. Neither seemed to understand the other's needs.

Suggestions for Overcoming the Obstacle:

- Help the husband to understand that his wife's need for connectedness is not unreasonable.
- Help the wife to understand her husband's need for independence.
- Help each to understand the need to be influenced by the other.
- Try to get each spouse to avoid assuming (mind reading) what the other is thinking or feeling.

3. *Both partners exhibit different styles of communication.* Some couples have very different styles of communication, for example, one partner may be more expressive than the other (Markman et al., 1994). Different styles of communication are often related to family history, culture, and personality. For example, if one partner was raised in a family where members were not allowed to express anger, then any expression of dissatisfaction by the other partner could lead to misinterpretation.

Suggestions for Overcoming the Obstacle:

- Help couples to become aware of their differing styles.
- Help each partner to understand the history related to the other's style of communication.
- Help each to accept differences in the other.

4. *The couple's problems cannot be resolved.* Many couples report that their problems have gone on too long and cannot be resolved. This often occurs when one or both partners believe the other cannot change because of his or her personality (Weiner-Davis, 1992). For example, partners may often be described as "angry," "hateful," "disrespectful," "uncaring," or "insensitive," as if their behavior was the result of some ingrained personality trait. Unfortunately in such cases, the other partner begins to expect such behavior and responds accordingly. This becomes a self-fulfilling prophecy, where partners expect the worst. Consequently, such expectations often are communicated to the partner. For example, if a wife expects her husband to be angry she will communicate as if he is angry, whether he feels that way or not. This often prevents the possibility for effective communication.

Suggestions for Overcoming the Obstacle:

- Help each partner to vary his or her behavior to elicit a more positive response.
- Get the couple to change the environment in which they discuss issues.
- Do not accept their view that their partners will not change.

CONCLUSION

The ability to communicate effectively is a key element of a satisfying marital relationship. In good marriages, couples tend to have clear communication, flexibility, recognition of individual differences, cooperation, and acknowledgement of successes. Partners are able to deal directly with conflict and request changes from each other in a constructive manner. While there are several obstacles (such as gender and power issues), couples may overcome these obstacles by practicing rules for effective communication.

KEY POINTS

- Communication is of great importance to healthy family and couple functioning.
- In a healthy relationship, partners are able to speak openly and directly about conflicts.
- All marriages develop a culture of their own that differs from that of their families of origin.
- Gender issues—including ignorance of the other's experience, premature problem solving, negative expectations, and differences in timing between partners—may block the expression of empathy within the relationship.
- Coaching communication is an important element in therapeutic change strategies and is effective for both couples and divorced parents.

MARITAL SKILLS INVENTORY

Please check when you have completed this proceeding.

Coach Communication

_____   Model the desired behavior.

_____   Provide instructions.

_____   Practice the behavior.

_____   Provide feedback.

Teach Rules for Effective Communication

_____   Speak in first person.

_____   Level with each other.

_____   Listen to each other.

_____   State the complaint concisely.

_____   Describe what you need; avoid mind reading.

_____   Show appreciation.

_____   Start softly.

_____   Apologize (as appropriate).

Overcome Obstacles to Effective Communication

_____   When one or both partners fail to listen.

_____   When partners have different expectations for intimacy or independence.

_____   When partners exhibit different styles of communication.

REFERENCES

Becvar, R. J. (1974). *Skills for effective communication.* New York: Wiley.

Bergman, S. (1991). Men's psychological development: A relational perceptive (Works in Progress No. 48). Wellesley, MA: Stone Center Working Paper Series.

Brown, J., Brown, C., & Portes, P. (1991). *The families in transition program.* Louisville, KY: University of Louisville.

Goldstein, A. (1973). *Structured learning therapy.* New York: Academic Press.

Gottman, J. (2000). *Clinical manual for marital therapy: A scientifically-based marital therapy.* Seattle, WA: The Seattle Martial and Family Institute, Inc.

Gottman, J. (1999). *The marriage clinic: A scientifically-based marital therapy.* New York: Norton.

Gottman, J. (1994). *Why marriages succeed or fail.* New York: Simon & Schuster.

Gottman, J., Markman, H., & Notarius, C. (1997). The topography of marital conflict: A sequential analysis of verbal and nonverbal behavior. *Journal of Marriage and the Family,* 461–477.

Hansen, J., Pound, R., & Warner, R. (1976). Use of modeling procedures. *Personnel & Guidance Journal, 54,* 242–245.

Hare-Mustin, R. T., & Marecek, J. (Eds.). (1990). *Making a difference: Psychology and the construction of gender.* New Haven, CT: Yale University Press.

Hosford, R., & de Visser, C. (1974). *Behavioral counseling: An introduction.* Washington, DC: American Personnel & Guidance Press.

Jacobson, N. S. (1981). Marital problems. In J. L. Shelton & R. L. Levy (Eds.), *Behavioral assignment and treatment compliance* (pp. 147–166). Champaign, IL: Research Press.

Jacobson, N. S., Waldron, H., & Moore, D. (1980). Toward a behavioral profile of marital distress. *Journal of Consulting & Clinical Psychology, 49,* pp. 269–277.

Jacobson, N. S., Waldron, H., & Moore, D. (1981). Martial problems. In J. L. Shelton & R. L. Levy (Eds.), *Behavioral Assignments and Treatment Compliance* (pp. 147–166). Champaign, IL: Research Press.

Jeter, K. (1982). Analytic essay: Intercultural and interracial marriage. In G. Crtser & J. Leon (Eds.), *Intermarriage in the United States.* New York: Haworth Press.

Jordan, J. V., Kaplan, A. G., Miller, J. B., Stirer, I. P., & Surrey, J. L. (1991). *Women's Growth in Connection: Writing from the Stone Center.* New York: Guilford Press.

Karpel, M. A. (1994). *Evaluating Couples.* New York: Norton.

Krumboltz, J., Varenhorst, B., & Thoresen, C. (1967). Nonverbal factors in effectiveness of models in counseling. *Journal of Counseling Psychology, 14,* 412–418.

Markman, J. H., Stanley, S., & Blumberg, S. L. (1994). *Fighting for your marriage: Positive steps for preventing divorce and preserving a lasting love.* San Francisco: Jossey-Bass.

Markman, J. H. (1981). The prediction of marital distress: A five year follow-up. *Journal of Consulting and Clinical Psychology, 49,* 760–762.

Miller, S., Nunnally, E. W., & Wackman, D. B. (1976). A communication training program for couples. *Social Casework, 57,* 9–18.

Riskin, J. (1982). Research on non-labeled families: A longitudinal study. In F. Walsh (Ed.), *Normal family processes* (pp. 67–93). New York: Guilford Press.

Rappaport, A. F. (1976). Conjugal relationship enhancement program. In D. H. L. Olson (Ed.), *Treating relationships* (pp. 41–66). Lake Mills, IA: Graphic Publishing.

Satir, V. (1972). *Peoplemaking.* Palo Alto, CA: Science & Behavior Books.

Tannen, D. (1990). *You just don't under-stand: Women and men in conversation.* New York: Morrow.

Warner, R., & Hansen, J. (1970). Verbal-reinforcement and model-reinforce-ment group counseling with alienated students. *Journal of Counseling Psychology, 14,* 168–172.

Warner, R., Swisher, J., & Horan, J. (1973). Drug abuse prevention: A behavioral approach. *NAASP Bulletin, 372,* 49–54.

Weiner-Davis, M. (1992). *Divorce busting.* New York: Summit Books.

8

✳

Building Trust
and Intimacy

CHAPTER OBJECTIVES

Upon completion of this chapter, the reader will be able to describe:

1. Strategies that therapists can employ to promote trust in a relationship.
2. Differences in how men and women view intimacy.
3. Steps for enhancing intimacy in couples.
4. Barriers to intimacy between partners.

INTRODUCTION

A typical question for marital therapists is, "What is the glue that makes for a successful marriage?" While there are many factors that contribute to a successful marriage, trust and intimacy are absolutely necessary for a long-lasting, loving relationship, with mutual care and respect. This chapter will address ways to assist couples to build trust and intimacy in their relationship.

TRUST

Trust refers to reliability, fairness, and faith in one's partner. Without trust, closeness and intimacy are not possible in the relationship. In a marriage, trust means that one is able to count on the other partner being there

(Markman et al., 1994). The most satisfying, healthy marriages are characterized by trust.

Karpel (1994) describes trust as a "relational resource" that makes for an easier and richer relationship. He further states:

> Trust allows us to feel safe and secure in a relationship. Without it, self-disclosure, vulnerability, spontaneity, and vitality are inconceivable. Without it, communication is futile, commitment is uncertain, and intimacy elusive. It is the foundation upon which any satisfying and stable relationship is built. Trust is impossible without trustworthiness, which refers to the overall level of merited trust in a relationship (Boszormenyi-Nagy & Krasner, 1986; Boszormenyi-Nagy & Ulrich, 1981). Trustworthiness involves an ongoing effort to try and be reliable and fair. Trust refers to the individual's capacity to believe and rely on his or her partner; trustworthiness refers to whether or not (or more accurately, to what degree) such trust is merited. Merited trust is based on past actions and predicts future ones. It is based not on what a person says he or she will do but on what he or she actually does. (p. 110)

Another kind of trust is residual (Boszormenyi-Nagy, 1987), which refers to the trust that remains when the rules of the relationship have been violated. Karpel (1994) gives the following example:

> For example, imagine that you are sitting with a couple who are angry, mistrustful, and stuck. The husband says, "If I had known you really wanted to go, I would have been more willing to at least consider it." You turn to the wife and ask if she believes what the husband has just said. Now imagine two different possibilities. In one case, she says, "No, I don't believe a word he says. He wouldn't know the truth if it fell on him." In a different case, she answers, "Yes. I know he wouldn't make it up. If he says it's true, it's true." The latter is an expression of residual trust, and the task of working with the second couple will probably be considerably easier than working with the first. (pp. 110–111)

Partners who do not trust each other are less likely to commit themselves to the marriage. Trust and commitment are highly correlated—the more partners trust each other, the more they will commit to the relationship.

BUILDING TRUST

There are several strategies that therapists can employ to promote trust in the relationship:

1. *Help couple accept partner's view of the problem.* Gottman (1994) underscores the importance of partners accepting each other's attempts to maintain communication. It is important to remind partners that they are allies who share each other's best interest.

2. *Trust is a slow process.* Therapists should remind the couple that trust takes a long time to build and rebuild. When the trust is violated, such as in an affair, it must be restored. The marriage contract needs to be renegotiated. The couple must understand that this does not happen overnight.

3. *Back up words with actions.* Trust is a process that happens in small steps. Partners can begin to restore trust by backing up their words with actions. For example, if a husband says he will be home by 6:00 p.m. and arrives at that time, he has taken a small step toward building trust and safety in the relationship.

4. *Spend enjoyable time together.* Trust is more likely to be restored when a couple spends some enjoyable time together (Weiner-Davis, 1992). When partners are able to spend pleasant time together, they are likely to feel better about each other and trust each other's motives more. The therapist should make sure that the partners in a couple are able to enjoy each other before trying to restore trust.

5. *Help couples understand their reciprocal obligations.* When couples are able to "give and take," they are more likely to build trust into the relationship (Karpel, 1994). This requires helping the couple to understand their obligations and their personal responsibilities to meet them. A wife who works to support her husband's education expects some repayment for her sacrifice. Such repayment helps to build trust in her husband and the marriage.

Case Study

A couple sought therapy after five years of marriage because each spouse was having an affair. Both had started their extramarital relationships within two years of the time they married and neither had ever felt "secure" in the relationship. From the beginning of the marriage, both spouses had maintained contacts with old friends and each had spent more time with premarriage friends than with each other. Consequently, the marital bond was weak, and the talks they had with each other about the situation only led to conflict and more distance. Each felt that the other could not be trusted.

The therapist proceeded by helping each spouse to understand the other's point of view, recognizing that it would take time to restore trust in each other. The therapist asked each spouse to suspend outside relationships and to focus on the marriage. The therapist also helped the couple look for small ways to restore the trust (arriving home at the expected time, keeping promises) and helped them find ways to spend more time with each other.

In this example, the couple have to reestablish trust because both have been involved in extramarital relationships. The first step in reestablishing this trust is for both to suspend any extra relationships and recommit themselves to their relationship. An additional step is for the couple to spend more time together.

Through positive time spent together, the spouses develop and reexperience positive feelings upon which to strengthen their relationship.

Gottman (1999) suggests that the two necessary factors in successful marriages are an overall level of positive affect, and an ability to reduce negative affect during conflict resolution. First, couples must have established a friendship and ongoing positive affect. The couple described above did not have a sound friendship or a sense of "we-ness." They had not established what Gottman (1999) refers to as a "love map," or a knowledge of the spouse's likes and dislikes, and they did not have a strong "fondness and admiration" system, where they gave frequent spontaneous expressions of love and caring. Without these basics during nonconflictual situations, couples have difficulty during conflictual situations because they are more likely to interpret comments from the other spouse as negative, even when they are neutral. Gottman calls this "not having enough emotional money in the bank" (p. 105).

Treatment for this couple would involve the development of friendship, getting to know each other at a deeper level, and making more frequent deposits in the "emotional bank account"—more frequent expressions of positive affect.

INTIMACY

In his book *Successful Marriage* (1985), Robert Beavers provides the following description of marital intimacy:

> The pursuit of emotional heath and personal enjoyment by couples involves intimacy—the joy of being known and accepted by another who is loved. There is no intimacy except when there is equal overt power. This idea can be supported both logically and empirically. If one is superior to another in station and authority, he or she must not express such human feelings as fear, loneliness, wistfulness, uncertainty. Conversely, if a person is inferior to another, he or she must not show certain human characteristics that would be "uppity" such as assertiveness, a desire for respect, potent anger. Only when two people approach each other with the assumption of equality can they hope to know and be known by each other. (p. 52)

The author suggests that only when there is equal overt power can there be expression of openness, vulnerability, and innermost thoughts and feelings. When there is a power differential, partners may be isolated by fear of anger, domination, and exposure of weakness.

Fusion versus Intimacy

There seems to be confusion between fusion and intimacy. Such confusion is reflected in the common cultural and religious expression, "and then they were one." Often repeated in marriage ceremonies, the phrase is based on the assumption that an individual can become complete by "fusion" with another person. Bowen (1978) suggests the contrary. He writes that couples who are fused have failed to differentiate from their families of origin and do not feel free to develop a separate intimate relationship with another. They are afraid to accept differences in the other because these differences would be too great a threat to their own poorly developed "self."

When two people are fused, they often fail to take responsibility for themselves in the relationship. In a fused relationship, each spouse feels that his or her happiness is the other person's responsibility, and often blames the other for problems in the relationship. It is common for a spouse to feel that if the other spouse would change his or her behavior, the problem would go away, and they would be happy. When spouses blame each other, they are failing to take responsibility for themselves in the relationship.

Couples who are fused also have trouble negotiating intimacy or closeness in the relationship. Negotiation means that each spouse must give in to some degree. A spouse who is fused in the relationship often fears that "giving in" means "caving in" and risking the fearful emotions of losing one's identity. Thus, fusion inhibits couples from sorting and resorting priorities, and from developing spoken and unspoken rules about how they want to be together. Moreover, such couples even have difficulty resolving mundane issues such as whether the toilet seat should be up or down, who puts the dishes away, or who takes out the trash. Such minor issues become identity struggles. Couples must develop rules for closeness and cooperation. Each spouse must know what is important to the other and appreciate the other's thoughts and feelings, even when they are different.

The net result of fusion is that neither partner communicates directly with the other because each is fearful that their relationship will turn out like their parents' relationship. Thus, communication becomes more distorted as each tries to become fulfilled through the mate. Ultimately, neither spouse is happy because the couple is unable to negotiate what they want in the relationship. With less support from the family and community, spouses often find themselves isolated and dissatisfied with the marriage.

Gender Differences

Men and women often view intimacy differently. Women view intimacy as sharing personal conversation (feelings), while men do not use conversation to get close. Rather they can become close by doing things without discussion (Tannen, 1990). Wives often complain that their husbands never talk and when they do, it is often about topics such as sports, business, or cars (Weiner-Davis, 1992). Weiner-Davis further states:

> Another difference I've observed in male and female conversational styles which coincides with Tannen's observations is that when talking about personal problems, women say they want to feel understood. In contrast to women's desire for empathy when talking about personal problems, men feel the need to fix things, and do so by offering solutions. These solutions

are usually not well accepted because they give the message, "So do something about it" rather than "I know what you mean." Women then attack men for not listening, not caring and being insensitive. Men recoil from this attack, confused by their partner's response to their helping efforts. (p. 49)

In short, there are times when men would be better off listening than trying to solve the problem.

Carter and McGoldrick (1999) further elaborate:

Men, of course, often confuse intimacy with sexuality, partly because they are not particularly comfortable with, nor know much about, the former (Pittman, 1993). Telling another the details of one's life is a common experience for women. At an early age, girls are encouraged to share their thoughts and feelings with others, and boys are discouraged from such intimacies (Tannen, 1990). Women have also learned that real closeness with men is likely to demand sexual as well as emotional intimacy, and they play by these gender rules. Not to do so would often spell the end to a relationship that they wish to maintain. In recent years, as men and women have interacted in more equal relationships in school and the work place, it has become more common for platonic friendships to be maintained between sexes and to be tolerated more easily by both of the friends' significant others. (p. 130)

Moreover, the norms for emotional intimacy are different today from twenty-five years ago. Traditional gender roles that have in the past served as a guide for marriage are no longer accepted, leaving young adults in a quandary on how to manage emotional intimacy (Carter & McGoldrick, 1999). Defining the parameters of emotional intimacy thus becomes a difficult task, often leading to separation and divorce. The therapist often must challenge the traditional norms of masculinity and femininity to help a couple achieve closeness.

In intimate relationships, both partners are able to understand their differences and work together to deal with them. A husband will respond to his wife's need for affectionate conversation, while the wife will understand that her husband's need for closeness may be expressed through an activity (such as a walk in the neighborhood) or physical closeness (such as sitting on the couch together). Husbands who claim that their wives "nag them all the time" need to understand the wife's desire for more attention or time together. Wives need to understand that some husbands feel threatened and often have a greater need for independence. Greater understanding in both cases leads to a closer relationship.

ENHANCING INTIMACY

L'Abate (1977) lists several steps for enhancing intimacy:

1. *See the good in self and other.* Each partner should be able to look for the good in himself or herself and the other partner. This requires each spouse

to look for opportunities to show appreciation or affirmation of the other. It also requires substituting criticism with appreciative remarks. For instance, if a husband admits to his wife that he wrote a bad check, the wife might, instead of being critical, tell him that she appreciates his honesty. Gottman (1994) suggests that by focusing on what a partner "most wants or deserves to hear" in a specific situation, he or she can receive appreciation rather than criticism. Moreover, if one cannot think of anything nice to say in a specific situation, one might try asking the other spouse what he or she would most like to hear. Similarly, partners can help each other by revealing what they need as well (p. 206).

Therapists can help partners express the good they see in the other by asking the following questions:

- What is it you appreciate about your wife/husband?
- What was the last thing your husband/wife did to make you feel special?
- What do you think your husband/wife needs most from you now?

2. *Caring for the Other Partner.* Caring can be expressed in a number of ways, depending on the needs of the couple. This requires a spouse to be less preoccupied with himself or herself and to become more tuned in to the partner. Partners can show they care for each other by asking questions about the other's day, job, or family. Partners need to ask the fundamental question: "What does my spouse need from me now?" In some cases, a partner may first state his or her care needs: "I wish you would cook dinner when I have to work late," or "I like it when you show interest in my work."

Therapists can help partners express care for each other by suggesting the following:

- What could your husband/wife do that would be most helpful right now?
- Find out how your husband/wife is feeling now.
- What could she/he do to show you that he/she cares for you?

3. *Protecting Your Relationship.* Couples must protect their relationship by keeping other things—friends, family, and children—out. This requires each spouse to separate from their family of origin and establish a marital bond where the role of son or daughter becomes secondary to the role of husband or wife. The couple must negotiate boundaries with extended families, relatives, and friends.

Establishing a strong marital bond to protect the relationship requires each spouse to value "us" over "me." The therapist can help couples protect their relationship with the following questions:

- What can you do to keep others from taking time away from your relationship?
- How can you manage the kids and still have time for yourselves?

4. *Enjoying One's Self and the Relationship.* Happily married couples can achieve closeness through pleasurable activities. Markman et al. (1994) examined a number of variables and found that fun shared by both partners emerged as the strongest factor contributing to overall marital happiness. The time that couples spend in enjoyable activities enhances intimacy and strengthens the marital bond. Couples should be encouraged to negotiate activities that are pleasurable to both partners. This requires setting time aside without interferences. Some questions to help couples begin to arrange pleasurable activities in their lives follow:

   - Sit down and make a list: what things would you like to do together?
   - What do other couples do for fun that interests you?
   - Pick three activities and set time aside for each activity. What can each of you do to make sure you spend this time together?

5. *Taking Responsibility.* Intimacy can only be achieved when each spouse takes personal responsibility for the relationship's failures. This requires partners to avoid blaming the other partner for the problem. Taking responsibility requires trying to understand the other partner's view and why he or she might be upset. It means being accountable for specific aspects of the problem. In some cases it means one spouse must acknowledge responsibility, even when he or she is not sure about what he or she did to upset the other. For example, the therapist can help a partner acknowledge responsibility with questions such as the following:

   - Can you see why your wife/husband might be upset with you?
   - Can you see your part in this problem?
   - Can you think of something that you would like to change here?

6. *Sharing Hurt.* Intimate relationships are characterized by sharing feelings of vulnerability. Sharing feelings such as hurt, resentment, frustration, and guilt promotes empathy and understanding—cornerstones for a close and intimate relationship. Sharing without attacking the other partner is the first step. Sharing feelings of hurt is more effective when it is done without blame. Partners should be encouraged to use "I-statements" rather than "you-statements" to put the focus on the partner's feelings, rather than the other partner's shortcomings (Gottman, 1998). That is, rather than saying, "You make me feel guilty," one would preferably say, "I feel guilty when _____." The therapist can facilitate partners sharing the expression of underlying feelings with prompts such as:

   - Tell your husband/wife how this affects you.
   - What lies behind your anger?
   - What kinds of feelings do you experience when he/she criticizes you?

7. *Forgiveness.* In an intimate relationship, partners will become angry with each other. In instances where one or both partners have acted in ways

that are hurtful, it is important for each partner to forgive the other. When partners fail to forgive each other, resentment builds, conflict becomes greater, and ultimately a state of hopelessness becomes pervasive (Markman et al., 1994). Forgiveness requires that beyond giving a simple apology ("I'm sorry"), the partner should accept responsibility for his or her behavior ("You're right. I had no right to say that to you.").

Partners who fail to forgive fail to restore intimacy, and put themselves at risk for additional physical and psychological problems. Markman et al. (1994) state that saying, "I'm sorry. I was wrong. Please forgive me," is one of the most healing things that can happen between two people (p. 227). The authors also suggest that in addition to asking forgiveness, the partner should make a commitment to change the offending behavior. The therapist can facilitate forgiveness by posing the following questions:

- Have you apologized for hurting your partner?
- Did you take responsibility for this act?
- Have you done anything to change your behavior?

Case Study

Mr. and Mrs. Duncan had been married for five years. Both sought marital therapy because each felt alone in the marriage. Mr. Duncan had always felt a need to please his mother. He had been triangulated into his mother and father's conflict and continued to have a close relationship with his mother through his adult life. Mrs. Duncan's father died when she was six, and she lived with her mother and older sister until she was married in her early twenties. She complained that Mr. Duncan was "unavailable to her emotionally" and that her efforts to get support from him pushed him further away. She further reported feelings of "inadequacy" and tended to withdraw at such times.

Mr. Duncan could not understand his wife's problem and thought that she was expecting too much of him. The therapist helped to create an atmosphere for change by discussing what each appreciated in the other and soliciting examples of things each did to make the other feel special. He also helped the wife to be more specific about what she needed emotionally from her husband and what she could do to help him get closer to her. Finally, the therapist discussed what the couple might do to keep others (such as Mr. Duncan's mother) from taking time away from their relationship. This process included individual sessions with Mr. Duncan on how he could stay connected with his mother while moving closer to his wife.

In this case, Mr. Duncan's overinvolvement with his mother and Mrs. Duncan's expectations for more time with him led to emotional isolation in the marriage. The therapist helped each spouse to focus on those things that each appreciated in the other. This produced more positive feelings and helped each of them to focus more on the needs of the other than his or her own needs. Finally, the therapist helped Mr. Duncan protect his relationship with his wife by being less involved with his mother.

BARRIERS TO INTIMACY

Most couples want to be close but run up against a number of barriers. It is critical that the therapist identify the barriers and provide suggestions to the couple for overcoming them. Below are some typical barriers and suggestions for overcoming them.

1. *Fear of Intimacy.* Many couples have a fear of becoming more intimate. In some cases partners believe that it is important to handle their own emotions and be independent. Such fears may result from child rearing that emphasized self-reliance and provided little support from parents. Such marriages are characterized by emotional distance where couples lead parallel or independent lives (Weeks & Treat, 1992). Thus, when a problem arises, rather than turning to each other for support, partners often try to cope with the problem on their own.

   Proposed Solution:

   It is important for the therapist to help both partners understand their unconscious fears. This often means examining each partner's role in her or his family of origin and what messages each received about expressions of intimacy, closeness, and distance. It is important to normalize these fears and help each to understand how they developed. In such cases, the therapist should help the couple decide one step that each could take that would help the couple overcome their fear. Partners need to learn to ask for closeness and trust each other with their feelings.

2. *Inability to Receive Intimacy.* Some couples have much difficulty with intimacy. They are typically characterized by a limited ability to receive mutual affection or support. When one partner attempts to provide nurturance or affection, the other partner does not receive it. Karpel (1994) elaborates:

   > . . . whatever the surface fluctuations, the underlying rule seems to be that no situation can exist in which one person offers warmth, affection and love and the other receives it. Novice therapists are often confused by these couples because they assume that both partners want intimacy and will welcome efforts to help them achieve it. However, when intimacy is problematic, it is often because it is deeply threatening to one or both partners. The therapist's—and the partners'—efforts to enhance intimacy increase the unconscious sense of dangerous vulnerability and contribute to unconscious attempts to obstruct or prevent it. (p. 161)

These couples, according to Karpel, differ from couples who are unable to negotiate differences. In fact, their efforts to oppose intimacy often result in a therapeutic impasse.

Proposed Solution:

To assist such couples, the therapist must first understand the protective function of the symptom (Karpel, 1994). For example, one partner's problem with closeness may serve to protect the other partner. In such cases, the therapist should help the couple understand how avoidance or disagreement about intimacy functions in the relationship (for example, whether one partner is serving as a caretaker for the other). Each partner needs to check out how the other feels, and then listen nondefensively (Gottman, 1998).

3. *Acceptance of Differences.* Partners sometimes believe it is too risky to talk about certain subjects. Partners from different religious or cultural backgrounds often avoid discussing their differences, for fear that each will be unaccepted by the other ("Will I still be accepted if my spouse knows about my past?"). Inability to discuss such fundamental issues creates distance and prevents the couple from talking about other topics such as money, sex, and politics. Partners must learn to avoid criticizing or judging the other's feelings.

Proposed Solution:

In such cases, the therapist should help the couple understand that such differences—ethnic, cultural, or otherwise—cannot be changed. Rather than view them as internal problems, the couple should see the differences as an external problem or threat to the relationship. Both parties should be encouraged to discuss how they might overcome such problems to protect the marriage.

4. *Hidden Issues in the Relationship.* Some couples avoid topics because of hidden issues in the relationship. Markman, Stanley, and Blumberg in their book *Fighting for Your Marriage* describe hidden issues as "deeper, fundamental issues that can come up with any issue or event" (p. 123). Behind common issues such as money and sex are often deeper issues such as control, acceptance, and fairness. In such instances, partners have grown up with an authoritarian parent. Often, hidden issues of control, acceptance, and fairness are expressed in the form of covert questions, such as: who is most important in the relationship, or does one partner's needs count as much as the other partner's needs. Such questions often affect more simple issues such as where the couple will eat tonight, or where they will spend the holidays. Resolution of hidden issues is critical to the integrity of the marriage.

Proposed Solution:

Therapists first need to help couples recognize a hidden issue when it arises. When a hidden issue is identified, the therapist should help the couple understand it. Understanding the issue is a precondition for problem solving. Markman et al. (1994) suggest that the deeper the issue, the less likely that problem solving will be the preferred solution. Rather, what each partner needs to do is listen to the other without interrupting, and then restate the other's concerns. Such interactions help partners accept each other and resolve hidden agendas. Couples must be willing to share responsibility for the problem and work toward a solution.

CONCLUSION

Trust and intimacy are critical factors in a successful marriage. Trust develops slowly as couples spend enjoyable times together, strive to understand each other, back up their actions with words, and fulfill their obligations to each other.

Intimacy can only occur when each partner has a clear sense of himself/herself as separate from the other. An intimate relationship develops from a choice to be together, rather than a need to fulfill one's self through another. In an intimate relationship, partners bring out the best in each other, care for each other, and enjoy the relationship. They also take responsibility for the relationship, protect it, and share their joys as well as their hurts. The therapist should help couples develop trust and overcome barriers to intimacy.

KEY POINTS

- Trust and intimacy are the building blocks of any relationship.
- Intimacy can only occur when each partner has a clear sense of one as separate from the other.
- Trust develops slowly as couples spend enjoyable times together, strive to understand each other, back up their actions with words, and fulfill their obligations to each other.
- Without trust, closeness and intimacy are not possible in the relationship.
- People who have failed to differentiate from their families of origin do not feel free to develop a separate intimate relationship with another.
- Men and women view intimacy differently.
- In intimate relationships, both partners are able to understand their differences and work together to deal with them.
- Partners who fail to forgive, fail to restore intimacy and put themselves at risk for additional physical and psychological problems.
- Most couples want to be close but run up against a number of barriers.

MARITAL SKILLS INVENTORY

Please check when you have completed these procedures.

_____   Teach skills for building trust and enhancing intimacy.

_____   Build trust in the relationship.

_____   Examine gender differences in the relationship.

_____   Enhance intimacy in the relationship.

_____   Overcome barriers to intimacy in the relationship.

REFERENCES

Beavers, W. R. (1985). *Successful marriage: A family systems approach to couples.* New York: Norton.

Boszormenyi-Nagy, I., & Krasner, B. (1986). *Between give and take: A clinical guide to contextual therapy.* New York: Brunner/Mazel.

Boszormenyi-Nagy, I., & Ulrich, D. (1981). Contextual family therapy. In A. Gurman & D. Kniskren (Eds.), *Handbook of Family Therapy.* New York: Brunner/Mazel.

Boszormenyi-Nagy, I. (1987). *Foundations of contextual therapy: Collected papers of Ivan Boszormenyi-Nagy.* New York: Brunner/Mazel.

Bowen, M. (1978). *Family therapy in clinical practice.* New York: Aronson.

Carter, B., & McGoldrick, M. (1999). *The expanded family life cycle: Individual, family and social perspectives* (3rd. ed.). Needham Heights, MA: Allyn & Bacon.

Gottman, J. (1999). *The marriage clinic: A scientifically-based marital therapy.* New York: Norton.

Gottman, J. (1998). *Clinical manual for marital therapy: A scientifically-based marital therapy.* Seattle, WA: The Seattle Marital and Family Institute.

Gottman, J. (1994). *Why marriages succeed or fail.* New York: Simon & Schuster.

Karpel, M. A. (1994). *Evaluating couples: A handbook for practitioners.* New York: Norton.

L'Abate, L. (1977). *Enrichment: Structural/interventions with couples, families and groups.* Washington, DC: University Press of America.

Markman, H., Stanley, S., & Blumberg, S.C. (1994). *Fighting for your marriage: Positive steps for preventing divorce and preserving a lasting love.* San Francisco: Jossey-Bass.

Tannen, D. (1990). *You just don't understand: Women and men in conversation.* New York: Morrow.

Weeks, G. R., & Treat, S. (1992). *Couples in treatment: Technique and approaches for effective practice.* New York: Brunner/Mazel.

Weiner-Davis, M. (1992). *Divorce Busting.* New York: Summit Books.

9

✳

Handling Unresolvable Problems

CHAPTER OBJECTIVES

Upon completion of this chapter, the reader will be able to:

1. Understand the difference between solvable and unsolvable problems.

2. Ask questions and present the problem as external to the couple.

3. Describe four strategies for promoting emotional acceptance.

4. List the key elements for promoting emotional acceptance.

INTRODUCTION

Many couples come to therapy with long-term problems that seem unsolvable. In such cases, both partners seem to believe that nothing can be done to help them. Perhaps because the problem has gone on for years, the couple believes that it is unchangeable. They fail to understand that relationships and people can change despite the fact that the problems are long-standing.

Although most problem behaviors can be resolved in some way, however, there are some that are unresolvable. This chapter will focus on a discussion of those problems and strategies for handling them.

UNCHANGEABLE PROBLEMS

A number of problems that confront couples are not responsive to traditional change-oriented strategies. For example, differences in personality, temperament, culture, or ethnicity are not amenable to change. Culture and ethnic differences lead to differences in expectations and attitudes about marriage. The greater the difference in cultural background, the more problems couples will experience in adjusting to the marriage (McGoldrick & Preto, 1984). The authors state:

> For example, a WASP/Italian couple might run into conflicts because the WASP takes literally the dramatic expressiveness of the Italian whereas the Italian finds the WASP's emotional distancing intolerable. The WASP may label the Italian "hysterical" or "crazy" and in return be labeled "cold" or "catatonic." Knowledge about differences in cultural belief systems can be helpful to spouses who take each other's behavior personally. Couples may have a sudden and remarkable shift in response when they can come to see the spouse's behavior as fitting into a larger ethnic context rather than as a personal attack.
>
> Ethnic differences often become personal differences. Families at times may use their ethnic customs or religious beliefs selectively to justify an emotional position within the family or against outsiders. But the opposite problem can be equally difficult. That is, couples often react to each other as if the other's behavior is a personal attack rather than a difference rooted in ethnicity. Typically we tolerate differences when we are not under stress—and in fact, find them appealing. However, when stress is added to a system, our tolerance for difference diminishes. We become frustrated if we are not understood in ways that fit with our wishes and expectations. WASPs tend to withdraw when upset, to move toward stoical isolation, in order to mobilize their powers of reason (their major resource in coping with stress). Jews, on the other hand, seek to discuss and analyze their experience together; Italians may seek solace in food, emotional and dramatic expression of their feelings, and a high degree of human contact. Obviously, these groups may perceive each other's reactions as offensive or insensitive, although within each group's ethnic context, their reactions make excellent sense. In our experience, much of therapy with intermarried couples involves helping family members recognize each other's behavior as a reaction from a different frame of reference. (pp. 73–74)

Differences in ethnic or cultural backgrounds often produce unresolvable conflict definitions of sex roles and relationships of partners to their family, friends, and coworkers. For example, in Japanese families, it is often expected that the wife will become part of the husband's family, while for other ethnic groups (WASPs, Irish), the couple boundary can be strong, with advice from parents viewed as interference. Thus, what seems normal to each partner is based on different perceptions and experiences.

Externalization of the Problem

One of the ways to handle unresolvable problems is to externalize the problem referring to it as if it rests outside the couple (White, 1988). In such cases, the therapist might ask, "How long have you struggled with this problem? How does the conflict affect you? What do you do when you are being influenced by the conflict? Has the conflict been dominating your relationship? How would things be different if this problem didn't exist?" Such questions move the problem outside the couple so they can take action against it. If the problem is external to the couple, the therapist can help them work together as a team to overcome it (White & Epston, 1990). If an individual's spouse has been identified as having the problem, the therapist must help the spouse to work toward solving the problem rather than becoming defensive.

It is helpful for the therapist to assess the influence "the problem" has on the couple and then assess what influence the couple has on the problem (Brown & Christensen, 1999). The therapist might ask questions such as: "What do you both do that seems to overcome the conflict? What kind of influence do you have on the conflict?" The therapist searches for examples where the couple has ameliorated the problem and prevented it from influencing their lives.

If the therapist is successful in getting the couple to see how they can influence the problem, he or she can help them look forward to a time when they can have more control over this situation. Here the therapist helps the couple to recognize when they are able to control the problem. The couple works closely together to reduce the influence of the problem on their relationship. Questions such as "What do you imagine your relationship will be like when you no longer have this problem?" or "What do you want to be doing when this problem doesn't exist?" help the couple to think about the future. The therapist helps the couple to recognize small steps of progress that lead to new patterns in the relationship.

Consider the following example:

> Tom and Wilma sought therapy because both were dissatisfied with their relationship. Neither felt understood by the other. Moreover, each complained that the more they talked about their problems (including the lack of respect for each other, and Wilma's need to feel closer to Tom), the more distant they felt. Both reported that they felt alone in the marriage. When the therapist asked them what they wanted in the marriage, neither of them could express his or her desires without putting the other down. Tom and Wilma agreed that they felt more comfortable discussing problems than how each could make the other happy. In the first session, the therapist asked them how long they had struggled with the problem and how the conflict affected them. Neither could remember how long the problem had affected them but agreed that it had gotten worse the last two years of their marriage. Both reported that they felt lonely. At this point, the therapist discussed how the problem influenced each of them and how things might be different if this problem did not

exist. Although they were more comfortable discussing problems, they concurred that they needed to work more together and discuss solutions.

In this case, the therapist helped the couple move from a problem-saturated discussion to a discussion of solutions. The therapist was able to help them create a new reality where both spouses must work together and talk about how they *wanted things to be* versus how they *did not want things to be.*

ACCEPTANCE

Partners who present themselves with unchangeable problems—problems based on differences in personality, ethnicity, and culture—must learn to accept each other's view of the problem. That is, each must become more compassionate and "soften" his or her position on the other's behavior before any change can take place (Christensen, Jacobson, & Babcock, 1995). If the spouse is not able to understand the other's position, marital gridlock occurs and change is unlikely to happen. For example, if partners are unable to understand how ethnic or cultural traditions affect the other's behavior, then each will not see the other's concern as valid or see how each other's behaviors cause pain for their partner.

PROMOTING ACCEPTANCE

To handle unresolvable issues, both partners must learn to emotionally accept the other's position or view of the problem. Emotional acceptance according to Christensen et al. (1995) refers to marital interaction where each partner experiences a negative behavior in a different way. That is, if a problem in the past was unacceptable and aversive, such behavior in the present becomes tolerated and acceptable. For example, partners may not be able to accommodate to their ethnic/cultural beliefs and behavior, but they may be able to change the way they view it or live with it.

Case Study

Clara and John had been married for fifteen years. While John had always been a faithful husband and a good provider, he was not an affectionate person and rarely paid Clara a compliment. Clara had hoped for a very romantic husband and frequently touched and kissed John. Although he typically accepted her affection, he never initiated any on his own. Because of Clara's increasing concern and complaints about this, John finally agreed to attend therapy with her. The therapist helped them recognize personality differences and talked with them about how one partner is supposed to know the other cares about them. John said, "I'm here, aren't I? Haven't I always taken care of you and been faithful to you?" Clara said a spouse should not only show love but also verbalize it.

Couples must then learn to accept what they can not change in the spouse and thereby learn to live with the problem. Christensen, Jacobson, and Babcock (1995) utilize four strategies to promote acceptance of unresolvable problems. A brief description of each strategy follows.

Emotional Acceptance Through Empathic Joining Around the Problem

Partners who come to therapy often view each other as uncaring, selfish, dependent, hostile, or emotionally disturbed. They believe that such qualities or traits are a part of one's personality. When partners experience themselves in this way, acceptance is difficult and behavior change is unlikely to occur. The authors suggest that when partners experience each other in this way, an implicit or explicit hierarchy is often created between them, bringing out statements like: "I'm okay. She is compulsive," or "He is controlling. I am not."

Couples often need to review the problem in a different way before accepting it. For example, partners in therapy often view their spouses as insensitive, uncaring, angry, or unloving. When partners view each other in this manner, acceptance is often quite difficult. Christensen et al. (1995) suggest that acceptance is limited, when one partner views the problem as residing within the other partner rather than in the relationship. ("He has the problem but I'm not a part of it.")

In order to create acceptance, the therapist must reframe the marital problem as one of common differences between people and each partner's emotional reaction to these differences (Christensen et al. 1995). The authors further emphasize the pain each partner experiences and their ineffectual efforts to deal with it. Often pain will lead to personal attacks by partners, thus leading to marital dissatisfaction. However, when each partner can express their pain without personal attacks and blame, the couple is more likely to accept the differences between them.

For example, the therapist might help partners to express their own experience by saying the following:

Therapist: John, I would like you to talk about your own experience without blaming Clara. Talk how the problem affects you.

John: Clara, you spend money like it grows on trees.

Therapist: John, what I want you to do is describe what Clara does and how it makes you feel.

John: When you go out and spend a lot of money without telling me, I get mad.

Therapist: That's better. What is it that upsets you?

John: She doesn't feel it's important enough to tell me. As Rodney Dangerfield says, "I don't get any respect."

Therapist: So it's more than being mad. You feel she doesn't respect you enough to tell you.

John: Yeah.

Therapist: So it hurts when she doesn't respect you.

Clara: I would show him more respect if he would show some appreciation and concern for me.

Therapist: Tell John when you don't feel appreciated.

Clara: I don't feel appreciated when you never show any affection or attention.

Therapist: It sounds like you are different. You each have different needs. This is pretty normal.

In this case, the therapist is asking the husband to express his dissatisfaction to his wife without turning her off, and the wife to express dissatisfaction to her husband without turning him off. The therapist helps them see that the best way a partner can express dissatisfaction with the mate is through letting the mate know what he or she is doing and how it affects the other person. The therapist helps the couple reframe their behaviors as a common difference in personalities and instructs them to practice ways to express their hurt and dissatisfaction without blaming (which often leads to further arguments and dissatisfaction). Clara was able to tell John that she felt more loved and appreciated when he complimented her or showed affection. John was able to tell Clara through an "I" message that he was bothered when she did not show respect for him.

The therapist can further assist each spouse to talk about their feelings by suggesting that the couple should:

- Express their hurt, pain, disappointment, and doubts, rather than anger and resentment.
- Decide what made them feel that way.
- Express dissatisfaction with the other partner through an "I" message.
- Verbalize the disliked behavior, the feeling it produces, and how one partner would like the other to behave.

The therapist should help each spouse to express their fears and vulnerabilities without personal attack, allowing one spouse to hear the other without becoming defensive, thus leading to greater acceptance.

Key Elements of the Therapeutic Strategy

- Reframe the problem and the partner's behavior in terms of common differences.
- Emphasize the pain each partner experiences to accommodate to the other.
- Help each partner talk about his or her own experience rather than talking about the other.
- Emphasize the use of "soft" feelings (vulnerability, hurt, or fear) rather than "hard" feelings (anger, resentment).

- Create a safe atmosphere where soft feelings can be expressed.
- Encourage active listening in situations where partners seem to misunder-stand each other.

Emotional Acceptance
Through Detachment From the Problem

The first strategy emphasizes acceptance through empathy and understanding for each other, while the second strategy enhances acceptance through detach-ment from the problem (Christensen et al., 1995). One of the ways to detach is to refer to the problem as "it." For example, the therapist might say, "Has 'it' (the yelling problem) been dominating your lives in ways that you feel is unfair?", or "What would you be doing more of in your relationship if 'it' was not trying to destroy your lives?" Such questions help the couple to define the problem externally: if the problem is outside of the couple, then they can work together to overcome it, thus freeing them to work against the problem rather than spending their energy defending themselves.

With this strategy, the therapist avoids evaluating or assigning responsibil-ity for change to one partner. Rather, the emphasis is on detached patterns of behavior. The therapist helps the couple view the interaction, which triggers the problem as an "it" that confronts both partners. The couple is encouraged to view the problem as a challenge that they must overcome to restore their relationship.

Key Elements of the Therapeutic Strategy

- Discuss basic differences and conflictual interaction sequences that surround them.
- Discuss a forthcoming event that may trigger the problem.
- Discuss recent positive events that are related to the problem.
- Discuss recent negative events that are related to the problem.
- Use an inanimate object to refer to the problem.
- Refer to the problem as an "it."
- Use humor to describe the problem as long as it does not show disrespect or minimize the problem.

Case Study (Continued)

Therapist: John, would you like to respond to Clara's message about attention and affection?

John: I do care about Clara.

Clara: I don't feel appreciated when you never show me any affection or attention.

Therapist: It's good that you are able to share how you feel. When does it [the problem] seem worse?

Clara: On weekends. I would like to do more things with John, but he doesn't seem interested.

Therapist: Do you ask him?

Clara: No. I can tell that he wants to be by himself.

Therapist: John expresses his caring by taking care of you. You express your caring through affection. The problem seems to be related to differences in showing caring. So let's pretend that this cup is the problem (moves the cup to the center of the table). It is in the center of the table and it is up to the two of you to get it off the table.

The therapist externalized the problem of John and Clara by referring to it as "the difference in showing caring." By asking them how they could deal with "their difference in showing caring" problem, they began to see it as outside of themselves and discussed ways to deal with it. John indicated to Clara that he had strong feelings of love even though he didn't express it the way she liked.

Emotional Acceptance Through Tolerance Building

The third therapeutic strategy is designed to help the couple tolerate the problem. This means that each partner must learn to tolerate or live with the other partner's negative behavior. Christensen et al. (1995) suggest that this can only occur when partners spend endless time and energy to prevent or escape the other partner's behavior. Tolerance requires partners to be less reactive to the problem. The therapist will know that the partners are tolerant if each is able to let go of his or her efforts to change the other's behavior.

Christensen et al. (1995) list three procedures for helping spouses to develop tolerance:

Positive Features of Negative Behavior   The therapist can build tolerance by helping each spouse to identify the positive features of the negative behavior. This is somewhat different from "positive connotation," which only refers to the positive aspects of the behavior. For example, if a wife is very angry and critical of her husband because he is unavailable, the therapist who wants to give this a positive connotation might say, "Your wife's criticism is her way of letting you know who much she loves you and wants to stay involved with you. This is her way of ensuring that you will communicate." In contrast, the therapist who wants to show the positive features of negative behavior would not discount the wife's anger, but might say, "Your wife's criticism and anger is coming from a deep hurt that she is experiencing, and whether it is true or not, she thinks this is the only way she can get your attention." In short, the therapist strives to interpret negative behavior as partly positive. Even if the behavior cannot be reframed as positive, the therapist can at least point out that differences can be complementary, and can create balance in a relationship. (Both the spouse who is very emotional and the spouse who is very objective and detached have good qualities. The one expresses feelings very easily; the other sees things from an objective stance. Both characteristics are very positive and important in a relationship, but each spouse has too much of only one of these qualities. A blending or moving toward the middle would be helpful.)

During the interview, if the couple begins to describe each other's differences, the therapist might note that this creates balance. Some common examples occurring in couples are: active versus passive, dominant versus submissive, stable versus unstable, and emotional versus rational. Differences are often pieces of a jigsaw puzzle where the various pieces fit or complement each other (Colapinto, 1991).

Role-Playing or Behavior Rehearsal of Negative Behavior   The therapist can also facilitate tolerance through behavioral rehearsal. Here the therapist attempts to help the couple find a new way to discuss the problem—often going beyond traditional ways of communicating with each other. For example, to build tolerance, the therapist helps the couples to identify old problematic patterns (such as criticism and blame). By asking the couple to rehearse these patterns (such as husband attacking a wife for asking too many questions), the therapist can help the couple to identify thoughts and feelings that contribute to the conflict. The purpose of the behavioral rehearsal, thus, is to get the couple to discuss their problem without destructive thoughts and feelings that often lead to personal attacks and defensiveness. The exercise is similar to stress inoculation where couples become desensitized to each other's behavior.

Fake Incidents of Negative Behavior   In some cases the therapist can encourage acceptance of differences by asking the couple to fake the negative behavior (criticism) when they do not feel that way. For example, a husband may criticize his wife for spending so much time at work when he is not upset with her. By faking the negative behavior, the spouse can observe the partner's hurt and prevent escalation of the conflict (Christensen et al., 1995). To ensure that conflict does not escalate, the therapist should encourage the spouse to reveal his/her intentions. Faking the behavior can help couples build tolerance in several ways. First, the partner who is the recipient of the negative behavior never knows whether the negative behavior is being faked or whether it is intentional. Second, faking the behavior helps to view the problem differently, since the couple interacts without the negative emotions, thus increasing tolerance of the behavior. Finally, faking the behavior helps to desensitize the couple to the problem, making it easier to accept the problem.

Key Elements of the Therapeutic Strategy

- Point out the positive features of each partner's negative behavior.
- Remind couples that they are likely to relapse and fall back into old patterns.
- Prepare couples to handle relapse by asking them to rehearse it.
- Ask couples to express their feelings rather than act them out.

- Ask couples to fake incidents of the negative behavior when they are not predisposed to act that way.
- Ask the faking partner to express negative emotion with the behavior.
- Suggest that the faking partner remain calm so he or she can observe the reactions of the other partner.
- Ask the faking partner to reveal the fake immediately to prevent escalation and facilitate healthy discussion.

Case Study (Continued)

Therapist: Okay. I would like to rehearse this problem as if it were Saturday morning and you, Clara, want to go out and do something, and John, you want to do something else. John, what do you normally do on Saturday mornings?

John: I usually read the paper.

Therapist: Okay. So you are reading the paper and Clara, you are getting ready to go out. How does John respond?

Clara: He doesn't even look at me. When I say I'm leaving, he mumbles, "Okay." He doesn't say anything affectionate. He doesn't kiss me.

John: I love Clara very much, but I'm someone who just doesn't show affection by mushy talk or a lot of kissing.

Clara: John, I think it's important for Clara to hear this, but it's also important for you to be available for her. She doesn't always feel that love and she needs you to show it by being more verbal about your feelings and by being more affectionate. Clara, it is important for you to remember that John expresses love through being faithful and providing well for you.

When John indicated that he had strong feelings of love, but did not see himself as an affectionate person, the very act of explaining this helped Clara to accept the situation. The therapist also emphasized the positives that John had stated and emphasized his way of expressing love—that of being faithful and providing well. This helped Clara change her perceptions of John's feelings for her and helped her deal with the fact that he may never be as affectionate as she would like. Through the sessions, she became better able to accept John as he was, understanding that he might never change in the way she would like.

Emotional Acceptance Through Greater Self-Care

Spouses need to develop ways to care for themselves to protect themselves in helpless struggles with each other. By fostering self-acceptance, self-control, and self-awareness, the therapist helps the couple to be more tolerant of each other's problems. Spouses who are able to forgive themselves for not being perfect can risk more intimate self-expression with each other. As they learn to tolerate conflict, their acceptance of themselves and each other generalizes to their children. Interactions become opportunities for family members to be heard and understood, rather than being controlled or judged.

There are several ways to care for oneself:

- Calming down by taking your pulse every five minutes during difficult discussions.

- Taking a time out if your heart rate goes ten percent above the resting rate (an increase of 8–10 beats of a minute) (Gottman, 1994).

- Relax by taking a bath, stretching, going for a walk, listening to music, or calling a friend.

- Replace self-defeating thoughts with positive thoughts ("When she uses that tone of voice, what do you tell yourself?" or, "How might this be useful to you?").

- Identify the benefits of the partner's behavior. Every behavior has costs and benefits.

Thus, when a wife complains that her husband leaves during their arguments, the therapist might help the couple to identify those situations where leaving is useful (for example, when there is potential for violence.) Self-care requires each spouse to take responsibility for himself or herself when the spouse is unable to meet his/her needs.

Key Elements of the Therapeutic Strategy

- Help partners explore alternative means for meeting their needs.

- Discuss personal responsibility for meeting needs with each partner.

- Remind partners that their problems will likely occur again and that each partner must protect himself or herself from escalating conflict.

- Discuss how each partner might protect himself or herself (such as leaving the situation or calling someone for support).

- Discuss the consequences of the protective behavior to prevent escalation of the problem.

Case Study (Continued)

Therapist: When you are really frustrated, what do you do to calm down and take care of yourself?

John: I don't think we do anything.

Therapist: Each of you needs to take responsibility for meeting your needs when your spouse is unable to do so.

Clara: Like how? John never wants to talk about anything. What could I do?

Therapist: What is something that you really like to do—something that calms you when you are upset?

Clara: I like to garden.

Therapist: So gardening is a treat for you and gives you a sense of well-being. Are there other things that help?

Clara: I enjoy being with friends.

Therapist: So maybe when you're feeling low about not getting attention from John, you might spend some time with friends, or you may garden.

Clara: I would enjoy those things.

Therapist: I think it would be helpful for both of you to work on things we've talked about—you, Clara, showing more respect for John; and you John, showing more affection for Clara. Sometimes, however, one or both of you may not get the change you want.

Clara: So when that doesn't happen, I should find something that is relaxing and can put me in a better mood.

Therapist: That's right!

CONCLUSION

There are a number of marital problems that are unresolvable. Personality and ethnic and cultural differences often have a negative impact on couples and are not amenable to traditional change strategies. Rather, the therapist can be most helpful by helping the couple emotionally to accept the behavior of the other partner. The therapist can enhance emotional acceptance through the following strategies: (1) empathic joining around the problem, (2) detachment from the problem, (3) tolerance building, and (4) greater self-care. These strategies help the couple be less sensitive to the problem so they can live with it.

KEY POINTS

- Some problems that confront couples are not responsive to traditional change-oriented strategies.
- Differences in ethnic or cultural backgrounds often produce unresolvable conflict.
- One of the ways to handle unresolvable problems is to externalize the problem, or refer to it as if it exists outside the couple.
- If the therapist is successful in getting the couple to see how they can influence the problem, he or she can help them look forward to a time when they can have more control over the situation.
- Partners who present themselves with unchangeable problems must learn to accept each other's view of the problem.

- In order to create acceptance, the therapist must reframe the marital problem as one of common differences between people and each partner's emotional reaction to these differences.

- Acceptance can occur when each partner learns to tolerate or live with the other partner's negative behavior.

- The therapist can help the couple become more tolerant of each other's problems by fostering self-acceptance, self-control, and self-awareness.

MARITAL SKILLS INVENTORY

Please check when you have completed the procedures below.

_____ Determine whether the problem is solvable or unsolvable.

_____ Externalize the problem.

Promote acceptance for unresolvable issues:

_____ Reframe the marital problem as one of common differences.

_____ Refer to the problem as though it were an inanimate object.

_____ Point out positive features of each partner's negative behavior.

_____ Prepare couples to handle relapse by asking them to rehearse it.

_____ Help the couple replace self-defeating thoughts with positive thoughts.

_____ Help partners explore alternative means for meeting their needs.

REFERENCES

Brown, J. H., & Christensen, D.N. (1999). *Family therapy: Theory and practice* (2nd ed.). Pacific Grove, CA: Brooks/Cole.

Christensen, A., Jacobson, N. S., & Babcock, J. C. (1995). Integrative behavioral couple therapy. In N. S. Jacobson & A.S. Burman (Eds.), *Clinical handbook of couple therapy* (pp. 31–64). New York: Guilford.

Colapinto, J. (1991). Structural family therapy. In A. S. Gurman and D. P. Kniskern (Eds.), *Handbook of family therapy* (Vol. 2). New York: Brunner/Mazel.

Gottman, J. (1994). *Why marriages succeed or fail.* New York: Simon & Schuster.

McGoldrick, M., & Preto, N. G. (1984). Ethnic intermarriage: Implications for therapy. *Family Process* 23(3): 347–362.

White, M. (1988). *The externalizing of the problem.* Adelaide, Australia: Dulwich Centre.

White, M., & Epston, D. (1990). *Narrative means to therapeutic ends.* New York: Norton.

10

✳

Building Support
for Marriage

CHAPTER OBJECTIVES

Upon completion of this chapter, the reader will be able to:

1. Identify sources of support for the marital relationship.

2. List guidelines for helping couples to assess shared areas of interest.

3. Ask questions to help couples develop their own rituals.

4. Ask questions to help couples develop a set of shared beliefs.

5. Identify strategies for sources of support.

6. Specify obstacles to getting support.

INTRODUCTION

The purpose of this chapter is to assist the therapist in identifying sources of support and resources for a couple. Sources of support vary along a continuum, beginning with the marital subsystem and moving outward to larger social systems. Sources of support might include: (a) nuclear or immediate family (children, parents, household members), (b) relatives (blood and marriage), (c) informal network members (friends, neighbors, coworkers, and others), (d) social organizations (church and clubs), (e) educational organizations and agencies (family agencies, health organizations, schools, and day-care centers), (f) professional services (counseling and early intervention services), and (g) policy making groups and individuals (agency directors, school boards, and county and state governments) (Dunst, Trivette, & Deal, 1988).

The value of support may differ for husbands and wives. Friendship networks may be more important for women than men. Monica McGoldrick (1999) states the following:

> Friendship is an extremely important resource for women throughout the life cycle. From earliest childhood, girls concentrate more energy on working out friendships than boys do. Girls assess activities in terms of their impact on relationships, whereas boys usually subordinate relationships to the games they are playing. Throughout life, women tend to have more close friends than men do, but the relationships that women have are often not validated by the larger society (Antonucci, 1994). Schydlowsky (1983) shows that the importance of women's close female friendships diminishes from adolescence to early adulthood, as they focus on finding a mate and establishing a marriage, and then increases throughout the rest of the life cycle. Close female friendships were reported to be more important than close male friendships throughout the life cycle, second only to good health in importance for life satisfaction. (p. 119)

In a satisfying marriage, partners respect the friendship systems of their mates, and couples who have friendships outside the marriage are more likely to have satisfying marital relationships.

NEED FOR SUPPORT

Friends and family outside the marriage can be helpful to the couple to express and resolve negative feelings about the marriage (Gottman, 1994). It is critical for couples to find persons or groups for trust and support. It is usually advisable to draw on informal or natural supports before utilizing professional support and resources. Natural supports are people who are resourceful and empathic to the couple. Professional support personnel should not replace natural supports; rather, they should strengthen these relationships. Natural supports offer opportunities for reciprocal aid, a critical element in empowering couples. When partners can repay the support person, it strengthens their sense that they have to give as well as take.

Consider Bill and Sally, a couple who had been married seven years and had two children, ages 5 and 2, and came to therapy because Sally felt lonely in the marriage.

Therapist: So, Sally, tell me more about the loneliness you feel.

Sally: I don't know how to describe it. It just seems like the last few years, I have felt trapped. I am always taking care of the children, and Bill is busy with his work.

Bill: She's right. I'm on the road a lot with my job. Sometimes we see each other only on weekends.

Sally: It's not Bill's fault. He has to travel to different offices with his sales job.

Therapist: Do you ever get out with friends?

Sally: I used to, but the only time we get out now is when Bill has a sales meeting and the representatives bring their wives.

Therapist: How often does that happen?

Sally: Not much. Maybe once every three or four months.

Therapist: So, did you have more friends before you were married or had children?

Sally: Yes. Before we had children, I did. We also lived near my sister and mother then.

Therapist: So you moved.

Sally: Yes. When Bill took his new job, we moved and I don't see my family much.

Therapist: What kinds of things did you do before you had children?

Sally: Well, I played tennis and I was pretty involved at church.

Therapist: What keeps you from doing those things now?

Sally: It is a lot more difficult to get away now that I have children.

Therapist: Is Bill gone every night? Could you get a sitter?

Sally: Bill is home some nights but I can't predict which nights those will be. I really don't like getting a sitter.

Therapist: Bill, do you know in advance which nights you will be gone?

Bill: I could plan in advance. What night is the tennis league?

Sally: Wednesday.

Bill: I'm home most Wednesdays, except when the sales representatives come to town. I could take the kids over to church on those nights.

Bill and Sally are in a classic traditional marriage where the only outside contact the wife has is with her husband's friends. Here the therapist elicited the husband's cooperation and helped the wife make plans for developing outside friendships and activities.

SOURCES OF SUPPORT

There are a number of sources of support for couples. A brief discussion of each source follows.

Church and Religious Groups There is a clear body of research to support the fact that church and synagogue members have a higher level of mental health than nonmembers do. Likewise, the divorce rate is lower for couples who participate in religious activities than for couples who do not. Markman, Stanley, Blumberg (1994) suggest that religious and spiritual groups provide "natural points of connections" (p. 291) for couples. These points include: (a) regular meetings for specific activities, (b) spiritual activities (such as worship, prayer, reading and discussion groups), (c) social activities (coffee hours, ice cream socials, picnics, dinners, and recreational activities), and (d) service activities (building houses, food drives, and visits to nursing homes). Church and religious activities, by their very nature, place great importance on marriage.

Marriage Enrichment Groups The primary goals of marriage enrichment groups are to promote self-awareness, empathy, self-disclosure, increased intimacy, and development of communication and problem-solving skills with ongoing support group activities (Hof, Epstein, & Miller, 1980). The most common type of support group is the weekend retreat. During these weekends, group leaders help couples evaluate their relationships and determine how they want to enrich them. Couples are encouraged to share private areas of their relationships, both in the group and privately. Ongoing groups provide maintenance and support of newly acquired skills and healthy marital practices.

Recreational Activities The amount of time that couples spend in having fun is related to their overall level of marital satisfaction. When couples are able to set time aside for fun, it strengthens the bond for both partners. Couples may participate in yoga, exercise, or computer classes, or more simple things such as walking, gardening, or going to the movies. Some couples set aside one night each week as "date night" to get away. The therapist should remind couples that this time should be set aside for fun, not conflict. Couples should set aside special times to resolve problems. Trying to resolve conflict during a recreational activity undermines the enjoyment value and benefits to the relationship (Markman et al., 1994).

Hobbies and Individual Interests The therapist can also help the couple build support for the relationship by helping each partner to pursue his or her own interests. Partners obviously do not have to do everything together, and in fact, each must take some responsibility for making himself or herself happy. Partners should have areas of interest that they share, while at the same time exploring their individual interests. Weiner-Davis (1992) suggests that staying home consistently because the partner does not want to go out is a guaranteed way to destroy a marriage. Resentment will build unless partners are encouraged or at least given permission to be different and subsequently take some responsibility in meeting their own individual needs. Hobbies such as golf, gardening, and hiking will help each partner to develop his or her own interests and build support for a happy relationship.

ASSESSING AREAS OF INTEREST

The following guidelines will be useful in helping couples to assess shared areas of interest:

1. Ask each partner to generate a list of interests.

2. Ask each partner to prioritize his or her interests.

3. Request that partners exchange their lists and circle those interests they share with their partner (minimum of five).

4. Ask the couple to set a specific time aside for enjoyment.

5. Ask the couple to pick an activity to share during that time.

6. Ask the couple to plan the activity. (Who will make reservations? Who will get a baby sitter?)

7. Ask the couple to decide how they will protect this time against outside interference.

8. Ask each partner how he or she supports each other's individual interests.

9. Ask each partner to respect the other's differences.

10. Ask each partner to describe his or her hopes and dreams for their shared experience.

DEVELOPING RITUALS

Newly married couples must create rituals as a way of completing developmental tasks (Imber-Black, 1999). Sometimes, couples skip important developmental milestones that later become metaphors for the presenting problem. For example, when couples elope or forego a honeymoon, marital therapists may use this as a metaphor for skipping some important developmental task, such as creating a sense of attachment and tradition. As a couple identifies elements of the marriage that were skipped and need to be developed, the planning of a honeymoon or special anniversary celebration can symbolize the completion of that relationship task.

Creating rituals can be particularly difficult when the partners come from different cultures or religious backgrounds. Gay and lesbian couples may also have difficulty developing rituals, since society and often their families of origin do not affirm their relationship. For such couples, the therapist's role must be to help them develop rituals that strengthen the relationship and draw the partners closer together.

Sometimes, rituals are developed through celebrations, traditions, and routines for handling holidays and meals. Gottman (1998) provides a set of questions for couples to develop their own rituals:

1. How do we or should we eat together at dinner? What is the meaning of dinnertime? How was dinnertime handled in each of our families while we were growing up?

2. How should we part at the beginning of each day? What was this like in our families while we were growing up? How should our reunions be handled?

3. How should bedtime be? What was this like in our families while we were growing up? How do we want this time to be?

4. What is the meaning of weekends? What was this like in our families while we were growing up? What should weekends be like?

5. What are our rituals about vacations? What was this like in our families while we were growing up? What should they mean?

6. Pick a meaningful holiday. What is the true meaning of this holiday to us? How should it be celebrated this year? How was it celebrated in each of our families while we were growing up?

7. How do we get refreshed and renewed? What is the meaning of these rituals?

8. What rituals do we have when someone is sick? What was this like in our families when we were growing up? How should it be in our family? (p. 276)

The answers to these questions will help couples build meaning and support for their relationship. Rituals create positive memories and a relationship history that couples can draw upon in times of stress.

Examples of rituals for specific marital issues follow:

1. A dual-career couple that works late hours establishes a "date night" once a week.

2. A couple who experienced a separation lists all of the negative memories of the separation and burns the list.

3. A newly married stepfamily shares traditions for celebrating a Thanksgiving meal.

4. A couple that has been married for thirty-five years decides to renew their vows and invite family and friends.

5. A couple who shares little in common decides to buy new bicycles and plan a trip together.

6. A couple establishes a ritual of preparing noodle soup for a partner who felt ill.

7. Partners who grew up in different cultures decide to have a reunion, where members of each side of the family share a favorite story about the family.

8. Gay partners who decide to "come out" to their parents plan their "coming out" communication.

9. A couple from different religious backgrounds plans an interfaith wedding.

10. A couple that eloped plans a special anniversary celebration to mark the first year of marriage.

11. A couple who skipped the honeymoon plans a "belated honeymoon"
     ten years later.

The above-mentioned rituals contain symbols, metaphors, and actions to
mark a life cycle transition or a special event in the couple's relationship. Many
of these rituals provide support from family and friends for the couple's relationship. Imber-Black (1999) suggests that rituals are a powerful way to connect persons to a community of support.

DEVELOPING SHARED BELIEFS

Another way for couples to build support for their marriage is to develop a
shared meaning in their relationship. Couples who share basic common values
have less conflict and more satisfying marriages. For example, couples who
share core religious beliefs or philosophy have a set of guidelines for use in
dealing with both expected problems such as life transitions as well as unexpected problems, such as illnesses or loss of job.

A therapist can help couples develop shared beliefs by asking the following
questions:

1. What are some common values that are important to you?
2. How do you act in ways to support these values?
3. What are your beliefs about loyalty? Trust? Commitment? Respect?
    Responsibility? Intimacy?
4. How do your values/beliefs differ from those of your partner? How do
    you handle these differences?
5. What are your thoughts about other people? Do you share the same
    appreciation for others?
6. Describe those values/beliefs you share with your partner.
7. Describe how those values create meaning in your relationship.

The ability to find shared beliefs helps couples deal with everyday problems
and issues.

STRATEGIES FOR IDENTIFYING
SOURCES OF SUPPORT

1. *Ask the couple who they usually call on to help them resolve problems.* The fol-
    lowing questions are useful in assessing the couple's *existing network:*

    ▪ Who else is concerned about this problem?
    ▪ How do you know they are concerned?
    ▪ With whom do you discuss the problem?

- What kind of help do you want from her or her? Does that help? How so?
- What do they expect from you?
- Is this a person who could be helpful to you here?

2. *Brainstorm a list of persons from the community who are in regular contact with the couple.* The therapist might ask, "Are you involved with _____?" or "Who are you in contact with at this agency?" It is important to identify all professionals (social workers, ministers, therapists, and so on) who come in contact with the couple.

3. *Identify neighbors or friends who can meet needs that cannot be met by the couple.* The therapist might ask, "Is there someone else in your neighborhood who can help you with _____?" or "Is there anyone who could help you when your husband/wife is gone?"

4. *Ask the couple if there is anything that would stop them from asking a resource person for help.* A couple may be able to identify people who could help them but may be reluctant to ask for the support. Perhaps a partner does not want to be indebted or dependent on others. In other cases, the couple may desire to approach others but lack the prerequisite skills to do so. Identifying barriers to utilizing resources assists the therapist in dealing with these obstacles.

Consider the case of a newly married couple, Jake and Jackie:

Therapist: Who else is concerned about your relationship?

Jackie: No one. This is not a problem that we would feel like discussing with our friends.

Therapist: I think the kind of conflicts you are experiencing are pretty typical of newly married couples.

Jake: I guess . . . but I, for one, don't feel like talking to anyone else.

Therapist: Do you feel comfortable talking to me?

Jake: Yes, but you're older and you're trained to handle these kind of problems.

Therapist: Are there other people like myself with whom you share your concerns?

Jackie: They have a "marriage mentoring" program at our church. I hadn't thought of using it though.

Jake: What do they do?

Jackie: The mentors are older couples who have been married for some time . . . and they pair these couples up with younger couples like us.

Jake: So what do they do?

Therapist: Basically, from what I know, they listen to your issues and provide support. You might want to get some more information about the program.

Jackie: That's a possibility.

Jake: Yeah, I wouldn't mind trying it. It would be easier to talk to an older couple than to our friends.

Here the therapist was able to help the couple identify a potential source of support where none existed. Couples who are learning new behaviors need support to recognize that some of their concerns and conflicts are quite normal, and that they can be resolved.

It is usually advisable to draw on informal or natural supports before utilizing professional supports and resources. Natural supports are people who are resourceful and empathic to the couple. Professional support personnel (such as family life educators, and ministers) should not replace natural supports; rather, they should strengthen these relationships. Natural supports offer opportunities for reciprocal aid, a critical element in empowering couples. When one or both partners can repay the support person (someone who listens or offers encouragement), it strengths their sense that they have to give as well as take.

SPECIFYING OBSTACLES
TO GETTING SUPPORT

In spite of the benefits of informal supports, the therapist should also be aware that there are several legitimate obstacles to their use.

1. The couple may not have the skills to develop relationships with others.
2. The couple may be embarrassed to ask for help.
3. The couple may be unwilling to approach others whom they do not know.
4. The couple may prefer to rely on themselves and not depend on others.
5. The couple may be closed-off and reluctant to let others know their business.
6. The couple does not believe they can be helped.
7. The couple believes that talking to others will make things worse.
8. The couple believes that no one can understand their problems.

In such cases, the couple must use the therapist for support. The therapist should then help them acquire the competencies to obtain support from other sources. While the therapist can help couples learn new behaviors, there also must be ways to maintain that behavior; natural support in a couple's everyday environment is helpful in this regard. As the therapist works toward this end, collaboration with other professionals may also be helpful.

Case Study—Jeff and Wendy

Wendy and Jeff, a couple who have been married seven years, entered therapy because of increasingly frequent arguments. Jeff reported that Wendy appeared depressed and disinterested in being involved with him. He added that she was always trying to please her mother. Wendy indicated that she felt stuck between her husband and mother.

Wendy: I feel like I have to be perfect with everyone. I have been depressed before . . . and I feel it coming back.

Therapist: How so?

Wendy: I'm not dealing well with our son. I feel like a poor mother and Jeff says I'm unavailable for him.

Jeff: She's a good mother, but her own mother criticizes her a lot.

Therapist: So how do you deal with your mother, Wendy?

Wendy: I don't, I just listen. I know she's right sometimes, but at other times, she criticizes when she doesn't know the situation.

Therapist: Can you think of a time when you were able to explain the situation to your mother?

Wendy: Once . . . when Jeff helped me deal with her.

Jeff: Her mother just needs to back off.

Therapist: What did Jeff do that helped you deal with her?

Wendy: He listened and reminded me that I'm a good mother and that my mother wasn't there to know the whole situation.

Jeff: When her mother criticizes her, she gets "down" and that affects us.

Therapist: Who else can you talk with to get support?

Wendy: We really don't spend much time with others, and I don't like to discuss family problems.

Therapist: What keeps you from doing that?

Wendy: I feel like I'm inadequate if I can't even handle my own child.

Therapist: Do you know anyone you could open up to?

Wendy: I don't know. I have an aunt I really like, but her children are older.

Therapist: My guess is that she dealt with similar issues in her marriage when her children were young. It might be interesting to find out what she did.

Wendy: Yeah. I haven't spoken to her for a while, but I'd like to talk with her.

Therapist: There is also a "mother's group" at the community center. It meets weekly and mothers talk about concerns they have with their children and how they deal with those. There are no experts telling how it should be—just a group of mothers who talk about what works for them.

Wendy: That sounds interesting.

Wendy and Jeff's case is typical of couples who need support. Their problems with Wendy's mother and Wendy's feelings of inadequacy kept her from reaching out to others (such as her aunt) who could support them. In this case, the therapist listened and provided support for Wendy. He also helped Wendy to understand how her aunt could be supportive to her and suggested other supports as well (the mother's group). When the partners in a couple can get support from the therapist for their problems, it often opens the door for other kinds of support.

CONCLUSION

Couples who have satisfying marriages get support for their relationships. Friends, family, relatives, and coworkers can be crucial in supporting a relationship. Furthermore, spiritual and recreational activities, marriage enrichment groups, and professional people such as therapists can provide support as well. The therapist should help the couple identify sources of support, develop rituals, and develop a set of shared beliefs that can help strengthen the relationship. As a part of therapy, the therapist should assess the couple's support system and determine if there are any obstacles for their use. If so, he or she should provide support to the couple while helping them overcome some of the obstacles.

KEY POINTS

1. All couples need support. Meeting this need is critical to the well-being of the marriage.
2. It is usually advisable to draw on informal or natural supports (friends and family) before utilizing professional support and resources.
3. Newly married couples must create rituals as a way of completing developmental tasks.
4. Rituals can be developed through celebrations, traditions, and routines for handling holidays and meals.
5. Couples can build support for their marriage by developing a shared meaning in their relationship.
6. It is important for the therapist to help the couple identify sources of support.
7. There are a number of obstacles (lack of skills, reluctance) to "hooking up with" informal supports.

MARITAL SKILLS INVENTORY

Please check when you have completed the procedures below.

Identify sources of support, including:

_____ Church and religious groups.

_____ Marriage-enrichment groups.

_____ Recreational activities.

_____ Hobbies and individual interests.

Assess areas of interest by asking:

_____ Partners to generate areas of interest.

_____ Partners to prioritize their interests.

_____ Partners to exchange their lists and circle those interests they share with their partner.

_____ Partners to pick an activity to share during that time.

_____ Partners to plan an activity.

_____ Partners to decide how they will protect this time against outside interference.

_____ Partners how they support each other's individual interests.

_____ Each partner to respect the other's differences.

_____ Each partner to describe their hopes and dreams for their shared experiences.

Develop rituals by asking:

_____ Each partner the meaning of dinnertime.

_____ Each partner how they should part each day.

_____ Each partner about the meaning of weekends.

_____ Each partner about rituals about vacations.

_____ Each partner about the meaning of holidays.

_____ Each partner how he or she gets refreshed and renewed.

_____ Each partner about rituals around the illness of the other.

Develop shared beliefs by determining:

_____ Common values that are important to the couple.

_____ Ways the couple supports these values.

_____ Beliefs about loyalty and trust, commitment, respect, responsibility, and intimacy.

_____ Values/beliefs that are different for each partner, and ways they handle those differences.

_____ Values/beliefs partners share with each other.

Identify a support network by:

_____ Asking the couple what they have done to resolve their problems.

_____ Brainstorming a list of persons from the community who are in regular contact with the couple.

_____ Identifying neighbors or friends who can meet needs that cannot be met by the couple.

_____ Asking the couple if there is anything that would stop them from asking resource persons for help.

Check if the following are obstacles for getting support

_____ Couple does not have the skills to develop relationships with others.

_____ Couple is embarrassed to ask for help.

_____ Couple is unwilling to approach others whom they do not know.

_____ Couple prefers to rely on themselves and not on others.

_____ Couple is closed and reluctant to let others "inside."

_____ Couple does not believe there is help.

_____ Couple believes that talking to others will make things worse.

_____ Couple believes that no one can understand the problems faced.

REFERENCES

Antonucci, T. C. (1994). A life span view of women's social relationships. In B. F. Turner & L. E. Troll (Eds.), *Women growing older.* Thousand Oaks, CA: Sage.

Dunst, C., Trivette, C., & Deal, A. (1988). *Enabling and empowering families: Principles and guidelines for practice.* Cambridge, MA: Brookline Books.

Gottman, J. (1994). *Why marriages succeed or fail.* New York: Simon & Schuster.

Gottman, J. (1998). *Clinical manual for marital therapy: A scientifically-based mar-*

ital therapy. Seattle, WA: The Seattle Marital & Family Institute.

Hof, L., Epstein, N., & Miller, W. R. (1980). Integrating attitudinal and behavior change in marital enrichment. *Family Relations, 29,* 241–248.

Imber-Black, E. (1999). Creating meaningful rituals for new life cycle transitions. In B. Carter & M. McGoldrick (Eds.). *The expanded family life cycle: Individual, family and social perspectives* (3rd Ed.). Needham Heights, MA: Allyn & Bacon.

Markman, H., Stanley, S., & Blumberg, S. L. (1994). *Fighting for your marriage: Positive steps for preventing divorce and preserving a lasting love.* San Francisco: Jossey-Bass.

McGoldrick, M. (1999). Women through the family life cycle. Chapter 6 In B. Carter & M. McGoldrick (Eds.). *The expanded family life cycle: Individual, family and social perspectives* (3rd ed., pp. 106–123). Needham Heights, MA: Allyn & Bacon.

Schydlowsky, B. M. (1983). *Friendships among women in midlife.* Unpublished dissertation, University of Michigan, Ann Arbor.

Weiner-Davis, M. (1992). *Divorce-busting: A revolutionary and rapid program for staying together.* New York: Summit Books.

PART IV

＊

Evaluation of Treatment Outcome

11

✳

Evaluating
for Termination
and Follow-Up

CHAPTER OBJECTIVES

Upon completion of this chapter, the therapist will be able to help the couple:

1. Rate their relationship on a variety of dimensions.
2. Record their own behaviors on a graph.
3. Develop a plan for termination.
4. Develop a plan to transfer learning.
5. Develop a plan for relapse prevention.
6. Decide whether to continue therapy if goals have not been reached.
7. Decide whether individual or conjoint therapy is warranted.

INTRODUCTION

Termination of marital therapy should occur when the couple has reached their goals and do not wish to work on any related concerns. Any discussion to terminate should be made both by the therapist and the couple, and termination should occur when there is some way of evaluating the results of therapy. This chapter focuses on ways to evaluate the progress of therapy, guidelines for termination, and methods for preventing relapse.

EVALUATIVE DATA IN MARITAL THERAPY

Research on marital intervention has consistently provided positive results. In fact, Jacobson and Addis (1993) reported that all of the published studies of marital treatment showed more positive effects for couples in treatment than for couples in no-treatment control groups. However, they suggested that these differences might be related more to the deterioration of marriages in the no-treatment control groups than in improvement in the couples in treatment. They further suggest that most tested treatments report no better than 50 percent success, that all treatments help *some* couples, and all tested treatments appear to have about the same success rate. Furthermore, while about 50 to 75 percent of couples in therapy make initial gains, a large number of these couples relapse within two years.

Before Gottman's published research work in 1998, much of the research suggested that there was not a single factor or set of factors that accounted for success; that is, interventions did not appear to be differentially effective. Gottman's research (1998), however, was designed specifically to determine dysfunctional patterns in "bad" marriages, positive behaviors in satisfying marriages, and the cause of dysfunctional patterns. He discovered that to have any lasting effect in behavioral marital therapy, the intervention must have two prongs: to increase everyday levels of positive affect, and to reduce negative affect during conflict resolution.

EVALUATING PROGRESS IN THERAPY

Evaluating the progress of couples in therapy can be difficult because of the ambiguity regarding success and failure; in fact, researchers have had difficulty defining treatment success. For many researchers, the measure of success is lowered divorce rates. For others, success may be defined as increased marital satisfaction (by self-report), more harmonious communication (by self-report or therapist observation), or decrease in conflict. Continuation of a marriage is generally viewed as a successful outcome of therapy; however, in some cases, divorce may be the most positive outcome. Perhaps the most effective way to assess success is by setting goals with the couple and determining the extent to which the goals were met.

Gottman (1999) has also provided some process tools that are useful in evaluating the progress of therapy. His research for the past several years has focused on predictions of couples who will divorce, and he has discovered that the two major points when couples divorce are in the first seven years of marriage and around 16–20 years into the marriage. His research indicates that the best predictor of divorce in the early stages is the pattern of negative interaction he refers to as "Four Horsemen of the Apocalypse"—criticism, defensiveness, contempt, and stonewalling—and the best predictor for the later stage is the absence of positive affect. He has been able to make such predictions with over 90 percent accuracy (Gottman & Levenson, 1992; Buehlman, Gottman & Katz, 1992) and has replicated these findings in two additional longitudinal studies (Gottman, 1994).

Gottman (1999) has developed a marriage contract that contains seventeen areas of a marital relationship. These include:

- Staying emotionally connected
- Handling job and other stress effectively
- Handling issues or disagreements well
- Having a romantic, passionate relationship
- Sex life
- Dealing with important events
- Child issues
- Major issues re in-laws, relatives
- Jealousy
- Resolving differences
- Similar values/goals
- Handling very hard events (violence, drugs, affair)
- Working as a team
- Power and influence
- Handling finances
- Having fun together
- Similarities in spirituality (pp. 363–369)

Such a contract can serve as a pre-post test of marital change. At the beginning of treatment, the couple completes a checklist of the seventeen items. They read the item, discuss how they are doing, and determine if changes are desired. If so, they discuss how they want things to be and write the agreement in the space provided. Upon completion of the checklist, the couple has determined various areas in their relationship that they think need to be changed. This, then, becomes the therapist-couple contract, and completion of the goals would suggest success.

Self-Evaluation

Self-evaluations reflect the couple's perception of change in therapy. The assumption here is that if the couple is making progress or has reached the stated goals, they will report it to the therapist ("We both seem to be making time for each other. We're getting along well now"). Likewise, if a couple perceives that there has been no change or that the relationship is even worse, they might say, "Things are no different," or "We don't seem to be able to work things out." One way to help couples assess progress is through a questionnaire administered prior to, during, and following treatment. This can be done with a Likert rating scale, having couples rate their relationship on a variety of dimensions from 1–5, with 1 being "poor," 3 being "fair" and 5 being "excellent." A sample questionnaire is given in Figure 11.1.

Rate your current relationship on the following dimensions.	Poor		Fair	Excellent	
	1	2	3	4	5
1. Quality time spent together. Comments:	1	2	3	4	5
2. Feeling close to each other Comments:	1	2	3	4	5
3. Handling conflict successfully Comments:	1	2	3	4	5
4. Trusting one another Comments:	1	2	3	4	5
5. Sexual Relationship Comments:	1	2	3	4	5
6. Feeling respected Comments:	1	2	3	4	5
7. Handling stress in the relationship Comments:	1	2	3	4	5
8. Feeling important in the relationship Comments:	1	2	3	4	5
9. Getting support for our marriage Comments:	1	2	3	4	5
10. Sharing core beliefs and values Comments:	1	2	3	4	5
11. Tolerating unsolvable problems Comments:	1	2	3	4	5
12. Talking openly about problems Comments:	1	2	3	4	5
13. Feeling heard by partner Comments:	1	2	3	4	5
14. Working together as a team Comments:	1	2	3	4	5
15. Having fun together Comments:	1	2	3	4	5

FIGURE 11.1 Sample Marital Self-Report Questionnaire.

While rating scales are a cost-effective method for evaluating the effectiveness of therapy, they have several limitations. First, self-evaluation is open to bias because couples will often report what they think is pleasing to the therapist. Furthermore, self-evaluation is subjective and may not accurately reflect the couple's progress in treatment. Secondly, self-evaluation is often an unreliable measure of progress because couples rate themselves differently from day to day, depending on the circumstances (stress at a given time). Finally, self-evaluation is nonstandardized, has no norms, and includes language that may have different meanings in different cultures. Therefore, the therapist must consider multiple measures and view self-report as only one of these.

In some cases, the couple might not agree on specific items in the rating scale. In such cases, the therapist might respond as follows:

Therapist: We've been meeting for eight weeks now, and each of you indicates that your relationship is better. So . . . I would like you to take fifteen or twenty minutes together and rate yourself on each of these items. You may not agree on how to rate some of the items. If so, rate each separately and put your name next to the rating. Also, if you have anything to add or are having difficulty rating the item, indicate so in the "comments" section.

The self-evaluation thus provides a general measure of the couple's progress in treatment. It also helps the therapist and couple to determine whether treatment should be terminated or continued.

Observation

In addition to rating scales, the therapist may ask the couple to observe their behavior. In such cases, the therapist may ask the couple to record a baseline rate of the behavior (quality time spent together, number and length of positive interactions, and so on). The therapist might practice with the couple by asking them to record behavior during the session or observe videotape of a marital interaction. The couple should be asked to record their observations on a prepared form. The form should include the date, spouse's name, and target behavior for observation. The couple should be asked to observe their behavior over the course of a week, or at least with enough time to obtain an accurate level of the behavior. Once the baseline is completed, the therapist and couple can set a realistic objective. For example, if the couple is averaging two minutes of positive interactions a day for one week, the therapist might ask the couple if they could increase their average level to ten minutes of positive interactions per day.

In some cases, the therapist may ask the couple to plot the time on a graph. The therapist should record the time (minutes, hours, days) on the horizontal axis and the target behavior on the vertical axis (See Figure 11.2).

If the baseline shows sharp fluctuations, behavior should be recorded until there is some degree of stability (in some cases, an event such as being out of town or attending a celebration may greatly influence the rate of behavior). In

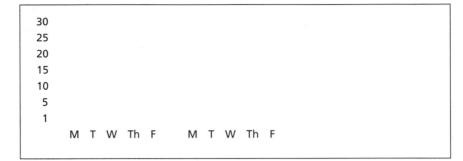

FIGURE 11.2 Illustration of Observation Graph

such cases, the therapist should ask the couple to continue recording their behaviors.

Self–observation has several limitations. First, the observation may serve to raise the couple's level of awareness and thus serve as an intervention. Secondly, one or both partners may fail to follow through with the recording because it is too much trouble. This often occurs when the therapist has not discussed the purpose and procedures for recording. Finally, as in the case of self-evaluation, the couple may provide more favorable data to please the therapist.

Termination of Therapy

As stated above, any discussion to terminate should be made both by the therapist and the couple. However, this does not always occur, for several reasons. The couple may feel that therapy is not helping or they may become angry with the therapist. Occasionally, the couple may be unwilling to change some of their behavior. Unless the therapist works through these concerns early in therapy, termination may be premature. In order to ensure that termination occurs as goals are achieved, the therapist should be aware of and follow the guidelines suggested by Hanna and Brown (1999, pp. 278–279). They are as follows:

Plan for Termination in Advance The therapist should be careful not to withdraw therapy abruptly because in such cases the problem behavior generally returns to the pretreatment level. Couples should be given an estimate for the length of therapy. The use of a contract specifying a fixed number of sessions ensures a periodic review of therapy (Barker, 1981). Setting a specific time for termination helps the couple and therapist plan for change. The therapist should be flexible about the frequency of sessions, depending on the nature of the problem. The frequency of sessions should decrease when initial goals have been met (Wright & Leahey, 1984).

Plan to Gradually Withdraw Therapy If couples have been heavily dependent on therapy (as sometimes happens in cases of severe crisis), they are less likely to resist termination if therapy is withdrawn gradually. One method of gradual withdrawal is to increase the amount of time between sessions (perhaps to between three and five weeks). This step should be taken if couples are unsure they can maintain the desired changes. Todd (1986) discusses this withdrawal process as follows:

> As therapy begins to be successful in achieving the agreed upon goals, the sessions are usually spaced at wider time intervals, such as moving to alternate weeks and progressing to once a month. This allows the spouses to do more of the work themselves and helps ensure that they can maintain the changes without the therapist. (p. 81)

Wright and Leahey (1984) suggest that couples are more likely to believe they have the resources to deal with their problems when the therapist gives them credit for change. If couples believe they are responsible for alleviating the presenting problem, they are likely to be more confident that they can handle future problems. Statements such as, "You handled this well. You'll be able to handle a similar problem if it comes up," help the couple believe in their abilities outside of therapy.

Summarize the Major Themes In terminating, the therapist should summarize the major themes of therapy and observe closely to see whether the couple agrees or disagrees with the summary statement. If the couple disagrees, the therapist should note this and give them the opportunity to discuss their views. On some occasions, the therapist may ask the couple to summarize the therapy.

Ask the Couple to Decide What Needs to Happen for Them to Return to Therapy It is important for the therapist to help the couple decide when they can no longer manage the problem and need to return to therapy. The therapist might say, "What would be the first sign that you can no longer handle this problem?" Tomm and Wright (1979) suggest that the therapist ask, "What would each of you need to do to bring this problem back?" Such questions should help family members understand the specific changes they have made in therapy. The therapist should help the couple understand that returning to therapy does not mean the couple has failed. Instead, a follow-up session can be framed as a booster shot to help the couple maintain desire changes. Then, if further services are sought, the therapist can reiterate that this is not an indicator of failure; instead, additional therapy sessions are likely to be brief because the couple has demonstrated an ability to solve their problems (Todd, 1986).

Reassure the Couple That They Have the Strengths and Resources to Deal with Future Problems In some cases, a couple presents a new problem at the time of termination. If the problem is not serious, the therapist must reassure the couple that they have the skills to deal with this situation on their own. Sometimes, the therapist might have difficulty letting go of the couple (the therapist may get special nurturance and support from the couple or may need the couple to work out some unresolved issue). In this case, he/she should discuss such matters in supervision to minimize the couple's dependence on him/her as well as his/her dependence on the client.

Plan Transfer of Learning

Before termination, it is important for the therapist not to assume that the couple's newly acquired behaviors will generalize to new situations. Treatment effects may be situational. For example, a couple may be taught how to interact positively with each other in therapy, but once they leave, they are unable to interact positively at home and in social situations. Thus the therapist and couple should discuss specific steps for trying out new behaviors in extra-therapy situations. Communication/problem solving skills learned in therapy could be tried out with specific people each partner sees daily.

There are several things the therapist can do to facilitate generalization of learning.

Approximate the Conditions the Couple Will Encounter in Real Life
For example, a couple may learn new rules for negotiating conflict. Unless the couple tries out the new behavior outside the therapy session, however, the therapist will not be able to incorporate extra-therapy factors (e.g., interference, limited time, etc.) into treatment. Homework assignments help the therapist to modify treatment accordingly so that changes will transfer outside of therapy.

Plan Treatment With More Than One Treatment Agent Practicing new behaviors (e.g., listening, problem solving, etc.) with friends, co-workers, family and others increases the probability that changes will generalize.

Transfer Control of New Behaviors to Others Who Can Support the Couple It is critical that the couple is able to identify others (friends, family, mentoring couples) who can support the couple's new behavior and recognize their progress. Marital satisfaction is likely to be greater when each partner has the support of others for the relationship.

Teach the Couple to Monitor and Control Their Own Behavior Several studies have indicated that couples can monitor and control their own performance, and in turn decrease problem behaviors (Bray & Jouriles, 1995). On the other hand, a couple who cannot monitor and record their own behavior probably cannot control it. Thus, self-monitoring is a prerequisite condition for successfully transferring the control of the treatment program to the couple.

Case Study: Jim and Sandy

Therapist: You seem to be able to negotiate conflict in the session. How are you doing at home?

Sandy: Every time we sit down to talk about something, we get a phone call or the kids want something.

Therapist: So how do you handle this?

Jim: We just never seem to get around to talking about things.

Sandy: We want to . . . you would just need to be at our house to understand.

Therapist: Help me to understand.

Sandy: Everyone seems to be on different schedules so it's hard to plan a time to sit down together.

Therapist: When do the two of you have time alone?

Jim: When the kids go to bed.

Therapist: When is that?

Sandy: We try to get them to bed by 10:00 p.m.

Jim: It's hard to do that sometimes.

Therapist: Are you pretty exhausted?

Jim: Yeah, we both work so we're ready for bed at that time too.

Therapist: That isn't the best time to talk about an issue.

Sandy: No, I just like to take a bath and wind down then.

Therapist: Do you have any time after dinner? Can you tell the kids that you need some time for yourself?

Jim: I guess we could . . . they have homework. Maybe that would be the best time.

Therapist: Why don't you start with a half-hour. When do you finish dinner?

Sandy: We normally put the dishes away by 7:00 p.m. We could start then.

Therapist: Great! Let's start with an issue you can handle.

Sandy: Okay. The decision about whether to have another child wouldn't work.

Therapist: What about the issue of how you spend time together?

Jim: That's something we can talk about.

Sandy: Sure. I think we need to talk about the other things with you.

The therapist needs to ensure that the issues Jim and Sandy start with are issues they can successfully resolve. Whether or not to have a baby (especially when one partner is opposed) would be so emotionally laden that successful resolution would be too difficult to start with.

Relapse Prevention

Termination raises the issue of relapse. While marital therapy may be effective in the short-term, maladaptive behaviors are likely to reoccur unless relapse prevention is incorporated into the treatment plan. Bray and Jouriles (1995) state the following:

Prominent marital therapy researchers suggest that booster sessions may be necessary to maintain the gains established during initial treatments (Jacobson & Addis, 1993). A reasonable question is whether it is realistic to expect that one round of therapy is enough to last a lifetime, particularly for some individuals who may bring significant and unresolved psychological and family of origin issues into their marriages. It is clear from longitudinal studies of other mental disorders, for example, depression and physical disorders, for example, hypertension, that there are repeated relapses and that monitoring and ongoing treatment may be necessary through the life cycle. A family life cycle approach may be a useful framework within which to conceptualize the long-term process of marital relations. (pp. 461–473)

Christensen (1998) lists four steps for relapse prevention. A brief description of each step follows:

Step 1. Help Couples Recognize Their Patterns Couples need to understand their maladaptive patterns. They need to understand what triggers problem behavior and what maintains it. For example, a husband needs to know when his tone of voice triggers an angry response from his wife and when this withdrawal maintains the conflictual interaction. Awareness of these patterns will help the couple to identify conditions (such as the time of day) when these patterns are most likely to occur. Recognizing conditions that lead to problematic patterns helps the couple to exercise control over their interactions.

Step 2. Help Couples Learn the Details of Their Pattern One of the ways to get couples to prevent relapse is to get them to pay attention to the details of daily life events and their relationship to problematic interactional patterns. Problematic patterns occur in four phases:

1. In the early build up phase, triggering events occur such as negative thoughts ("He doesn't care about me," or "We'll never make it.") and blaming statements begin to escalate and lead to tension.

2. In the late build up, tension builds and is often manifested in physical signs (such as muscle tension and rapid heart rate).

3. The third phase is often characterized by a harmful incident (such as a personal attack, alcohol abuse, withdrawal, or infidelity).

4. The justification phase includes denial, excuses, or guilt for what was done or said.

The use of assessment questions can help couples recognize their problematic patterns. The two most common types include questions that help the couple to scale small increments of change and time-oriented questions that offer a comparison between one time and another.

Step 3. Help Couples Practice Small Steps Toward Change In step three, the couple learns to practice alternative behaviors to the old pattern.

This first requires each spouse to recognize how he or she contributes to the problem and what specifically he or she can do to prevent it. For example, a husband who yells at his wife needs to be aware of alternative behaviors he can substitute for the yelling. Likewise, the wife, although not responsible for her husband's yelling, needs to recognize how her behavior (silence and withdrawal, or screaming) is not useful. To learn alternative behaviors, the therapist must help the couple to learn three basic skills: (a) to avoid high risk situations (discussing problems late at night when both partners are tired), (b) to intervene in high risk situations (calling time out when either partner loses control of their behavior), and (c) to escape high risk situations (going for a walk) to reduce the level of stress.

Step 4. Help Couples Create a Plan to Prevent Relapse The therapist should help the couple develop a plan for relapse. First, the therapist should remind the couple that relapse is normal and does not represent failure. Rather, the goal is to accept the likelihood of relapse and to develop a plan to reduce its frequency, intensity, and duration. Successful plans identify: (a) early warning signs of a problem, (b) problem behaviors, maladaptive or inappropriate ways of coping with the problem, and (c) warning signs that the problematic pattern is likely to reoccur. The therapist should help the couple practice each of these steps so that each partner will understand what they must do when relapse occurs. Finally, the therapist should help the couple celebrate success when they have been able to prevent relapse.

> *Case Study: Ron and Candy*
>
> **Therapist:** Let's talk a little bit about what would happen to make this problem reoccur and how you might handle it.
>
> **Candy:** What do you mean?
>
> **Therapist:** Well, things have been going pretty well the last two weeks, but let's say that you begin to experience this problem again. What would be the first sign that a "war," using your words, was about to begin?
>
> **Ron:** When Candy gets real quiet.
>
> **Therapist:** What do you mean "real quiet"? When she doesn't talk to you?
>
> **Ron:** It's more than that. She doesn't want to be in the same room with me.
>
> **Therapist:** You mean when you walk in a room, she walks out.
>
> **Ron:** Sometimes.
>
> **Therapist:** When is that most likely to occur?
>
> **Candy:** When he has been out and he doesn't tell me where he is . . . doesn't let me know when he is coming home.
>
> **Therapist:** Anything else that makes you leave the room?

Candy: Sometimes I'm tired from work and don't want to deal with him.

Therapist: What do you mean you don't want to deal with him?

Candy: He wants to know what's wrong.

Ron: I bug her. She won't respond and I keep asking because she won't talk and then she blows up and we're into it.

Therapist: How do you bug her?

Candy: He just keeps saying, "What's wrong? What's wrong?"

Therapist: And then you blow up . . . How do you do that?

Candy: I start yelling for him to get out.

Therapist: And what do you do, Ron?

Ron: I generally start yelling back at her.

Therapist: What do you say?

Ron: I ask her to tell me what's wrong.

Therapist: Does she tell you?

Ron: No . . . so I just keep asking and she gets angry.

Therapist: Then what?

Ron: I generally tell her to "go to hell" and leave.

Therapist: So what could you do to avoid these situations?

Ron: I don't know.

Candy: I agree we should talk things over but I don't feel like doing it early in the morning when I'm getting ready for work . . . and besides, just because I'm silent doesn't mean that I'm angry with him.

Therapist: How would Ron know that you are not angry with him?

Candy: I'll just tell him that I'm not mad at him.

Therapist: What if you are mad at him?

Candy: Then we can talk about it when I get home.

Therapist: When?

Candy: After dinner.

Therapist: How does that work for you, Ron?

Ron: Fine, but how do I know you will?

Candy: I'll write it down on the planner on the refrigerator.

Therapist: Will that work?

Ron: I don't know, but I'm willing to try it.

Therapist: What happens if things get out of control?

Candy: We call time-out, like we discussed earlier.

Therapist: What will you do then?

Candy: I'll read or go for a walk.

Ron: It helps me to go out and work in the shop.

Therapist: When will you get back together?

Candy: We'll either talk about it later if we are ready or we'll reschedule the next night at the same time.

Ron: Sometimes it's hard for me to cool off. So—the next night works best for me.

Therapist: I've written your plan down. Can you put it somewhere where you can refer to it?

The case above gives a good example of a couple who has made progress but who are likely to experience difficulties when they try to communicate at home. By expecting that there may be times of conflict and planning ways to deal with this, the couple is establishing techniques that will help them to resolve problems as they arise. When they see the therapist next, they will have a chance to discuss how these plans worked. If they worked well, the therapist will compliment them. If they did not, they will make additional plans for how to handle conflictual situations.

DECIDING WHEN TO TERMINATE THERAPY
IF GOALS HAVE NOT BEEN ACHIEVED

There are times when a couple has clearly not reached their goals; yet the therapy seems to "be stuck" and quite unproductive. In fact, there are times when therapy is clearly not working, and the ethical approach is to consider termination. Sometimes the obstacles rest in the couple and cannot be overcome. Other times, the problem may be a personality conflict between the therapist and one or both partners. In either case, before termination is effected, there are several situations that should be considered and evaluated. These are situations that are likely to preclude success in therapy and may warrant termination.

One or Both Partners Are Not Committed to The Relationship When one or both partners are unable to commit to marital therapy, the therapist should let the couple know that marital therapy would not be productive and that they need to make a decision about their relationship.

Long-Term History of Conflict That Cannot be Resolved It has been the authors' experience that couples who have a long-term history where positions are polarized do not benefit from marital therapy unless each is able to see some merit in the other's position.

Lack of Fondness and Admiration for Each Other When couples lose a sense of fondness and admiration for the other, marital therapy will not be beneficial (Gottman, 1998) unless each can engender more positive thoughts about the other.

High Degree of Mistrust Between Partners In some cases, mistrust is so great one or both partners are unable to overcome it. Previous separations, infidelity, and secrets often contribute to deep feelings of mistrust. Without trust there can be no intimacy in the relationship.

Lack of Connection Between the Therapist and One or Both Partners
When the therapist has not developed an alliance with one or both partners, it will be difficult to establish a therapeutic relationship. Unless the therapist can connect with both partners, it is unlikely that they will be engaged in the treatment process.

In general, it is unwise to terminate marital therapy if the therapist believes that there is potential for violence. In fact, it is unwise to terminate prematurely without assessing for potential violence or possible self-injury. In cases where one partner is seriously depressed and reports that he or she "cannot live without him or her," the therapist should consider individual treatment until such time the partner is stabilized. Assessing for potential danger is critical before recommending termination.

DECIDING WHETHER TO SEE
PARTNERS INDIVIDUALLY

In some cases it may be advisable to see partners individually. This could be done while seeing the couple, or it could be that the couple has reached their goals and one partner needs individual treatment before termination. If the following conditions exist for one partner, he or she may require individual therapy:

- A chronic mental health problem (for example, depression, anxiety, or a phobia, which may also require medical attention);
- Substance abuse or alcohol problems which may require referral to outside services;
- Ambivalence about the marriage and issues around whether to separate or divorce;
- Other individual problems (e.g., affective disorders, sexual dysfunction, personality disorders) that may affect the relationship.

Once a decision has been made to see a partner individually, the therapist must determine whether to see the couple concurrently. Karpel (1994) lists several factors to consider when making this decision (adapted from pp. 113–136):

1. The needs and desires of the partner that is being seen individually—is the partner so overwhelmed with his or her own problems that he or she is unable to focus on the other partner?

2. The needs and desires of the other partner—does he or she worry that the problems of the partner in individual therapy will have a long term effect on the relationship?

3. The lasting effects of the individual's problem on the marital relationship—is it possible to make progress with the couple while still seeing an individual partner?

4. The resources required for therapy—does the couple have sufficient time, money, and energy for both individual and marital therapy?

If in doubt, the therapist may want to avoid termination and continue to see the couple, in order to monitor the effects of individual treatment on the couple's relationship.

Plan and Execute Follow Up

Once termination has been discussed, a follow-up date should be set. Follow-up allows the therapist to find out how the couple is progressing and provides a time to discuss new problems if some have developed. In addition, it often helps facilitate the couple's implementation of skills. Short-term follow-up should occur two to four weeks after therapy, and long-term follow-up should occur three to six months after treatment to evaluate the effects of therapy.

Follow-up interviews or phone calls provide an opportunity for the couple to discuss what is working and what still needs to change. Interviews are helpful for reinforcing new behaviors and problem solving when necessary. In some cases, a phone call from the therapist may help to determine the effectiveness of therapy and/or whether a follow-up interview is necessary.

CONCLUSION

Evaluation is critical to the treatment of couples. Developing a method for evaluating marital therapy helps the therapist to gather information to meet the needs of the couple better. Evaluation also allows the therapist to assess the therapy's effectiveness. Funding sources and HMOs are increasingly requiring therapists to demonstrate their effectiveness through various positive behaviors that do, in fact, take place as a result of marital therapy.

KEY POINTS

- Termination of marital therapy should occur when the couple has reached the established goals and do not wish to work on any related concern.

- Research on marital interventions has consistently provided positive results.
- A marriage contract (in the manner of Gottman's model) can serve as a pre-post test of marital change.
- Self-evaluations reflect the couple's perception of change in therapy.
- Termination should be a planned withdrawal and agreed upon by both the therapist and couple at the point when there are resources to deal with future problems.
- Before termination, it is important for the therapist not to assume that the couple's newly acquired behaviors will generalize to new situations.
- The therapist can facilitate generalization of learning by approximating the conditions the couple will encounter in real life.
- While marital therapy may be effective in the short term, maladaptive behaviors are likely to reoccur unless relapse prevention is incorporated into the treatment plan.
- Even if positive changes have not occurred, termination is warranted when there is a lack of commitment to the relationship and a long-term history of conflict.

MARITAL SKILLS INVENTORY

Please check when you have completed the procedures below.

Evaluate Therapy

_____   Rating scales

_____   Self-observation

Plan Termination

_____   Plan for termination in advance.

_____   Plan to gradually withdraw therapy.

_____   Summarize the major themes.

_____   Ask the couple to decide what needs to happen for them to return to therapy.

_____   Reassure the couple that they have the strengths and resources to deal with future problems.

Plan Transfer of Learning

_____   Approximate the conditions the couple will encounter in real life.

_____   Plan treatment with more than one treatment agent.

_____ Transfer control of new behaviors to others who can support the couple.
_____ Teach the couple to monitor and control their own behavior.

Plan for Relapse Prevention

_____ Help couple recognize their patterns.

_____ Help couple learn the details of their patterns.

_____ Help couple practice small steps toward change.

_____ Help couple create a plan to prevent relapse.

Decide When to Terminate Therapy

Yes   No

_____ _____ Partners are committed to the relationship.

_____ _____ Long term history of conflict that cannot be resolved.

_____ _____ Lack of fondness and admiration for each other.

_____ _____ High degree of mistrust between partners.

_____ _____ Lack of connection between the therapist and one or both partners.

Decide Whether to See Partners Individually

Yes   No

_____ _____ Chronic mental health problems.

_____ _____ Substance abuse or alcohol problems.

_____ _____ Ambivalence about the marriage.

_____ _____ Other individual problems.

Plan and Execute Follow-Up

Yes   No

_____ _____

REFERENCES

Barker, P. (1981). *Basic family therapy.* Baltimore: University Park Press.

Bray, J. H., & Jouriles, E. N. (1995). Treatment of marital conflict and prevention of divorce. *Journal of Marital and Family Therapy, 21,* 451–473.

Buehlman, K., Gottman, J. M., & Katy, L. (1992). How a couple views their past predicts their future: Predicting divorce from an oral history interview. *Journal of Family Psychology, 5,* 295–318.

Christensen, D. N. (1998). *Solution focused based casework.* Class handout, University of Louisville, Louisville, KY.

Gottman, J. M. (1994). *Why marriages succeed or fail*. New York: Simon & Schuster.

Gottman, J. M. (1998). *Clinical manual for marital therapy: A scientifically-based marital therapy.* Seattle Marital and Family Institute. Seattle, WA.

Gottman, J. M. (1999). The marriage clinic: A scientifically-based marital therapy. New York: Norton.

Gottman, J. M., & Levinson, R. W. (1992). Marital processes predictive of later dissolution: Behavior, physiology, and health. *Journal of Personality and Social Psychology, 63,* 221–233.

Hanna, S. M., & Brown, J. H. (1999). *The practice of family therapy. Key elements across models.* Belmont, CA: Wadsworth.

Jacobson, N. S., & Addis, M. E. (1993). Research on couple therapy: What do we know? Where are we going? *Journal of Consulting and Clinical Psychology, 61*(1), 85–93.

Karpel, M. A. (1994). Evaluating couples: A handbook for practitioners. New York: Norton.

Todd, T. C. (1986). Structural-strategic marital therapy. In N. S. Jacobson & A. S. Gurman (Eds.). *Clinical handbook of marital therapy* (pp. 71–106). New York: Guilford.

Tomm, K. M., & Wright, C. M. (1979). Training in family therapy: Perceptual, conceptual and executive skills. *Family Process,* 18, 227–250.

Wright, L., & Leahey, M. (1984). *Nurses and families: A guide to family assessment and intervention.* Philadelphia: Davis.

PART V

Techniques in Practice

12

✳

Case Studies
of Special Populations

CHAPTER OBJECTIVES

Upon completion of this chapter, the reader will be able to:

1. Tell how marital-therapy concepts and techniques can be applied to these populations:

   - Unfaithful partners
   - Divorcing partners
   - Remarried partners
   - Gay and lesbian partners
   - Couple in which one partner is addicted
   - Couple in which one person is chronically ill
   - Dual-career couples

2. Discuss specific marital issues peculiar to the special populations listed above.

INTRODUCTION

In this chapter, we will provide case studies of special marital problems: infidelity, divorce, remarriage, gay and lesbian couples, addiction, and chronic illness. Problems related to dual-career couples will also be addressed. The case studies will enable the reader to see how the therapist integrates concepts and skills, and applies them to specific problems. The cases reflect typical problems that are frequently noted in clinical practice. Each case contains a dialogue between the therapist and clients in the left column and a description of therapeutic skills and methods in the right column. The first case—Al and Wanda—focuses on marital infidelity.

MARITAL INFIDELITY—
THE CASE OF AL AND WANDA

Therapist: I'm glad we could get together.

Wanda: Yes. I'm sorry that I canceled our last appointment, but I had to pick my child up from school.

Therapist: Okay . . . and I asked that both you and Al attend the session.

Wanda: Yes . . . I know. When I called, you wanted to see both of us . . . but I just wanted to see you by myself during the first session.

Therapist: So, Al doesn't know you are here?

Wanda: That's right.

The client, Wanda, has called to schedule the appointment and has given marital difficulties as the presenting problem. The therapist has requested that she bring her husband, but she has decided not to— because she has a "secret" to discuss.

Therapist: Well, tell me what's going on—why you decided to come.

Wanda: (Sighs) Well, this is hard for me to do.

Therapist: Yes.

Wanda: Al and I have drifted apart and just don't have anything in common anymore.

Therapist: Has this been gradual or can you think of when the change occurred?

Wanda: Oh . . . maybe two years or so . . . I'm not sure.

Therapist: Maybe longer?

Wanda: Um . . . I think two years.

Therapist: That's when you first recognized that you were drifting apart?

Wanda: Yes.

Therapist: What seemed different?

The therapist determines that Wanda's husband is unaware that she is coming to therapy and questions her about her reasons. He asks various questions to assess exactly what the problem area is, how long the problem has been going on, and what specifically is different now, both in their everyday lives and their relationship.

Wanda: I'm not sure. It seemed different when Charles—our youngest son—left for college.

Therapist: Then it was just the two of you.

Wanda: Yes. The one thing we always had in common was our children, particularly Charles.

The therapist noted that some changes occurred at a particular developmental stage when the last child left home.

Therapist: Why Charles?

Wanda: He was into sports . . . so we were together a lot to go to his games.

Therapist: Were those the only times you went out together?

Wanda: Pretty much. Occasionally, we go to a movie, but that's about it.

Therapist: So now you don't do much together.

Wanda: Right.

Therapist: How has this affected your relationship?

Wanda: Well, as I said, we have just drifted apart. I think the kids were about all we had in common.

Therapist: Is that why you're here—you want to reconnect with Al?

Wanda: I guess.

The therapist begins to assess the client's motivation for therapy.

Therapist: If that's the case, I'm not sure why you wanted to see me alone.

Wanda: I'm just not sure where I am with the marriage and . . . (sighs) I've been seeing someone else.

The client begins relating the real reason she didn't bring her husband.

Therapist: How long have you been seeing this person?

Wanda: Oh, about three months. I didn't intend for this to happen, but . . . I met him at work and one day he asked me if I wanted to go to lunch. We then started going to lunch together several times a week. Then . . . I started seeing him after work. I don't know. I wish it never happened, but it did. I'm sure you've seen situations like this before.

Therapist: Yes. Each one is different, however.

Wanda: I guess.

Therapist: So what are you wanting to do about this?

Wanda: I don't know.

Therapist: I assume Al doesn't know.

Wanda: That's right.

The therapist asks questions to see what the real purpose of therapy is— working on the marriage or ending it.

Successful marital therapy cannot occur when the therapist keeps important information about one partner (such as an affair) secret from the other. When one partner discloses information about the other partner, he or she is entering into a covert coalition with the therapist. Since we are discussing the initial interview, the therapist should take into account whether a client's spouse will eventually be engaged, and how the therapist will delay the potential alignment with the client until both partners are present. When an individual comes in without the other spouse, the strategy presented here is designed to help the therapist stay away from intimate content until the nature of the individual's significant relationship can be identified. Regardless, the therapist must be clear that he or she will not keep information about one partner secret from the other.

Therapist: I guess the real issue here is whether or not you want to work on the marriage.

Wanda: Yes . . . I wish it could work out . . . but I have my doubts.

Therapist: Why is that?

Wanda: I don't know. I'm not sure he would want to do anything about it.

Therapist: What makes you so sure?

Wanda: Well . . . maybe he would . . . but he just doesn't seem interested in anything anymore.

Therapist: Does that include you?

Wanda: Yeah.

The therapist begins to discover the client's goals. The client is not saying that she definitely wants to end her relationship; rather, she seems to think there's nothing she can do to get attention from her husband.

Therapist: What have you done to try to get him interested?

Wanda: Nothing recently.

Therapist: Is that because of your interest in the person at work?

Wanda: Probably . . . I mean he listens to me and acts interested in what I have to say.

Therapist: Is that all?

Wanda: Well, the relationship has gotten more serious and has become sexual as well as a friendship relationship. The whole thing just sort of happened gradually and I'm not sure how. I'm having a lot of doubts—about myself—about marriage and everything else.

The therapist discusses what Wanda has tried with her husband to get him more involved.

The therapist determines that Wanda's emotional needs are better met by the friend at work than by her husband. This gives a starting point for what needs to be changed in the relationship.

The therapist must make a decision here about whether he is working with an individual spouse about the affair, or whether the goal is to work on the marriage. The therapist must be clear that he or she cannot work on the marriage while he or she is colluding to keep a secret from a partner.

Therapist: Are you saying it was an accident?

Wanda: I don't know that it was an accident, but . . . uh, I don't think this would have happened several years ago.

Therapist: What are you saying—that things were better then and this could not have happened?

Wanda: Yes . . . I felt closer to Al then. I mean, it wasn't great but it was okay.

Therapist: If you could go back to the way things were, would you give up this new relationship?

Wanda: Yes.

Therapist: Then what keeps you from wanting to work on it?

Wanda: Well, I'm not sure what he would do if he found out.

Therapist: So if you had a way to tell him, what do you think he would do?

> The therapist wants to assess the reason for the affair—whether it was related to changes in the marriage or if the marriage has always been unsatisfying.

> The therapist explores with Wanda the value of the affair and her desire to keep the marriage together.

It is important here to assess the marriage for physical violence. Pittman and Wagers (1995) suggest that if the partner is potentially violent or unstable, the affair should not be revealed.

Wanda: I don't know . . . I know he would be angry.

Therapist: Do you think he could become violent or do anything to hurt you?

Wanda: No. Actually, I don't think he would say much. He would probably go off by himself. But why do I have to tell him?

Therapist: I can't work on a marriage with you because you and I have this secret that we share. It would get in the way of working with both of you.

Wanda: (Silence)

Therapist: I can't work with you, either, if you do not break off the affair.

> The therapist checked for the possibility of violence in the event Wanda told her husband about the affair.

> The therapist let Wanda know that he would not "keep her secret," nor would he work with her while an affair was in progress.

If marital therapy is to occur, the therapist must work with the individual to help her find a way to reveal the affair to her partner and end her relationship with the other party.

Therapist: What are you thinking?

Wanda: I just don't know whether he would want to come here if he knew.

Therapist: Maybe you should tell him here.

Wanda: What would I say?

Therapist: I think you need to be honest with him and take responsibility for your behavior.

Wanda: What would you say?

Therapist: I would tell him what happened—that it was wrong and that you are sorry.

Wanda: What if he asks me questions or wants to know if I had sex with him?

Therapist: I would tell him the truth—that you did have sex with him—but I wouldn't go into the details about how often you saw him or where you met.

Wanda: I don't know.

Therapist: I think the issue here is whether or not you want to save your marriage.

Wanda: Yes, I want to save the marriage, but I think I would rather tell him at home before we come to see you.

Therapist: That's fine. You need to know that this is going to take time. You can't earn his trust back over night.

Wanda: Yes.

Therapist: Okay. We had better stop for now. Will this time work for both of you?

Wanda: I'll call if it doesn't.

After the therapist determines that violence is not a likely possibility, he gives the client an option of telling her husband about the affair in the session.

The therapist helps Wanda have a realistic notion that change will be slow and that trust must be reestablished.

When the therapist meets the couple after the affair has been revealed, the therapist must provide support to the other partner. He or she must also help the couple decide how they want to handle the affair. The therapist must guard against any emotional threats or violence. Moreover, the therapist must provide hope that the marriage can be saved if the couple is willing to commit to working on it.

Therapist: Al, I'm glad you could come.

Al: I haven't been able to sleep or work since she told me.

Therapist: I'm sure it came as a shock.

The therapist tries to connect with Al and be empathic to his feelings. He then begins to assess Al's family of origin to determine what an affair might mean to him.

Al: Yeah, I knew things haven't been good between us, but I never believed she would do anything like that.

Therapist: Has anything like this ever happened in your family before?

Al: No, my family is quite religious.

Therapist: Tell me about your family.

Al: I was the oldest of the boys. We didn't have much money and had to work for everything. I didn't have much time for relationships.

Therapist: Where did you and Wanda meet?

Al: I met her in the library when I was in college. I was working at the desk and she frequently checked out books.

Therapist: How about your position in your family, Wanda?

Wanda: I was an only child. My mother raised me. My dad died when I was three years old.

Therapist: What do you remember about Al when you first met him?

Wanda: I thought he was attractive and very independent. I still feel that way.

Therapist: What about you, Al?

Al: I thought she was beautiful. We hit it off right away. How did we get where we are now?

Therapist: What are your thoughts about that? What do you think has happened?

Al: I don't know. I have to work all the time. I didn't know things were this bad. She never said anything.

Wanda: I didn't know what to say. I asked you several times if you wanted to do things, and you just didn't seem interested. I just figured you were busy and didn't care.

Al: I care . . . a lot. I guess I just don't show it.

Therapist: So, Wanda, what would you like Al to do?

Wanda: I want him to be interested in me—to ask me how things went at work—to ask me to go places.

The therapist gets the couple to recall the days they met and what each found attractive about the other.

The therapist begins a discussion of where needs are not being met, and what the couple can do to resolve the situation.

Therapist: What do you do to get him to do those things?

Wanda: I guess I don't try.

Therapist: Why not?

Wanda: I guess I expect him to be interested in me without asking.

Therapist: Since we are starting over, I think you will need to help each other. Al, what could she do to help you?

Al: If she just says, "Do you want to talk?"

Therapist: That sounds good, but it sounds like she thinks you're preoccupied and don't want to spend the time with her.

Al: I guess that's so.

Therapist: What do you do when you get home?

Al: Oh, I generally grab a newspaper and go to the family room.

Therapist: What if you were more available? What if you just put the paper down? Wanda, what are you normally doing when he gets home?

Wanda: I'm generally watering the plants or getting things ready for dinner.

Al: So—maybe I need to be with her rather than in the family room.

Wanda: I would like that.

> The therapist frames the situation as "starting over" which moves them away from "rehashing" things that have happened in the past and looking more toward what should happen in the future.

It is not uncommon for couples who have experienced infidelity problems to be angry and distrusting in the early stages of therapy. Even when the "wronged" spouse understands what has gone wrong in the relationship and the couple is working on changing this, resentment is common. In such cases, the therapist must help the couple understand that it will take some time for the resentment to go away, and for the trust that once existed to be reestablished.

Therapist: How did last week go?

Wanda: Not so well. I think Al is still angry about what happened.

Al: I just can't seem to forget it. I just wonder if she'll do the same thing the next time she feels lonely or frustrated.

> The therapist again helps the couple realize that regaining trust is a slow process.

Therapist: I don't think it's easy to forget, but I do think the resentment will go away over time. Have you been spending more time together?

Wanda: Yes. Al comes out in the yard or in the kitchen when he gets home. It's later on in the evening when we seem to have trouble.

Therapist: Like what?

Al: I just get to thinking about it and can't get it out of my head.

Therapist: That's pretty normal. What do you think would help?

> The therapist gets the spouse to think of ways to deal more effectively with his anger.

Al: I don't know.

Therapist: What do you do to relieve stress?

Al: I jog.

Therapist: Does it help?

Al: Yeah, most of the time.

Therapist: Can you jog when you start thinking about the affair? Is there anything Wanda can do to help?

Al: Sometimes I can jog. I can't think of anything Wanda could do to help.

Therapist: Is there anyone else you could talk to?

Al: I don't want to talk with anyone else about it.

Therapist: I understand . . . but I think it's important to find some ways to care for yourself right now.

Al: I know. It's just something I'll have to get over.

Therapist: How are things going otherwise?

Al: Things are better.

Wanda: (Nods head)

Al: It's when I start to resent the situation that I start asking questions.

Therapist: That will most likely not help. I think the more intimate time you spend with each other, the more likely you will be able to keep memories of the affair out of your relationship.

As the therapist begins to see progress in treatment, he or she must plan for relapse. This is particularly true for problems such as infidelity where memories and negative thoughts often trigger a destructive cycle of interaction between the partners.

Therapist: So it sounds like things are better.

Al: We are doing more things together.

Wanda: We talk more and we look for more opportunities to be together. When Al gets home, he comes and finds me . . . and I think I am doing better at asking him to do things. I know it will take time.

Therapist: Good. So you're taking it slowly and things seem to be going better. Sometimes with couples, things go along pretty well and then you fall into the old rut—in your case, not talking and each going your own way.

The therapist helps the couple have reasonable expectations and to plan for relapse.

Wanda: Um.

Therapist: What do you think it would take for things to go back to the way they were?

Wanda: Do you mean what would happen that would make us go back to the way we were before we came to the way we were?

Therapist: Yes, what would each of you be doing?

Al: I guess—for me—I still have bad memories of this.

Therapist: Okay. So you start thinking of the affair and then what happens?

Al: I don't know. Maybe I would ask Wanda a question.

Therapist: Like what?

Al: Oh, maybe like, "Do you ever think of him anymore?"

Therapist: And, Wanda, what would you say?

Wanda: "Why do you keep bringing this up?"

Therapist: Al.

Al: "Look, I can't help it. I didn't start this— run out and have an affair."

Wanda: "I can't do anything about what's over. I told you I'm sorry—and if I could take it back, I would."

Therapist: Al, what would you do or say then?

Al: I'd probably walk away.

Wanda: We wouldn't talk to each other for about two days.

Al: Yeah . . . things would be like they were.

Therapist: So what can you do to stop this pattern if it were to reoccur?

Al: I don't know. I could jog. That helps me get   things off my mind.

Therapist: Let's say you can't jog. It's raining or too cold. Then what could you do?

Wanda: Maybe I could calm him down rather than getting upset myself.

Therapist: How can you do that?

Wanda: I'm not sure.

Therapist: Is there something Wanda could do to help you when you get upset? How could she reassure you that things are ok, that she loves you, and wishes those thoughts would go away?

Al: I don't know if there is anything she can say . . . . maybe just give me a hug.

Therapist: You think a hug would help you feel better?

Al: I think so . . . maybe the thoughts wouldn't go away, but I could handle them better.

Wanda: I'll do that.

Therapist: It may take a while for the thoughts and resentment to leave—maybe six months—Maybe a year.

The therapist gets the couple to talk about how things might get back to the way they were and how they could respond to avoid their destructive pattern.

In this case, the therapist helped the couple to confront the affair and work on the relationship. Affairs create a lot of hurt and pain. The therapist avoided collusion by helping to reveal the affair to the partner. The therapist then helped them rebuild their relationship while at the same time monitoring the effects of the affair on both parties. The therapist helped the partner who did not have the affair to care for himself. As the couple progressed in treatment, the therapist helped the couple plan for relapse to prevent further problems from occurring.

Summary

Infidelity can have a major impact on marital relationships. A couple can survive an affair if they are willing to commit themselves to improving the relationship. The therapist must allow time (one to two years) for the couple to reestablish trust and heal the pain. The unfaithful partner must take responsibility for the affair while the other partner must get support and avoid bringing up the affair. The therapist must focus on the strengths of the relationship to give the couple hope that their marriage can be restored.

DIVORCE—
THE CASE OF ELANA AND MIKE

Considerable evidence exists that divorce can increase the likelihood of adverse effects on the psychological well being of families. Literature reviews and independent investigations illustrate the negative psychological impact on families, particularly families with children (Wallerstein, 1987). Currently, 45 percent of all first marriages will end in divorce (Lamb, Sternberg, & Thompson, 1997). Partners often experience stress because divorce requires all family members to adapt to rapid change. A client's decision to divorce is a major challenge for the marital therapist. Consider the case of Mike and Elana.

Elana: We just don't seem to get along anymore.

Therapist: What do you mean?

Elana: I'm tired of being criticized for everything I do.

Therapist: For instance . . .?

Elana: I don't know. It seems like everything— the way I look—the way I deal with the kids.

Mike: That's not true. I'm just concerned that you are always gone.

Elana: (Shakes her head)

Therapist: So (to Mike) you wish she were around more.

Mike: Yes . . . ever since she started spending time with Jackie, I never see her.

Therapist: Okay. It sounds like there are things bothering both of you. Elana, let's start with you first. Tell me more about what it is that you like to change in the relationship.

Elana: I don't have anything more to say. Jackie is a member of our church, and I enjoy being with her.

Therapist: Tell me two things that you would like Mike to do differently.

Elana: I want him to stop criticizing me, but I know that isn't going to change.

The therapist asks questions to determine the problem. He asks clients to be specific about concerns.

The therapist provides time for each spouse to relate his or her concerns about what is wrong in the relationship.

Again, the therapist works at getting clients to be specific.

Therapist: How long have you been married?

Elana: About six years.

Therapist: So was there ever a time he didn't criticize you?

The therapist checks to see if this has always been a concern or if the marriage has changed.

Elana: He's always been critical. That's the way he is. He's not going to change. (Turns head and looks out the window)

Therapist: You can't think of a time when things were different?

The therapist checks for exceptions.

Elana: Not really . . . I don't really care any more.

Therapist: Even from the beginning of the marriage, Mike has always been critical?

Elana: Look, I didn't want to come here in the first place.

Mike: She doesn't want to give me a chance.

Therapist: What do you mean?

Mike: Like I said before, ever since she started spending time with Jackie, she has been a different person.

Therapist: How is she different?

Mike: Well, Jackie is divorced and she doesn't have children, so Elana's always spending time with her. And when she's with Jackie, it's like she would rather be with her than me.

Therapist: What makes you think that?

Mike: If I ask her to do something, she says she's already made plans with Jackie.

It is not uncommon for spouses to come for marriage therapy with different agendas. In cases where there has been longstanding conflict, one spouse may want to work on the relationship while the other has disengaged. In some cases, the disengaged spouse may want to end the relationship but does not know how to do so. In other cases, they want to remove their guilt by saying they have tried everything to save the marriage. In such cases, the therapist must assess whether one or both spouses are working on the marriage or on a separation/divorce.

Elana: This has been going on forever. Right now there is nothing that I want from Mike.

Because Elana's and Mike's motivations seem different, the therapist asks to see them individually.

Therapist: I think it would help me to get a clearer picture of things if I could spend some time with each of you alone.

Mike: That's fine.

Elana: Uh huh.

Therapist: Elana, I would like to start with you. We'll go about 20 minutes and then I would like to see you, Mike.

Mike: Okay. (Leaves room)

Therapist: Elana, it seems like you have pulled away in the relationship.

Elana: I guess. I really don't want to be married to Mike.

Therapist: You don't believe that things can be different.

Elana: No . . . the only reason I've stayed this long is our two children. We've been married six years and all I've heard is criticism. We argue all the time, and it just isn't worth it.

Therapist: Mike says you have changed since you met Jackie. Is that true?

Elana: Maybe. At least I found someone I could talk to. Is that so wrong?

Therapist: No, but I think Mike believes that Jackie has influenced you.

Elana: Maybe. But I think I would have eventually made this decision anyway.

Therapist: So you are saying that you don't want to be married to Mike and that you don't want to work on making things better?

Elana: I want out.

Therapist: Do you think Mike knows that you want out?

Elana: He knows that I'm not happy, but I don't think he knows. No—he doesn't know.

Therapist: You don't think there is anything that can change your mind.

Elana: No . . . I really don't want to be around him. It's just gone on too long.

Therapist: So when were you planning to tell him?

Elana: I don't know. I know he is going to be upset. I thought maybe if we talked here, he would see that this will never work.

The therapist begins to assess whether or not Elana is committed to the marriage or if she's already decided to get out of it.

The therapist needs to be sure of the client's intentions.

The therapist checks to see if Elana has made plans to tell Mike she wants a divorce, and to discuss how she could do this.

Therapist: You were hoping, then, that therapy wouldn't work and that Mike would agree to a divorce.

Elana: Yeah, I guess. If I told him I wanted a divorce, I think he would just get angry and say that I didn't try to make the marriage work. But that's okay. He blames me for everything anyway.

Therapist: How does Mike express his anger?

Elana: He gets loud and obnoxious. If you're asking if he gets violent—no, he doesn't. He has never hit me and I don't think he would. He's just not like that.

The therapist assesses how Mike might react and whether or not violence could be an issue.

Therapist: So how do you want to handle this?

Elana: I guess I need to tell him now.

Therapist: Here?

Elana: What do you think?

In many cases, one partner will come to marital therapy for help in leaving the marriage. They may be afraid to tell the partner and want the therapist to be there when they announce it in case the reaction is volatile. In other cases, they may want the therapist to take care of the partner so they do not have to worry about him or her. In the United States and many European countries, between two-thirds and three-fourths of all divorces are petitioned by women. This may be due to women's increasing economic independence (Ahrons, 1999). Regardless, deciding to end the marriage is no easy task.

Therapist: I think Mike needs to know your position. Are you prepared to tell him?

The therapist discusses with Elana how to tell Mike.

Elana: How should I say it?

Therapist: Pretty much the way you said it to me.

Elana: Okay.

Therapist: If you are ready, I'll bring Mike in now and we'll discuss it. If you are not sure, I think we need to talk more about it.

Elana: No . . . I need to tell him.

Therapist: Mike, will you please come in now? Elana and I have been talking, and she felt that she needed to share something with you.

Elana: I've had a hard time telling you this . . . but I want out of the marriage. I want a divorce.

The therapist ensures that Elana is ready to tell Mike. He has not talked with Mike individually at this point; however, if Elana is not interested in continuing the marriage, Mike needs to know that. Obviously, there is no mutual contract to keep the marriage intact.

Mike: (Silence...looks down and then at Elana) I'm not surprised. You didn't really want to work on this. Did you just decide this?

Elana: I made up my mind some time ago . . . I just didn't want to tell you.

Mike: Did Jackie tell you to do this?

Elana: She has nothing to do with this.

Mike: Well, what do we do now? You know you didn't give me a chance. We came in here to learn to communicate better and now this.

Therapist: This must come as a surprise.

Mike: No, it's not a surprise. I just didn't think it would happen here.

Therapist: I think it's important to continue to meet to talk about how to handle various issues, and your children need to know what's going on. They need to hear from both of you why you are divorcing and they need to understand that it isn't their fault.

The goals have now changed from marital therapy to how to handle an "uncoupling" successfully.

It is critical for the therapist to continue meeting with both spouses to deal with the initial losses—dreams, roles, companionship, and trust. Couples who decide to divorce must give up lost dreams and fantasies such as the dream house, holiday celebrations, and time together with their children. Additional therapy sessions should be scheduled with both parents and children to deal with issues in the postdivorce relationship. Brown, Portes, and Christensen (1989) offer the following suggestions:

1. *Discuss issues raised in the literature on postdivorce relationships early in couple counseling.* The postdivorce relationship can be discussed with a couple as soon as they place their marriage in question. This can be done as part of the discussion about what needs to change in their relationship, regardless of whether they decide to divorce. Assuming the position early allows the couple to negotiate conflict while still keeping their options open. In so doing, they are also improving their chances for a healthy postdivorce relationship, should their efforts to change the marriage fail.

2. *Schedule sessions specifically for negotiating the new postdivorce relationship.* While clinicians may be able to work with only one spouse at the time of divorce, this activity can often indirectly contribute to improving the postdivorce relationship. Where possible, clinicians may find it useful to use their therapeutic leverage at the point of decision to divorce to structure the next month or two as a time to forge a postdivorce relationship. Couples must understand that they are not going to stop

relating as parents. Challenging them to be successful parents is difficult and often requires ongoing support counseling for the partner who is less happy about the divorce. The clinician must take the lead at this critical crisis point, however, to influence the formation of a healthy postdivorce relationship.

3. *Schedule sessions throughout the first year of divorce.* Clinicians may also wish to utilize their influence during the divorce crisis to schedule follow-up sessions throughout the first year after the divorce. Couples who are experiencing the pain and confusion of divorce will have difficulty working at the same time on their postdivorce relationship. The two tasks are often in conflict. The couple will, however, often accept the clinician's leadership to help stabilize the relationship. The clinician must think in terms of prevention versus remediation, and feel confident that proactive planning will lower the risk to the children's adjustment.

4. *Meet with each new branch of the family to discuss parent-child concerns.* The postdivorce relationship is often stressed because of the family's predivorce triangular relationships. For example, when a child and one parent are in conflict in the original family, the other parent is often brought into the interaction. This parent-child conflict does not usually get resolved; rather, it is simply diffused into the parental or marital relationship or even displaced to another child. These patterns are very tenacious and do not typically change with a divorce decree. If the couple is to have a stable postdivorce relationship, each parent must be able to work out the conflicts *within* his or her branch of the family without routinely engaging the other parent. So, while it is important to work with the couple dyad on coparenting issues, it is also helpful to work with each new branch of parent-child relationships (father and children, mother and children) to minimize the stress in the postdivorce parental relationship. This again is preventive planning, based on the clinician's judgment that there is reasonable concern that the children's adjustment will be at risk if the new family or families are left to muddle through on their own.

5. *Establish relationships with family mediators.* Whenever possible, encourage couples to use trained family mediators to settle divorce disputes. Many situations are made far more difficult by the litigation process while early involvement with a negotiated process can lower postdivorce conflict. A mediator's role is to help the couple settle disputes about property, custody and visitation; in the event the couple can negotiate these issues themselves, they will save money, emotional energy, and hopefully reach solutions which will be more positive for the family in the long run.

The research indicates that social support and involvement are highly related to low stress and better adjustment for both parents and children. Kurdek and Berg (1983) found that children's postdivorce adjustment is significantly related to their mother's use of social support systems. Likewise, therapists should help children increase contacts with additional adult caretakers, such as daycare professionals, baby sitters, adult relatives, friends, and neighbors (Santrock & Warshak, 1979). In short, parents' and children's postdivorce adjustment is associated with the extent to which family members develop and maintain support systems of friends and relatives.

Therapists who work with couples that are divorcing need to be aware of the emotional, economic, and legal processes (Ahrons, 1999). The therapist needs to help the couple forge a new postdivorce relationship. To do so, they need to separate as marital partners and reunite as coparents of their children. Divorce eliminates some of the rituals and rules that have previously helped the family function, and the therapist must help each of the parents establish new rituals and traditions. The therapist also needs to ensure that the new family has relatives and friends who will support them.

REMARRIAGE—
THE CASE OF JANET AND STEVE

Stepfamilies are fast becoming the most common type of family. Currently, half the marriages are remarried families and approximately 35 percent of children will live in a remarried family by the age of 18. In the future stepfamilies will likely become the most common form of family in the United States since 50 percent of first marriages end in divorce and approximately 70 percent of these people will remarry (Visher & Visher, 1996). There will soon be more stepfamilies than intact nuclear families.

Stepfamilies occur when at least one spouse has been previously married. It may be more difficult for remarried couples to complete the developmental tasks than it is for the original nuclear couples. While society focuses on the joys of marriage through advertising and television, remarried families often have difficulty adjusting to this pattern. Moreover, at the time of remarriage, spouses must deal with many of the issues unresolved in the previous marriage. Consider the case of Janet and Steve.

Janet: Everything just seems confused. I love Steve, and we thought this marriage would be great. But there are so many problems, and things just aren't working out.	The therapist asks for details about the presenting problem.
Therapist: Steve, when did your last marriage end? (Goes to the board to draw a genogram)	The genogram gives a visual picture of relationship history.
Steve: (Looks at the board) About nine months ago.	
Therapist: Do you think you had enough time to finish your last marriage?	Sometimes divorcing persons enter new relationships quite rapidly
Steve: Probably not. We were seeing each other before I was divorced.	and don't finish the

Janet: Our big problem is that his ex-wife just won't go away. She runs up these bills and expects us to pay them. I have two sons from my first marriage and they need things. Steve doesn't understand. My first husband died and didn't leave us anything.

Therapist: What are you saying—that Steve's money goes to his ex-wife and there isn't enough money for your children?

Steve: She doesn't understand. I've still got bills to pay and I have child support.

Janet: Then why did you buy Larry's (Steve's son) new tennis shoes last week? You know Chuck needs braces. Why can't the tennis shoes come from child support?

Steve: If I don't buy them, he won't have them. He needs the shoes for basketball.

uncoupling" tasks. Therefore, they bring some of the old issues into the new relationship.

Money is a typical concern in remarried families and there is frequently a dispute about a spouse's responsibility to his former family versus his or her current family.

Money often becomes a major issue in remarried families. It is common for stepfamilies to experience problems with child support and marital property. Resentment often builds when a wife feels that her husband has to pay both child support and other costs of children from the first marriage. Indeed, one or both parents generally enter the remarriage with financial obligations to their ex-spouse (Carter & McGoldrick, 1999). A husband who must pay child support to his first family as well as support his current family is in a difficult situation. The stepfamily is confronted with the question, "Do we support my children or your children?" This problem is likely to be more of an issue if the wife is not working or not receiving child support from her first marriage.

Stepfamilies that are formed after the death of a spouse present a unique set of issues. Children may see the stepparent as an intruder, particularly if the remaining parent does not provide enough time for the stepparent to get to know the children. Moreover, children may need to grieve the loss of their mother or father before they can accept someone else in the parent role. In some cases, there is a tendency for children to idealize the lost parent, particularly if the death was premature (Carter & McGoldrick, 1999). This makes it even more difficult for the stepparent to be accepted.

Steve: We have other problems also.

Therapist: Such as . . . .

Steve: I don't really have any authority or say with her children.

Therapist: I'm not sure what you mean.

Steve: They are always upset with me. If I try to discipline them, they just run to Janet.

The therapist listens for other issues.

Another typical problem in remarried families is who is allowed to provide

Therapist: You would like them to accept you as their father.

Steve: I know I'm not their real father . . . but they need discipline. They don't mind her . . . if she tells them to do something, they just ignore her. They know I'm tougher on them.

Janet: You need to explain things to kids—not just punish them.

Therapist: When you husband was alive, who did most of the disciplining?

Janet: My husband was real good with the boys. He could get them to do things I couldn't get them to do.

Therapist: What do you mean?

Janet: Oh, we might say the same things to them, but they would listen to him and not me. I guess I wasn't hard enough on them.

Therapist: You think your husband was a little firmer?

Janet: Yes, they knew they couldn't get away with anything from him.

Therapist: Can you see yourself being a little firmer with them?

Janet: I can if I have to.

Therapist: You think it works best if you discipline your children—maybe with Steve's support.

Janet: What do you mean?

Therapist: It sounds like you think since these are your children, you should set the rules. They are just getting to know Steve and are maybe having a hard time accepting him as their father. They really haven't had time to grieve the loss of their father—let alone accept Steve as his replacement.

Steve: I'm really not trying to be his replacement.

Therapist: I know, but they don't see it that way.

Steve: Sometimes I don't know whether I'm coming or going. I've got my own kids and problems with my ex-wife with child support and visitation.

discipline. It is important for a stepparent to become friends with stepchildren before taking on the role of disciplinarian.

The therapist gets Janet to talk about her effectiveness as a disciplinarian. He asks questions to point out that Janet needs support to follow through.

Therapist: That's right. That's why it might be better if right now, you concentrated on working out issues with your wife. When did you first meet Janet's kids?

The therapist helps the stepparent determine what his stepparenting role should be.

Steve: I guess it was about two months before we were married.

Janet: He came over to the house . . . I was having a tough time after my husband died. Steve and I knew each other in high school. I guess the children didn't have much time to get to know him.

Therapist: That's right. That's why it is important for them to spend time with you and get to know you before you try to be a parent to them.

A stepparent's role with children is often confusing unless the stepparent is properly integrated into the family. Often the stepparent is thrust into a parental role before he gets to know the children. Stepparents are often called upon to be the disciplinarians, only to find that the biological parent criticizes them when the children complain. If the stepparent is cut off from his own children or is having difficulties when his or her children visit, he or she may use excessive discipline with the stepchildren. In such cases, the children need time to get to know the stepparent (going out to eat, cooking a meal, and playing games) with the support of the biological parent. This process often takes longer when there is a wide discrepancy in the family life cycle—for example, a father with adolescent children married to a wife who is only slightly older than his children.

Therapist: It's going to take a while for you, Steve, to develop a relationship with Janet's children . . . but I think things are going to go better there if you can resolve some of the issues you have with your ex-wife around support and visitation. What seems to be the problem there?

The therapist moves back to the original issue of resolving issues with Steve's ex-wife.

Steve: She thinks I should be paying more child support.

Therapist: Are you now paying what you agreed to?

Steve: Yeah, that's what I don't understand. We agreed in court, and then six months later, she wants more. I think I give her enough. Plus—I buy things for the kids when we are together.

Therapist: Those things don't count toward your child support.

Janet: He's already giving her too much.

Therapist: That's something he needs to work out with his ex-wife. He needs your support to do this.

The therapist establishes a boundary around Steve and his ex-wife and the issues they need to deal with, apart from his current marital situation.

Steve: I'm not sure what to do.

Therapist: I believe you are a good father who wants to do the best for his children. Right?

Steve: Yes. If my children need more, I want to take care of them.

Therapist: How do you plan to handle the situation with your ex-wife?

Steve: I need to call her and talk about how the money is being spent—exactly what the boys need. I'm pretty limited right now, however, and I can't give much more.

Therapist: Is the money the major issue?

Steve: Yes, especially where Janet is concerned.

Therapist: After you talk with your ex-wife, can you discuss with Janet what is reasonable?

Steve: Yes, I'll try.

Therapist: What about visitation?

Steve: A few times I haven't been able to make it.

Therapist: Did you call?

Steve: Yes, but she was still upset.

Therapist: Why?

Steve: She said I didn't let her know . . . but I couldn't get away.

Therapist: Do you have a contingency plan if you are late?

Steve: No . . . but I probably need to develop one.

The integration of a new stepparent is more difficult when adolescent children are involved (Hetherington, 1990). Belonging in stepfamilies may take up to five years, particularly when the children involved are adolescents. This is often due to the incompatibility between the adolescent stage of development and the development of the remarried family. The adolescent wants more separation and independence while the stepfamily wants to pull together. This makes it particularly difficult for a stepparent to discipline an adolescent.

Therapist: It seems that you and Steve have some differences in childrearing.

Janet: Yes . . . he seems to think that they should be in early, and he wants to control everything they do. They're getting older and don't like that.

Steve: No, I just think you let them do anything they want.

Therapist: Give an example.

Steve: If they want to stay out late, she lets them.

Therapist: How late?

Janet: I think they're old enough to stay out until midnight.

Therapist: (To Steve) And you think they need to be in earlier?

Steve: It isn't that. They will just talk her into coming in whatever time they want to.

Janet: It would help if you were a little more supportive.

Therapist: What kind of support do you want from Steve?

Janet: I just wish he would back me up.

Therapist: That sounds reasonable. Steve, what do you need from Janet to help you back her up?

Steve: I wish she would let me know. I think she should at least talk it over with me.

Janet: I do tell you.

Steve: Afterwards. I feel like I have no say.

Therapist: So you would like to have a voice in when they come in?

Janet: I'd give you some say if you would listen.

Therapist: How so?

Janet: I would be happy to talk it over with him first if he would listen to what I have to say.

Steve: I'll listen.

Therapist: I think it's important at this stage for your boys to have some input into the time.

Janet: What do you mean?

The therapist leads a discussion of child-rearing techniques and helps Janet and Steve to agree on how they will deal with children. Janet now needs to reset boundaries to include Steve gradually.

The boundaries are set to allow Steve to give input and support Janet who actually sets the rules for the children. As the children begin to accept Steve, he can take a more active role in parenting.

The therapist helps Steve and Janet negotiate each other's roles and also the role the children have.

Therapist: If they want to come in at a certain time, they need to assure you that they will be safe. You need to give them a chance to do that.

Janet: I can do that. I just want to know that Steve is behind me.

Therapist: I think that's important. There may be times that you don't agree, but I think you need Steve's support to be firmer with the boys.

Janet: Yes.

Therapist: And, Steve, Janet seems ready to consult with you if she knows that you will listen to her.

In the above-mentioned case, the wife needs to help integrate the husband into the family. This is more difficult when the biological parent and children are close or have lived together for an extended period of time. The therapist in this case must help the biological parent (the wife, in this case) to restructure the boundaries to make room for the husband and let him become a part of the family. This process may take several years since children are often loyal to the biological parent who has left, in this case the deceased parent.

In this case, the therapist used a genogram to gather information about previous marriages. The therapist emphasized that the parents had not had enough time to develop into a new family. The children must have time to mourn the loss of their father, and the stepparent needed time to resolve issues of child support and visitation with his ex-spouse. Finally, the therapist help the step-couple to resolve differences in parenting—requesting that the biological parent become the primary caretaker while getting support from the stepparent.

LESBIAN AND GAY COUPLES—
THE CASE OF LAUREN AND LUCY

While all couples have problems, gay and lesbian couples experience a unique set of difficulties. Johnson and Colucci (1999) state the following:

> Coupling is a life endeavor that is filled with complexity for all couples, straight or lesbian/gay. But there are issues that are unique to lesbian and gay couples that derive from the special nature of same sex pairing and from the adaptation that lesbian/gay couples make to a devaluing larger culture. Specifically, there are no legal protections for lesbian/gay couples and no set of socially prescribed rituals to support and guide couple functioning. However, there are a couple of issues that lesbians and gays face in common with straight couples: the influence of the family of

origin, the impact of other external systems such as minority cultures and dominant culture, the prescriptions supplied by gender socialization, and the decision about whether or not to have children. (p. 351)

The most powerful factor in a gay/lesbian relationship is the family origin. Take the case of Lauren and Lucy:

Lauren: We just seem to be miles apart now.

Therapist: What do you mean by that?

Lauren: I don't know. Ever since we started living together three years ago, Lucy has her own friends and I'm alone most of the time.

Therapist: So you would like to be with Lucy more?

Lauren: Yes, I just feel excluded. She has friends at work but she never includes me.

Therapist: I see. What have you tried to do about this?

Lauren: I haven't tried much. Most of the time it just ends up in an argument.

Lucy: I tell her that just because we're living together doesn't mean that we can't go out with other people.

Lauren: I know, but that's easier for you than for me. I don't even have a family to go back to.

The therapist begins to assess the problem and what has been tried to resolve it.

Therapist: Tell me about that. (Goes to the flipchart to draw a diagram.)

Lauren: Well, we have been living together for three years. Prior to that we saw each other for about a year and a half. My parents were okay with that. But when we announced our relationship and that we were living together, they really got upset.

The therapist uses a genogram to provide a visual depiction of relationship histories. She begins with Lauren's family of origin.

Therapist: What is your relationship with them?

Lauren: We haven't spoken in the last year.

Therapist: How did you get along with them prior to the relationship with Lucy?

Lauren: It wasn't great. I had trouble being who I wanted to be. I knew that I was attracted to females, and I couldn't talk to them about that. But we always seemed to be arguing over what I wore or where I was going.

It is typical for some cut-off from families of origin when a child announces same sex preferences. The therapist is gathering information on Lauren's relationship with parents prior to their knowledge of her sexual preference.

Therapist: Would you like to have contact with your parents?

Lauren: Of course.

Therapist: Which parent are you closer to?

Lauren: My father. I think he would like to have contact with me, but my mother won't permit it.

Therapist: (Draws line between Lauren and her father on the diagram.) How are your mother and father different?

Lauren: My mother comes from a family with a lot of money. She went to a private school and I think she's embarrassed and doesn't want anyone to know that I'm a lesbian. My dad grew up poor, and I'm sure he doesn't like my relationship, but he doesn't worry about how it affects his social status.

The genogram continues to show where there have been close or distant relationships, including both parental and sibling relationships.

Therapist: Do you have brothers or sisters?

Lauren: Yes, an older sister.

Therapist: How old is she?

Lauren: 32.

Therapist: Do you talk with her?

Lauren: Yes, but not often. She lives in San Francisco.

Therapist: Is she married?

Lauren: Yes. She and her husband have two children.

Therapist: Who is she closest to?

Lauren: I guess my mom. She is a lawyer, and that really pleased my mother.

Therapist: (Records on genogram.) So your mother is most upset with your relationship?

Lauren: Yes. She was very angry.

Therapist: She was probably overwhelmed. Sounds like she runs the family.

Lauren: She does. She wants to control everything.

Therapist: Let's talk about some ways you can deal with this.

In some cases parents are supportive of their child's lesbian/gay relationship; however, in many cases, parents react negatively to such a relationship. In some instances, such as Lauren's relationship with Lucy, parents and siblings are divided about feelings. In Lauren's case, she has lost contact with her family of origin, primarily because of her mother's disapproval of the relationship. When the lesbian/gay child is cut off from the family, it creates pressures in other relationships.

Therapist: I think your cut-off from your family has created some pressure in your relationship with Lucy.

The therapist makes a link between the current situation and the family of origin.

Lauren: In what way?

Therapist: Well, for one, I wonder if you worry about other relationships. If your family can't accept your relationship with Lucy, can other people?

The therapist helps Lauren see that because her family of origin rejects her sexual preference, she assumes others will also.

Lauren: I suppose. Actually, I haven't told many people about our relationship. Only two people know.

Therapist: Maybe you're wondering what will happen if you tell people.

Lauren: Yes.

Therapist: Lucy, what are your thoughts on this?

Lucy: I guess I've never thought of what you said. My family is very supportive of me and Lauren. She's always welcome when I go home, and I don't really worry about whether other people accept me.

Lauren: I didn't have many friends when Lucy and I moved in together.

Therapist: Are both or either of you involved in a lesbian/gay community?

The therapist checks to see what kind of support systems Lauren and Lucy have established.

Lucy: Some, but not much. Many of the people we know have multiple partners. We see ourselves in more of a committed relationship.

Lesbian and gay couples need support from others. The lesbian/gay community can offer that support if the couple shares their values. In Lucy and Lauren's case, they prefer a monogamous relationship whereas in their community, many people have multiple partners. Regardless, it is important that the lesbian/gay couple have support from family and friends.

Lauren: I work in the schools, and I wouldn't want my colleagues to know about me.

Therapist: What is your job?

Lauren: I'm an elementary teacher. And I think if they knew, I'd probably keep my job, but I may be ostracized.

It is quite common for gay men and lesbians to have careers where their sexual orientation must be kept secret for some reason. In some fields, there may be reluctance to hire lesbians or gay men; in others, the gay or lesbian person may feel that secrecy is essential to avoid the stigma related to homosexuality, or that their potential to receive promotions may be hampered if they are known as homosexual.

In addition to the problems related to their careers, gay men/lesbians often lack rituals to symbolize their relationships. Since gay/lesbian marriages are not considered legal, gay/lesbian couples often lack the formal wedding ceremony to mark their rites of passage. If there is a ceremony at all, it frequently is not the happy event of a heterosexual couple where both partners' families are involved and supportive. Gay men/lesbians may have support from only one family of origin, or in some cases, neither.

Therapist: So (to Lauren) you don't feel you could get support from your work colleagues for your relationship.

Lauren: Oh, some of them would be fine. But I don't talk about it, because I know there would be some people who think it's terrible.

Therapist: How did you announce your relationship? Did you have any ceremony? Was it public?

The therapist explores how the couple established their current relationship and the rituals surrounding their entry into it. Specifically, the therapist explores the involvement of family and friends.

Lucy: Yes, we had a small ceremony, with only a few people. My mother helped plan it.

Therapist: Lauren, how were you involved?

Lauren: I wasn't very involved. I invited only one friend, and my family didn't come.

Therapist: Did you invite them?

Lauren: No, I knew they wouldn't come.

Therapist: Was this ceremony meaningful to you?

The therapist also explores the meaningfulness of the original ceremony.

Lauren: Yes, it was meaningful for me. But I wish more people could have shared it. I wish it could have been very public like my sister's wedding.

Therapist: If you were doing it over, would you do anything differently? I am asking both of you. Would you like to create a different kind of ceremony now?

Lucy: Another one?

Therapist: Yes, a ceremony to give your relationship new meaning.

A "new ceremony" can be a way of marking a new

Lauren: I guess I'd like to do something and invite my family. It's worth trying again. Maybe I could go and talk with my mom, dad, and sister separately and see how they react.

Therapist: How would you like this ceremony to be different? Or what things would you like to keep from the first one?

Lucy: It would be fun to do something different.

Lauren: Like what?

Therapist: Maybe it would be good to get some ideas from each of you and see if we can't put them together. Maybe each of you can think of rituals that were meaningful to you when you were growing up. Lauren, can you think of any?

Lauren: I'm not sure.

Therapist: Was there something you did regularly with your family that you really enjoyed—at bedtime, holidays, meals, etc.?

Lauren: When I was little, my mom and dad always read me a story at bedtime, and that meant a lot to me.

Therapist: So is this something you would like to incorporate into your ceremony?

Lauren: I'm not sure how it would fit.

Therapist: How about a story that the two of you write together?

Lucy: That sounds neat.

Lauren: Yeah . . . a story about us and how we got together.

Therapist: Lucy, how about you?

Lucy: Something I remember that I enjoyed was at Christmas when we would light the advent candles each week. I love candles.

Therapist: Would you like to have candles at your ceremony?

Lauren: Maybe we could light three candles— one for each year we've been together.

Therapist: So you'd like to read a story you have created and light three candles?

kind of relationship—one that is more public, for instance.

The therapist guides the couple in planning a different ceremony which would have special meaning to each partner.

Summary

Lesbians and gay men often lack support and validation by society for their relationship. While most heterosexual couples announce their engagement to the world, it is uncommon for extended family to have a shower or wedding celebration for same-sex couples (Imber-Black & Roberts, 1992).

ADDICTION—
THE CASE OF ROGER AND MINDY

Recent figures indicate that there are approximately 14 million alcoholics in America and that every alcoholic affects the lives of at least four to five people. Drinking is a significant factor in many fatal automobile accidents, traffic accidents, spousal abuse, manslaughter, and rapes (Hudak et.al, 1999). Yet, abuse of alcohol is often a secret problem within a family. In fact, when a couple comes to treatment, they are very likely to talk about problems with communication, money problems, or problems with children, and remain silent about any use/abuse of alcohol. At times, the therapist may have a sense that something in the puzzle does not fit but hasn't thought to explore the issue of alcohol or other drug problems. Treadway (1987) says that this may be for several reasons: (1) the therapist feels inexperienced in treating chemical dependency, (2) families or couples have become so used to the drinking that they do not even view it as an issue and never bring it up, or (3) the therapist has cultural stereotypes about problem drinkers ("falling down drunks who can't hold a job") and therefore does not consider that the person who seems to function relatively well could be abusing alcohol.

Many couples have become so used to organizing their lives around alcohol that they do not want to mention it as a possible problem. In fact, they may not see any relationship between drinking behavior and the presenting problems they bring to therapy. If they acknowledge that a partner (either one or both) is a problem drinker, they will then have to deal with an area where there may be little motivation to change.

Because so many marital problems are related to alcohol problems, it is the therapist's responsibility to assess this area. However, the therapist should also be aware that to push the alcohol issue might mean that the couple will leave therapy. Therefore, the challenging task becomes keeping the couple engaged while reducing their anxiety at the same time the alcohol situation is brought out into the open. Treadway (1987) suggests that the therapist should look for signs and ask questions related to alcohol use, both in the nuclear family and the family of origin, but to do this in a nonjudgmental way. If there seem to be signs of alcohol abuse, the therapist looks at how the presenting problem can be used to get help for the alcohol problem. He also stresses that the struggle around the presenting problem should be used to get the spouse to confront the partner's drinking rather than have the therapist confront this.

Consider the case of Roger and Mindy who have come to marital therapy because of the increasing number of conflicts they have.

Mindy: We simply can't talk with each other anymore. Every time I ask him to do anything, it turns into a big argument. I feel that he should help with things around the house, and every time I say anything, he calls me a nag and says he should have some time to relax and have a drink without me yelling at him.

The therapist lets the couple describe their concerns.

Therapist: Your concern, then, is what? Is it more that you can't talk, that you fight too much, or that he doesn't help you?

Mindy: Actually, I guess it's all of those things. But mainly, I need his help. I have a lot of things to do when I get home, but all he wants to do is sit in front of the TV. When he first gets home, it isn't so bad, but by the end of the evening, we're screaming at each other. I think it's getting worse. The other day, he even threatened me.

Therapist: Tell me about that.

Mindy: We got home at about the same time. I had to fix dinner and help the kids with their homework. I asked him to take out the garbage because the next day it would be picked up. He said, "I've had a bad day. I just want to relax, have a drink and watch the news." I guess that irritated me a little because I had also had a bad day but I didn't have the luxury to just sit down. I got testy and told him he's not a boarder—that he has some responsibilities. We kind of stopped at this point and I didn't say anything else until later when the kids had gone to bed. I asked if he took out the garbage and he just screamed at me. He said if I told him one more time to do something, he would slap me.

Therapist: What happened from the beginning of the evening to the time the two of you were yelling?

Mindy: Roger read the paper and watched the news. I prepared dinner and we ate. Then Roger watched TV some more and I gave the children a bath and put them to bed.

Therapist: Roger, do you share Mindy's concerns that the two of you argue too much?

Roger: She's right that we can't seem to talk with each other without arguing. She can be so persistent! She has to have me do things right when she says it. I really need time when I get home to unwind. I need a drink or two just to get rid of some of the stress of the day. She wants me to start working again immediately.

Therapist: So you don't mind helping. You just want to have some relaxing time at first.

Mindy: He wants to relax all the time he's home. If he had a drink and then helped, I'd be okay with that. He wants to continue drinking and relaxing the whole evening.

The presenting problem is arguments. The therapist asks questions to assess the extent of the drinking.

Therapist: So Roger's drinks and relaxation last a long time.

Mindy: Yes. I want him to spend some time with the children, but he's not much help.

Therapist: Why is that?

Mindy: When Roger has had a few drinks, he gets a little short with the children, and they really react to that.

Therapist: Are you saying that you think when Roger drinks to relax, he becomes less effective with the children.

Mindy: I think he's more irritable when he's had a few drinks.

Therapist: It sound like you're concerned about Roger's tendency to be short with the children, and you think it's related to the number of drinks he's had. Why don't you talk frankly with him about that now?

The therapist's aim is to have the wife confront the husband about his drinking.

The therapist must ensure that he or she has initially joined with the couple before issues about drinking and arguments have been brought up. He or she also must be aware of the amount of anxiety created by discussing drinking. In fact, this could easily make Roger stop attending therapy and make the arguments between him and Mindy much more intense. Therefore, the questioning should be slow and the issue should be addressed as a part of the presenting problem. Treadway (1987) also suggests that the therapist should anticipate that discussion of drinking may escalate problems and discuss with the couple or family whether or not they can handle talking about the drinking.

For instance, the therapist may say to Mindy, "Do you think Roger is concerned about how you feel about his drinking or will he be really angry with you tonight that you mentioned it?" At least, this way, it is brought out into the open, and the couple can discuss it.

Therapist: It sounds like Mindy needs some help and wants you to provide that, Roger. She wants help with the children and doesn't want you to be short with them. She thinks maybe you have too many drinks and that this interferes.

The therapist pursues Mindy's concerns about Roger's drinking by relating it to problems it creates in the family.

Roger: I do like to have a few drinks at night, but I don't think it hurts anything. And I need some time to myself after a stressful day. She always finds something to nitpick about, and now she's latched onto drinking. I will admit that I drink every day and that I sometimes have several drinks. I've never had any problem getting up and going to work, and I don't see how it hurts anything at home.

Mindy: The children say they don't like to be with you when you've had a lot of drinks. I don't like to be with you either when you've had a lot of drinks.

Therapist: Mindy, you need help with the children. You say when Roger drinks and relaxes, he's not very helpful and the children don't like being with him. Roger, you say you need to have a drink or two to relax. What do you think would be an acceptable amount to drink to relax you and not interfere with helping Mindy and spending time with the children?

The therapist moves in to keep an argument from escalating. He also begins to contract with Roger about a maximum amount of drinking which would not interfere with his helping with the children.

Roger: Drinking is not the problem. She just needs something to complain about.

Therapist: What would be a reasonable maximum of drinks you could have and not interfere with helping at home? If you drink no more than that, then you could assume that drinking is not the problem here.

Roger: How about a fifth of scotch?

Mindy: That's ridiculous!

Roger: I'm just kidding.

Therapist: Roger, I want you to decide what the maximum number of drinks a day will be. What amount is really all right for you? Whatever you decide, however, you need to be willing to stick with it.

Roger: I will say four drinks.

Mindy: I think that's too many.

Therapist: That seems like a lot to me also. However, right now, Roger has to make this decision on his own. You can give him your ideas on what is reasonable, but he should decide. Then if Roger keeps drinking more than he's committed to, it might indicate that he has a drinking problem that should be addressed. Also, we'll talk about this again next week and see how it's going.

> The therapist wants the maximum amount of drinking to come from Roger. Then, if that amount is exceeded, it provides an indication that there is a problem.

Conclusion

It is important for the therapist to stay out of power struggles with the client, and it is also important that the therapist not take the role of confronting the alcoholic. The alcoholic must determine that he or she wants to change because of the effects of such behavior on self and family. According to Treadway (1987), the family needs to stop either confronting or protecting the alcoholic. The alcoholic might be given the responsibility to decide and agree to a maximum daily limit of alcohol, and a violation of that standard, even once, indicates that he or she lacks control over the problem. This contract sometimes helps clients realize through their inability to stay within the limits they have set that they need to stop drinking. In other cases, the client may stay within his or her limit, but the pattern of use and amount set may be unacceptable to other members of the family. The spouse/family might then have the option of going to Al-Anon or taking other action. In any case, the problem of alcohol use/abuse is now out in the open and the family is no longer protecting the alcoholic and/or denying the problem.

CHRONIC ILLNESS—
THE CASE OF JUDY AND TED

The therapist who works with chronic illness must consider the interface between individual spouse's illnesses and the couple's developmental stage. Chronic illness is an unexpected stressor that interrupts the couple's development. Illness that occurs during the transition periods can have a devastating effect on the couple's relationship. In conducting a clinical assessment, the therapist must ask the basic question, "What is the fit between the psychosocial demands of a condition and family and the individual life structures and developmental tasks at a particular point in the life cycle?" (Rolland, 1999, p. 500). Consider the case of Ted and Judy.

Therapist: How long have you been married?

Judy: Five years.

Therapist: So, Ted, the onset of diabetes was quite sudden for you.

Ted: Yes, I knew something was wrong, but I didn't know what. I had very little energy, but the doctor said it may be due to the fact I am overweight. I didn't expect a diagnosis of diabetes.

The therapist collects initial information about the presenting problem.

Therapist: I believe diabetes is a hereditary disease. Did either of your parents or grandparents experience this?

Ted. Yes, my dad had diabetes, but he was older. Maybe they didn't detect it right away.

Therapist: What was your father's age at the time of detection? (Draws a genogram)

The genogram gives a visual picture of relationships and roles.

Ted: Dad was about 52 and Mom was 49.

Therapist: How old were you?

Ted: I was about 17.

Therapist: So you were about ready to leave home?

Ted: Yes, it happened my senior year in high school.

Therapist: How did your family cope with this problem?

Ted: It created some problems. Dad was a salesman and traveled a lot. He was taking insulin shots and I remember one night he was away from home and passed out. I guess his blood sugar was pretty low. Mom was really scared . . . and after that, he didn't travel as much.

The therapist gathers information about how illness was dealt with in Ted's family of origin.

Therapist: How did that affect your family?

Ted: Well, the diabetes didn't change things much. Dad was home more, but two years later, he had a mild stroke and never was the same. He died at the age of 56 of congestive heart failure.

Therapist: So how did this affect you?

Ted: I guess I grew up a little faster. I had more responsibility. It really scared me—the stroke. I took my dad to physical therapy. He never took care of himself though.

Therapist: What do you mean?

Ted: Well, he continued to smoke . . . and he was a pretty nervous guy—always worried about something.

Therapist: So—again, how did you deal with this?

Ted: I don't know. I guess I got some of it from him.

Therapist: (Making notes on the genogram) You got what from him?

Ted: I'm always worried something is going to happen.

Judy: Ted is always afraid of the worst.

Ted: Yeah, my dad was always talking about not having enough money . . . and I think he believed he would die at an early age.

In this case, the therapist constructs a genogram focusing on a previous illness in the family of origin and how the family coped with it. The marital therapist can learn a great deal about how a family copes with illness by trying to understand how they have coped with illnesses in the past. Patterns of coping with an illness can be transmitted across generations (Walsh & McGoldrick, 1991). Indeed, it is also helpful to find out if the family has dealt with other losses, such as divorce, unemployment, or death. Learning about what was helpful in coping with previous losses will help the therapist deal with current problems surrounding the illness.

Therapist: Tell me a little about how you coped with your father's death.

Ted: It was tough. I was in college and had to drop out and get a job. The job wasn't so bad, but we weren't sure we would have enough money.

Therapist: I see here on the intake form that you have two younger sisters.

Ted: That's right. I had to try and support the family. My dad didn't have much insurance at the time. So—what money Mom had left was pretty much taken.

Information about how Ted coped with the loss of his father may be translated into ways to cope with his own illness.

Therapist: How did your mom and sisters handle this?

Ted: Well, my sisters were pretty young. I don't know how much they remember. Mom never said much about it. She had to get a job. I know it wasn't easy for her, but she never complained—at least to me.

Therapist: So that helps me understand a few things. What helped you most to get through this?

Ted: I guess work—focusing on work. I had some good friends I could share things with. That's probably what's wrong here. We have just moved and we haven't met many people here.

Ted is beginning to recognize that his current lack of support makes his situation harder to accept.

Therapist: So Judy is your primary support.

Ted: Yes.

Judy: I don't mind that . . . I mean I want to be his primary support, but he complains all the time and worries that he will have a stroke and die, and I don't seem to be able to help him. I listen but . . . I don't know.

Therapist: What do you mean—you listen, but . . .?

Judy: I listen, but I find myself hearing the same thing over and over.

Ted: She tunes me out.

Therapist: Before we discuss this, I would like to know a little more about your situation, Judy. Tell me a little about your family and how you dealt with losses.

Knowledge of Judy's family of origin also helps the therapist understand how Judy deals with losses.

Judy: My father died suddenly . . . but that was after I left college.

Therapist: How many brothers and sisters do you have?

Judy: I have one younger brother . . . I pretty much had to look after him growing up.

Therapist: Why was this?

Judy: When I was in school, both of my parents worked long hours and weren't home much. I pretty much took care of myself.

Therapist: So you're used to handling things on your own. Sounds like both of you experienced losses at different stages of development.

Judy: I guess . . . but what I am having trouble with is Ted's fear . . . Just because he has diabetes doesn't mean he is going to have a stroke. His mood and everything have changed.

Therapist: Can you understand where some of his fear is coming from?

Judy: Yes, but he is not like his father. His father didn't take care of himself.

Ted: That's true, but I went through a lot at that time.

The therapist is helping both Judy and Ted understand the reasons for Ted's fears.

Rolland (1999) says that if a therapist can track the couple's coping abilities in the crisis, chronic, and terminal phases of the illness, they can uncover strengths as well as difficulties that might make them vulnerable at various phases of the current illness. As the therapist probes the couple's history, he or she should look for areas that might assist the couple with their current problem.

Therapist: Ted, how were you able to cope with your father's illness? What seemed to help?

Ted: I think I just focus on my work. I was taking a night course, also.

Therapist: So thinking about something else was helpful.

Ted: Yes, I felt more responsible when I was concentrating on my work. I felt like I was in control.

Therapist: Sounds like you overcame your fear and felt good about it.

Ted: Yes, I did. Looking back, I think I grew up. That part makes me feel good.

The therapist helps Ted recognize how he copes with illness and loss by recalling his coping skills when his father was ill.

Therapist: Do you think it's possible that you could overcome your fears now?

Ted: I'm sure it's possible. I know I complain a lot and that is what bothers Judy.

Therapist: Is that right, Judy?

Judy: Yes, he doesn't just worry about his illness. It seems to affect everything. His whole mood has changed.

Therapist: In what way?

The therapist encourages Ted to now use some of the coping tools he used earlier in his life.

Judy: He doesn't seem to be himself, and I can't do anything about it.

Ted: I didn't ask you to do anything.

Therapist: What about Judy's statement that you seem different?

Ted: Yeah, I suppose I haven't been myself. I get down about it—just thinking about it.

Therapist: When is that?

Ted: Most of the time, it's when I take my insulin shot. I really hate that. It gets to me. I wish I could take pills.

Therapist: Is that possible?

Ted: Maybe.

Therapist: I'm still intrigued how you were able to handle your father's illness by concentrating on your work. Do you see a possibility of doing that now?

Ted: I never thought about it. I'm pretty bored with my work. I guess I need to find something else.

The therapist must also be attuned to the role each partner played in his or her family of origin. Patterns and roles often get replicated. It is critical for the therapist to help the couple understand their experiences. Rolland states the following:

> Whether the parents (as children) were given too much responsibility (parentified) or shielded from involvement is of particular importance. What did they learn from these experiences that influences how they think about the current illness. Whether they emerge with a strong sense of competence or failure is essential information. By collecting . . . information about each adult's family of origin, one can anticipate areas of conflict and consensus. (p. 508)

Therapist: So, Ted, part of the problem is that you haven't found anything that interests you.

Judy: Or us . . . he isn't interested in going anywhere.

Therapist: Is that related to the illness or something else?

Ted: I guess Judy takes care of where we go and I just haven't been interested recently.

Therapist: Why not?

The therapist addresses withdrawal behaviors which are symptomatic of his fears.

Ted: I don't know. We have different interests, but it . . . um.

Therapist: I'm not sure what you're saying.

Ted: Sometimes I feel like going out, and other times I'm just not interested.

Therapist: So when was the last time you got interested in something?

Ted: I'm not sure.

Therapist: Think about it.

Judy: You used to like sailing.

Ted: Yes, but I sold my boat, and that just doesn't appeal to me anymore.

Therapist: So you don't find anything interesting?

Ted: Umm . . .

Judy: I've tried to get him interested in the theatre. We used to have season tickets and he liked . . .

Therapist: Judy, I think this is something Ted must figure out for himself. I think maybe you are playing the same role of caretaker here that you played in your family of origin.

The therapist instructs Ted rather than Judy to be responsible for finding something that interests him.

Judy: I'm not sure what you mean.

Therapist: Well, you took care of your family when your father died, and I think to some extent, you're taking care of Ted. Maybe you are too helpful. Ted never really has to figure out things for himself.

Judy: But I'm afraid he never will.

Therapist: I think that's when the trouble starts. You try to get him interested in something. He says he doesn't feel like it. Then you get upset, and he leaves the room.

The therapist points out the pattern of the couple and helps them see a way to behave differently.

Judy: So how should I handle it?

Therapist: How could Judy help here? I think she would like to spend more time with you. But when she tries, you seem to back off.

Ted: Sometimes I'm interested, but I just don't feel like it.

Dysfunctional complementarity that existed in the family of origin often gets replicated in the next generation. In this case, Judy becomes the helper and Ted the helpee. The therapist must be careful to recognize those instances when complementarity patterns are functional (assisting with his shots) and when they are dysfunctional (deciding what he should enjoy). Focusing only on the dysfunctional patterns presents a distorted pattern of the relationship and fails to build off the couple's strengths.

Therapist: How is Judy helpful to you?

Ted: Well, she helps me with my shots. She has everything ready and gives them to me at the appropriate times.

Therapist: What else?

Ted: Well, she's supportive. She's always optimistic that things will get better.

Therapist: How do you let her know when she is being helpful?

Ted: I'm not sure I do.

Judy: I know he appreciates it. He always thanks me.

Therapist: What you're saying is that there are times when you are very helpful and Ted appreciates it.

Ted: Yes.

Therapist: So how can Judy be helpful in finding an interest that would take your mind off the diabetes?

Ted: If she would let me be, I can do it.

Therapist: I think she can back off but I think she needs some reassurance that you will do something—preferably with her.

Ted: It isn't her. There are just times I don't feel like doing anything.

Therapist: I think she can live with it. You don't feel that way all the time?

Ted: No.

Therapist: What can she expect here? You said that when your father was sick, you focused on your work and that helped.

Ted: I know . . . and I think that would help . . . but . . .

Therapist: But, what?

Ted: I want to find something. I think if Judy will give me a chance . . .

Judy: I will, but I'd like to know that things will be different.

Therapist: Okay, we'll get back together in two weeks. Before we get back, Ted, I would like you to plan something for both of you—something you would enjoy.

The therapist instructs the couple to do two things: (1) Ted will take charge of planning something for them, and (2) Judy will let him.

Ted: When?

Therapist: I think you ought to plan it around time when you are feeling better. When is that?

Ted: I generally feel better about an hour after my shot.

Therapist: So that might be a good time to plan it. Judy, I think the hard part for you will be to sit back and let Ted make the plans. That will be a new role for you.

Judy: Yeah, it will be hard.

Therapist: What would help here?

Judy: To know that Ted would do it.

Therapist: How can you let her know that this will happen?

Ted: Maybe come up with a date and time.

Judy: That would be great. So when will it be?

Ted: How about next Saturday at 6:00? I will plan something.

Therapist: Good. I wouldn't expect things to change right away. You will probably be somewhat focused on the diabetes, but in time, I think this plan will work.

The therapist wants the couple to realize that this is only a start. Changes are relatively slow.

When symptoms have become chronic—such as when one partner (Judy) is trying to help the other (Ted) change—it is often wise to take a cautious position about the timing and amount of change. In such cases, restraining interventions may be used to help the therapist move at an optimal pace. In essence, the therapist is saying, "I'm not sure this change would be beneficial. I realize the problem has certain disadvantages, but there may be benefits to this situation that need to be identified first, so that improvement in one part of your life won't lead to unforeseen consequences elsewhere." What might happen if this problem were solved? As couples are encouraged to identify certain dilemmas that may have been covert, the therapist offers genuineness and warmth to the couple in addressing these unforeseen consequences before change occurs.

Summary

This case provides an example for using a developmental approach to examining chronic illness in a couple. The therapist focuses on each partner's role in his or her family of origin around illness and how these roles are enacted in the current relationship. Dysfunctional patterns and strengths are examined to understand how the couple is coping with the current problem. The therapist emphasizes current strengths to develop new interactional patterns around the illness. Finally, in the case of chronic problems, the therapist helps the couple to understand the consequences of their change.

DUAL CAREER COUPLES—
THE CASE OF LARRY AND SUSAN

Dual career couples present a special set of problems for the marital therapist. "Dual-career" refers to a couple who both have jobs that are fulfilling, require commitment, demand responsibility, and provide opportunities for "moving up." In such a marriage, both spouses work to experience self-fulfillment as well as economic rewards, and the jobs are equally important. That is, if one person is asked to transfer, the decision is not automatic, particularly if it interferes with the career of the other.

Recent statistics indicate that 20 percent of all working couples are dual career couples (Stolz-Loike, 1992). While those couples may earn more money, their lifestyles can be stressful and demanding, putting great strains on marital relationships. Although there are definite payoffs for each mate to have a satisfying and challenging career (more money, a better understanding of some of the stressors the other feels and therefore better ability to provide support, more stimulating conversations, and so on), the marriage may suffer at times, and each partner may experience some isolation. The couple must learn to deal with various stressors inherent in a situation where both partners have demanding careers.

In a dual career relationship, each partner has a role both as a mate and homemaker as well as a worker. In this situation, there's much potential for conflict, and in fact, divorce rates are higher for professional women and women with higher salaries. Some specific sources of conflict are experienced when couples have to deal with issues such as those below:

1. How are roles determined?

   The children have parent/teacher conferences. Both parents are busy. Who goes?

   Who is in charge of child care?

   Who takes care of household chores such as cooking, laundry, helping children with homework?

   Who takes care of the child who is ill?

   How were chores allotted in the families of origin?

2. Whose job takes priority?

   If one partner is offered a promotion in another city, does the other follow? How is this decision made?

3. How is time allotted?

   What takes priority—work duties or family activities?

4. How does the couple deal with work problems? Do those spill over into the home and create additional stress that ends in problems?

5. Do family problems cause difficulties at work?

6. With time constraints, how does the couple maintain time to enhance intimacy?

Larry and Susan, a dual career couple, have had to deal with many of these stressors. Larry works as a life insurance salesman with a large company and Susan is an independent interior decorator. They have been married three years and have a one-year-old child. They have come to therapy because both partners are feeling dissatisfaction in the marriage and report that they seem to clash on every issue they discuss.

Therapist: So what seems to be the problem?

Larry: I don't know. We just haven't been getting along for some time.

Susan: It's more than that.

Therapist: What do you mean?

Susan: We just don't seem to be happy. Well, I'm not happy . . . and we just don't ever talk to each other or have any fun.

The therapist initially probes to find out what the couple's concerns are. Later, the therapist will help them state the problem in operational terms.

Therapist: How long has this been going on?

Susan: It has gotten terrible over the past six months. Every time we say something to each other, it ends in a huge argument. We have a child who just had her first birthday, and I think the arguing is going to affect her.

Larry: It's been worse since we moved here.

Therapist: When did you move here?

Susan: About ten months ago. Larry got transferred, which meant I had to find a new job.

Therapist: What do you do?

Susan: I'm an interior decorator. I'm on my own now, but back in St. Louis, I worked for a department store. Larry sells life insurance.

Therapist: So you didn't have all the arguments before moving here.

Getting information about the history of the problem helps to understand it. In this case, changes seem to be related to the move and to additional responsibilities with the birth of a child.

Susan: We were happy there. Of course, we were both fairly settled since we had gone to school there and were very familiar with the area. And we both liked our jobs. When I got pregnant, we were both really happy and excited and Larry stayed very involved right until Megan was born. She has been a joy, but she has certainly changed our lives.

Larry: I think things were even more different than she's saying. She was a lot more supportive of me *and* my job, and seemed to understand how important it was for me to build a clientele. She had a job with set hours, and it was just easier. It seems like now that I'm again in a situation where I have to beat the bushes finding clients, she expects me to be home at a certain time, help take care of the house and the baby, and just ignore all the phone calls I should be making. It's almost like she expects me to put my career on hold so she can focus more on her own.

Susan: I do understand that your career is important, but I also have to build up a clientele, now that I'm on my own. And— if you remember, having the baby was a joint decision. We talked then about how we'll both have more responsibilities.

Therapist: It sounds like you have two issues going here—both of you trying to establish careers and both seeming overwhelmed with the responsibility of caring for the baby and household chores.

Larry: Right. I feel I should help some with the baby, but you know, my mother was a teacher, and she took care of the house and family and never expected my dad to be doing cooking—or laundry, of all things.

Susan: We talked about responsibilities with a new baby and Larry agreed that he should help. But now that the baby's here, he seems to have changed his mind.

Larry: I'm willing to help some. I just don't have the time to be doing laundry—or cleaning—or watching the baby all the time.

Here the therapist gets an idea of Larry's family of origin expectations of what a man does and what a woman does. Before the couple can resolve their conflict, they will have to negotiate new roles and perhaps be able to give up some of their old ideas. That is they must be willing to change sex-role

Therapist: It sounds like when you discussed the baby and agreed that both would be involved, that you had different interpretations of what that involvement would be.

Susan: I guess so. But even if we agreed on that, it just seems that there's not much good going on between us. There's almost no affection, and we never do anything together. We don't even talk—except to argue. I don't even know what's going on in his job now and he definitely doesn't know what I'm doing.

Therapist: So you would like to talk more, have more fun, and be more affectionate with each other.

Susan: Yes.

Larry: You know, I've talked with you about that. I feel like you have no time for me. When I have suggested we go out, you say you're too tired. When I've tried to talk with you, you won't talk. I asked you last Friday if you wanted to go to a movie and you said no.

Susan: We didn't have a baby sitter, and I was just exhausted. I had been up late the night before when Megan was sick.

Therapist: What did you want Larry to do?

Susan: I was hoping he would help with the baby and then maybe we could have done something at home if we couldn't go out. But since we didn't have a sitter and couldn't go out, he just read the newspaper and watched television.

Therapist: Did you ask him to help?

Susan: No, I could just tell he didn't want to do anything.

Therapist: Larry, would you have been willing to do something else if Susan had asked?

Larry: Sure. I get tired of sitting around by myself all the time.

Therapist: Would you have been willing to help Susan with some chores so the two of you could have done something?

definitions in a way that satisfies both parties.

Larry: Yes. She didn't ask me.

Therapist: It sounds like the two of you have experienced a lot of changes in the past year. You moved from an area you both liked, Larry has a new clientele base here, Susan has a job that requires more than her previous one . . . and on top of that, you have a new baby. Your lives have changed a lot, but you haven't talked or planned on how you can deal with these changes. In fact, it sounds like you have not talked about what each of you would like from the other.

Larry: Yeah, you're right. I guess I hadn't thought about all the changes, and it just seems like we've stopped talking.

If the therapist states the problem in ways that the couple will "buy" it, they will be more willing to work on a solution. By addressing it in terms of all the "changes," the couple is less likely to assess blame to each other and be more open to negotiation. The therapist may also relate to this couple that after the birth of a child, it is fairly normal for a couple to experience less marital satisfaction (Gottman, 1998), which may also contribute to some of their conflict.

It will also be essential for the therapist to confront ideas about gender-role expectations. Susan's expectation is that Larry will help while he obviously sees some tasks such as doing laundry or house cleaning as inappropriate for him. As the therapist deals with the gender-role conflicts, he or she must also treat this as a couple problem, rather than Larry's problem (that he's unwilling to help) or Susan's problem (that she expects too much).

Clients differ in their willingness to consider an equitable distribution of responsibilities, and the therapist must be somewhat cautious about bringing up this idea too soon. Some therapists prefer to use psychoeducational formats to address this issue because attitudes may be changed more effectively in a group setting where couples share how they divide up chores or deal with the needs of both spouses. One such workshop has been developed by Amatea and Cross (1983). In this format, couples discuss expectations and coping styles and learn how to make decisions jointly.

Another less threatening technique to use is to have partners complete surveys of gender roles and then discuss these. Young and Long (1998) give an example of such a survey which identifies various household chores and asks the partners to identify who performs the tasks (mainly man, mainly woman, together, or half/half). It also directs couples to talk about who did those kinds of tasks in their families of origin.

There is not a set formula for an effective resolution. Some couples may agree that chores should be divided equally while others may be able to function well with an unequal distribution. The important thing is to help the couple negotiate roles and responsibilities in a way that is acceptable to both.

Therapist: Let's see if I can summarize your concerns. Susan, you would like more help from Larry and you would also like to have a more affectionate relationship. Larry, you also would like to have more time with Susan since you're feeling neglected.

> The therapist begins to summarize concerns to prepare for prioritizing which areas need to be addressed first.

Susan: Yeah, I get really irritated sometimes when I'm doing most of the chores around home and I think Larry sees them as all my responsibility. I also resent that my job comes last. If someone has to stay home when Megan is sick, why is it always me?

Larry: Look, some days I'm putting in ten hours and am driving an hour to get home. So—I'm tired when I get home. And—when Megan's sick, you seem to want to be with her anyway.

Therapist: You both have stated that you want more time together and to get some of the fun and intimacy back into your relationship. What would help the two of you to work this out?

Larry: Well, I didn't know it was such a big deal to her. There are some things I'd be willing to do to help.

Susan: That would make me feel a lot better if you would take on some of the regular chores at home and if you would be willing to cook occasionally.

With the therapist's help, the couple has indicated that they are experiencing a "partnership" problem, with Susan having an unequal amount of responsibility and as a result doing little to support Larry. They have agreed that there are many day-to-day tasks that need to be done and that both should be responsible. The therapist's task at this point is to help the couple negotiate/problem solve how to get these chores done. Larry has assumed that because his mother did all the chores associated with children and housework, that his wife will also. Susan has been reluctant to talk with him about those things, and instead, has felt resentful that he has not helped.

After the chore distribution is made, the couple is then ready to deal with other concerns: how to have more time together, and how to bring back the fun and intimacy to their marriage.

Therapist: Susan and Larry, it seems that you have been so wrapped up in the everyday pressures of work and having a child that you have forgotten to be supportive and nurturing of each other. When was the last time you did something together that you really enjoyed? What made that happen?

Susan: We used to go out every Friday night, and it was great. It was the end of the week, we could let down, and it was a good time to just talk to each other about things that happened throughout the week. We just got into a habit of doing that.

Larry: Yeah, I really looked forward to Fridays.

Therapist: What happened to Fridays?

Susan: (Laughing) The baby!

Therapist: Is there some way you could continue those times? Is there someone you could get to baby sit on a regular basis?

Susan: Well, maybe I could get my niece. She likes Megan and I feel more comfortable leaving Megan now that she's a little older.

The therapist helps the couple reestablish some of the rituals that they had when they were first married. The therapist uses a solution-focused approach to emphasize positives and the possibilities for change.

The therapist continues to probe about rituals that the couple can establish to ensure that they have time together. If they can't have dinner together every night, they may be able to set aside a couple of nights a week. Friday night could be "date night." Rituals may be set up around successes at work—celebrations for promotions, a large sale for Larry, completion of a design project for Susan, or even a few minutes set aside at night to talk about the day.

The couple will also need to deal with ways to support each other in their careers and will need to reevaluate on a regular basis to ensure that they are continuing the rituals and negotiations. They will also need to identify ways to solve conflicts when their plans get derailed or do not work the way they had envisioned initially.

CONCLUSION

The dual-career couple is experiencing a lifestyle that is different from that of their parents. While this lifestyle has many rewards, it is also fraught with stresses and pressures. Both partners usually are committed to careers as well as relationships, and some of the conflicts they experience are quite different from those of other couples. Some basic issues they must resolve include whose career, if either, takes precedence; how they deal with everyday demands in the home and with children, if they have children; how they prioritize their time; and how they continue to support each other and nurture their relationship. The therapist who works with dual-career couples must be sensitive to expectations each partner has brought from his or her own family of origin, and be cautious but involved in helping the couple negotiate an equitable/workable division of labor and change some of those expectations of gender role.

In the case of Larry and Susan, the therapist helped the couple identify the area of conflict, express changes they would like, negotiate those changes, and build ways of maintaining a closer relationship through rituals and mutual support.

KEY POINTS

- Successful marital therapy cannot occur when the therapist keeps important information about one partner (such as an affair) secret from the other.
- It is critical for the therapist to assess the marriage for physical violence.
- As the therapist begins to see progress in treatment, he or she must plan for relapse.
- A couple can survive an affair if they are willing to commit themselves to improving the relationship.
- Considerable evidence exists that divorce can increase the likelihood of adverse effects on the psychological well-being of families, particularly those with children.
- In remarried families, the therapist must help the biological parent to restructure the boundaries to make room for the spouse, letting him or her become a part of the family.
- Lesbians and gay men often lack support and validation for their relationship by society.
- Because so many marital problems are related to alcohol problems, it is the therapist's responsibility to assess this area.
- The therapist who works with chronic illness must consider the interface between an individual spouse's illnesses and the couple's developmental stage.

REFERENCES

Ahrons, C. R. (1999). Divorce: An unscheduled family transition. In B. Carter & M. McGoldrick (Eds.). *The expanded family life cycle: Individual, family and social perspectives.* (3rd ed.) Needham Heights, MA: Allyn & Bacon.

Amatea, E. S., & Cross, E. G. (1983). Coupling and careers: A workshop for dual-career couples at the launching stage. *The Personnel and Guidance Journal, 62,* 48–52.

Brown, J. H., Portes, P. R., & Christensen, D. N. (1989). Understanding divorce stress on children: Implications for research and practice. *American Journal of Family Therapy, 17,* 315–325.

Carter, B., & McGoldrick, M. (Eds.)/ (1999). *The expanded family life cycle: Individual, family and social perspectives* (3rd ed.). Needham Heights, MA: Allyn & Bacon.

Gottman, J. (1998). Clinical Manual for Marital Therapy. Seattle, WA: The Seattle Marital and Family Institute.

Hetherington, E. M. (1990, March 23). *Remarriage, lies & videotape.* Presidential address to the Society for Research on Adolescence, Atlanta, GA.

Hudak, J., Krestan, J. A., & Bepko, C. (1999). Alcohol problems and the family life cycle. In B. Carter & M. McGoldrick (Eds.), *The expanded family life cycle: Individual, family and social perspectives.* (3rd Ed.) Needham Heights, MA: Allyn & Bacon.

Imber-Black, E., & Roberts, J. (1992). *Rituals for our times: Celebrating, healing, and changing our lives and our relationships.* New York: HarperCollins.

Johnson, T. W., & Colucci, P. (1999). Lesbians, gay men, and the family life cycle. In B. Carter & M. McGoldrick (Eds.). *The expanded family life cycle: Individual, family and social perspectives* (3rd Ed.), Needham Heights, MA: Allyn & Bacon.

Kurdek, L. A., & Berg, B. (1983). Correlates of children's adjustment to their parent's divorce. In L. A. Kurdek (Ed.), *Children and divorce* (pp. 47–60). San Francisco: Jossey-Bass.

Lamb, M., Sternberg, K., & Thompson, R. (1997). The effects of divorce and custody arrangements on children's behavior development and adjustment. *Family and Conciliation Courts Review, 35,* 393–404.

Pittman, F. S., & Wagers, T. P. (1995). Crisis of infidelity. In N. Jacobson & A. Gurman (Eds.), *Clinical handbook of couple therapy* (pp. 295–316). New York: Guilford Press.

Rolland, J. S. (1999). Chronic illness and the family life cycle. In B. Carter & M. McGoldrick (Eds.). *The expanded family life cycle: Individual, family and social perspectives.* (3rd Ed.) Needham Heights, MA: Allyn & Bacon.

Santrock, J. W., & Warshak, R. A. (1979). Father custody and social development in boys and girls. *Journal of Social Issues, 35,* 112–125.

Stolz-Loike, M. (1992). *Dual-career couples: New perspectives in counseling.* Alexandria, VA: American Association for Counseling and Development.

Treadway, David. (1987). The ties that bind: Both alcoholics and their families are bound to the bottle. Family Networker, July-August, 17–23.

Visher, E. B. & Visher, J. S. (1996) *Therapy with stepfamilies.* New York: Brunner/Mazel.

Wallerstein, J. (1987). Children of divorce: A ten-year study. In E. M. Hetherington & J. D. Aresteh (Eds.) *The impact of divorce, single parenting and stepparenting on children* (pp. 197–214). Hillsdale, NJ: Lawrence Erlbaum Asssoc.

Walsh, F., & McGoldrick, M. (1991). *Living beyond loss: Death and the family.* New York: Norton.

Young, Mark, & Long, L. (1998). *Counseling and therapy for couples.* Pacific Grove, CA: Brooks/Cole.

Appendix A

✳

CODE OF ETHICS AND STANDARDS OF PRACTICE OF THE AMERICAN COUNSELING ASSOCIATION

ACA Code of Ethics Preamble

The American Counseling Association is an educational, scientific, and professional organization whose members are dedicated to the enhancement of human development throughout the life-span. Association members recognize diversity in our society and embrace a cross-cultural approach in support of the worth, dignity, potential, and uniqueness of each individual.

The specification of a code of ethics enables the association to clarify to current and future members, and to those served by members, the nature of the ethical responsibilities held in common by its members. As the code of ethics of the association, this document establishes principles that define the ethical behavior of association members. All members of the American Counseling Association are required to adhere to the Code of Ethics and the Standards of Practice. The Code of Ethics will serve as the basis for processing ethical complaints initiated against members of the association.

ACA CODE OF ETHICS

Section A: The Counseling Relationship

Section B: Confidentiality

Section C: Professional Responsibility

Section D: Relationships With Other Professionals

Section E: Evaluation, Assessment, and Interpretation

Section F: Teaching, Training, and Supervision

Section G: Research and Publication

Section H: Resolving Ethical Issues

SOURCE: Copyright © ACA. Reprinted with permission. No further reproduction authorized without written permission of the American Counseling Association.

Section A: The Counseling Relationship

A.1. Client Welfare

a. Primary Responsibility. The primary responsibility of counselors is to respect the dignity and to promote the welfare of clients.

b. Positive Growth and Development. Counselors encourage client growth and development in ways that foster the clients' interest and welfare; counselors avoid fostering dependent counseling relationships.

c. Counseling Plans. Counselors and their clients work jointly in devising integrated, individual counseling plans that offer reasonable promise of success and are consistent with abilities and circumstances of clients. Counselors and clients regularly review counseling plans to ensure their continued viability and effectiveness, respecting clients' freedom of choice. (See A.3.b.)

d. Family Involvement. Counselors recognize that families are usually important in clients' lives and strive to enlist family understanding and involvement as a positive resource, when appropriate.

e. Career and Employment Needs. Counselors work with their clients in considering employment in jobs and circumstances that are consistent with the clients' overall abilities, vocational limitations, physical restrictions, general temperament, interest and aptitude patterns, social skills, education, general qualifications, and other relevant characteristics and needs. Counselors neither place nor participate in placing clients in positions that will result in damaging the interest and the welfare of clients, employers, or the public.

A.2. Respecting Diversity

a. Nondiscrimination. Counselors do not condone or engage in discrimination based on age, color, culture, disability, ethnic group, gender, race, religion, sexual orientation, marital status, or socioeconomic status. (See C.5.a., C.5.b., and D.1.i.)

b. Respecting Differences. Counselors will actively attempt to understand the diverse cultural backgrounds of the clients with whom they work. This includes, but is not limited to, learning how the counselor's own cultural/ethnic/racial identity impacts her or his values and beliefs about the counseling process. (See E.8. and F.2.i.)

A.3. Client Rights

a. Disclosure to Clients. When counseling is initiated, and throughout the counseling process as necessary, counselors inform clients of the purposes, goals, techniques, procedures, limitations, potential risks, and benefits of services to be performed, and other pertinent information. Counselors take steps to ensure that clients understand the implications of diagnosis, the intended use of tests and reports, fees, and billing arrangements. Clients have the right to expect confidentiality and to be provided with an explanation of its limitations, including supervision and/or treatment team professionals; to obtain clear information about their case records; to participate in the ongoing counseling plans; and to refuse any recommended services and be advised of the consequences of such refusal. (See E.5.a. and G.2.)

b. Freedom of Choice. Counselors offer clients the freedom to choose whether to enter into a counseling relationship and to determine which professional(s) will provide counseling. Restrictions that limit choices of clients are fully explained. (See A.1.c.)

c. Inability to Give Consent. When counseling minors or persons unable to give volun-
    tary informed consent, counselors act in these clients' best interests. (See B.3.)

A.4. Clients Served by Others

If a client is receiving services from another mental health professional, counselors, with
client consent, inform the professional persons already involved and develop clear agreements to avoid confusion and conflict for the client. (See C.6.c.)

A.5. Personal Needs and Values

a. Personal Needs. In the counseling relationship, counselors are aware of the intimacy and
    responsibilities inherent in the counseling relationship, maintain respect for clients, and
    avoid actions that seek to meet their personal needs at the expense of clients.

b. Personal Values. Counselors are aware of their own values, attitudes, beliefs, and behav-
    iors and how these apply in a diverse society, and avoid imposing their values on clients.
    (See C.5.a.)

A.6. Dual Relationships

a. Avoid When Possible. Counselors are aware of their influential positions with respect to
    clients, and they avoid exploiting the trust and dependency of clients. Counselors make
    every effort to avoid dual relationships with clients that could impair professional judg-
    ment or increase the risk of harm to clients. (Examples of such relationships include, but
    are not limited to, familial, social, financial, business, or close personal relationships with
    clients.) When a dual relationship cannot be avoided, counselors take appropriate profes-
    sional precautions such as informed consent, consultation, supervision, and documenta-
    tion to ensure that judgment is not impaired and no exploitation occurs. (See F.1.b.)

b. Superior/Subordinate Relationships. Counselors do not accept as clients superiors or sub-
    ordinates with whom they have administrative, supervisory, or evaluative relationships.

A.7. Sexual Intimacies With Clients

a. Current Clients. Counselors do not have any type of sexual intimacies with clients and
    do not counsel persons with whom they have had a sexual relationship.

b. Former Clients. Counselors do not engage in sexual intimacies with former clients
    within a minimum of 2 years after terminating the counseling relationship. Counselors
    who engage in such relationship after 2 years following termination have the responsi-
    bility to examine and document thoroughly that such relations did not have an exploita-
    tive nature, based on factors such as duration of counseling, amount of time since
    counseling, termination circumstances, client's personal history and mental status,
    adverse impact on the client, and actions by the counselor suggesting a plan to initiate
    a sexual relationship with the client after termination.

A.8. Multiple Clients

When counselors agree to provide counseling services to two or more persons who have a
relationship (such as husband and wife, or parents and children), counselors clarify at the
outset which person or persons are clients and the nature of the relationships they will have
with each involved person. If it becomes apparent that counselors may be called upon to
perform potentially conflicting roles, they clarify, adjust, or withdraw from roles appropriately. (See B.2. and B.4.d.)

A.9. Group Work

a. Screening. Counselors screen prospective group counseling/therapy participants. To the extent possible, counselors select members whose needs and goals are compatible with goals of the group, who will not impede the group process, and whose well-being will not be jeopardized by the group experience.

b. Protecting Clients. In a group setting, counselors take reasonable precautions to protect clients from physical or psychological trauma.

A.10. Fees and Bartering (See D.3.a. and D.3.b.)

a. Advance Understanding. Counselors clearly explain to clients, prior to entering the counseling relationship, all financial arrangements related to professional services including the use of collection agencies or legal measures for nonpayment. (A.11.c.)

b. Establishing Fees. In establishing fees for professional counseling services, counselors consider the financial status of clients and locality. In the event that the established fee structure is inappropriate for a client, assistance is provided in attempting to find comparable services of acceptable cost. (See A.10.d., D.3.a., and D.3.b.)

c. Bartering Discouraged. Counselors ordinarily refrain from accepting goods or services from clients in return for counseling services because such arrangements create inherent potential for conflicts, exploitation, and distortion of the professional relationship. Counselors may participate in bartering only if the relationship is not exploitative, if the client requests it, if a clear written contract is established, and if such arrangements are an accepted practice among professionals in the community. (See A.6.a.)

d. Pro Bono Service. Counselors contribute to society by devoting a portion of their professional activity to services for which there is little or no financial return (pro bono).

A.11. Termination and Referral

a. Abandonment Prohibited. Counselors do not abandon or neglect clients in counseling. Counselors assist in making appropriate arrangements for the continuation of treatment, when necessary, during interruptions such as vacations, and following termination.

b. Inability to Assist Clients. If counselors determine an inability to be of professional assistance to clients, they avoid entering or immediately terminate a counseling relationship. Counselors are knowledgeable about referral resources and suggest appropriate alternatives. If clients decline the suggested referral, counselors should discontinue the relationship.

c. Appropriate Termination. Counselors terminate a counseling relationship, securing client agreement when possible, when it is reasonably clear that the client is no longer benefiting, when services are no longer required, when counseling no longer serves the client's needs or interests, when clients do not pay fees charged, or when agency or institution limits do not allow provision of further counseling services. (See A.10.b. and C.2.g.)

A.12. Computer Technology

a. Use of Computers. When computer applications are used in counseling services, counselors ensure that (1) the client is intellectually, emotionally, and physically capable of using the computer application; (2) the computer application is appropriate for the needs of the client; (3) the client understands the purpose and operation of the computer applications; and (4) a follow-up of client use of a computer application is provided to correct possible misconceptions, discover inappropriate use, and assess subsequent needs.

b.   Explanation of Limitations. Counselors ensure that clients are provided information as a part of the counseling relationship that adequately explains the limitations of computer technology.

c.   Access to Computer Applications. Counselors provide for equal access to computer applications in counseling services. (See A.2.a.)

Section B: Confidentiality

B.1. Right to Privacy

a.   Respect for Privacy. Counselors respect their clients right to privacy and avoid illegal and unwarranted disclosures of confidential information. (See A.3.a. and B.6.a.)

b.   Client Waiver. The right to privacy may be waived by the client or his or her legally recognized representative.

c.   Exceptions. The general requirement that counselors keep information confidential does not apply when disclosure is required to prevent clear and imminent danger to the client or others or when legal requirements demand that confidential information be revealed. Counselors consult with other professionals when in doubt as to the validity of an exception.

d.   Contagious, Fatal Diseases. A counselor who receives information confirming that a client has a disease commonly known to be both communicable and fatal is justified in disclosing information to an identifiable third party, who by his or her relationship with the client is at a high risk of contracting the disease. Prior to making a disclosure the counselor should ascertain that the client has not already informed the third party about his or her disease and that the client is not intending to inform the third party in the immediate future. (See B.1.c and B.1.f.)

e.   Court-Ordered Disclosure. When court ordered to release confidential information without a client's permission, counselors request to the court that the disclosure not be required due to potential harm to the client or counseling relationship. (See B.1.c.)

f.   Minimal Disclosure. When circumstances require the disclosure of confidential information, only essential information is revealed. To the extent possible, clients are informed before confidential information is disclosed.

g.   Explanation of Limitations. When counseling is initiated and throughout the counseling process as necessary, counselors inform clients of the limitations of confidentiality and identify foreseeable situations in which confidentiality must be breached. (See G.2.a.)

h.   Subordinates. Counselors make every effort to ensure that privacy and confidentiality of clients are maintained by subordinates including employees, supervisees, clerical assistants, and volunteers. (See B.1.a.)

i.   Treatment Teams. If client treatment will involve a continued review by a treatment team, the client will be informed of the team's existence and composition.

B.2. Groups and Families

a.   Group Work. In group work, counselors clearly define confidentiality and the parameters for the specific group being entered, explain its importance, and discuss the difficulties related to confidentiality involved in group work. The fact that confidentiality cannot be guaranteed is clearly communicated to group members.

b. Family Counseling. In family counseling, information about one family member cannot be disclosed to another member without permission. Counselors protect the privacy rights of each family member. (See A.8., B.3., and B.4.d.)

B.3. Minor or Incompetent Clients

When counseling clients who are minors or individuals who are unable to give voluntary, informed consent, parents or guardians may be included in the counseling process as appropriate. Counselors act in the best interests of clients and take measures to safeguard confidentiality. (See A.3.c.)

B.4. Records

a. Requirement of Records. Counselors maintain records necessary for rendering professional services to their clients and as required by laws, regulations, or agency or institution procedures.

b. Confidentiality of Records. Counselors are responsible for securing the safety and confidentiality of any counseling records they create, maintain, transfer, or destroy whether the records are written, taped, computerized, or stored in any other medium. (See B.1.a.)

c. Permission to Record or Observe. Counselors obtain permission from clients prior to electronically recording or observing sessions. (See A.3.a.)

d. Client Access. Counselors recognize that counseling records are kept for the benefit of clients, and therefore provide access to records and copies of records when requested by competent clients, unless the records contain information that may be misleading and detrimental to the client. In situations involving multiple clients, access to records is limited to those parts of records that do not include confidential information related to another client. (See A.8., B.1.a., and B.2.b.)

e. Disclosure or Transfer. Counselors obtain written permission from clients to disclose or transfer records to legitimate third parties unless exceptions to confidentiality exist as listed in Section B.1. Steps are taken to ensure that receivers of counseling records are sensitive to their confidential nature.

B.5. Research and Training

a. Data Disguise Required. Use of data derived from counseling relationships for purposes of training, research, or publication is confined to content that is disguised to ensure the anonymity of the individuals involved. (See B.1.g. and G.3.d.)

b. Agreement for Identification. Identification of a client in a presentation or publication is permissible only when the client has reviewed the material and has agreed to its presentation or publication. (See G.3.d.)

B.6. Consultation

a. Respect for Privacy. Information obtained in a consulting relationship is discussed for professional purposes only with persons clearly concerned with the case. Written and oral reports present data germane to the purposes of the consultation, and every effort is made to protect client identity and avoid undue invasion of privacy.

b. Cooperating Agencies. Before sharing information, counselors make efforts to ensure that there are defined policies in other agencies serving the counselor's clients that effectively protect the confidentiality of information.

Section C: Professional Responsibility

C.1. Standards Knowledge

Counselors have a responsibility to read, understand, and follow the Code of Ethics and the Standards of Practice.

C.2. Professional Competence

a. Boundaries of Competence. Counselors practice only within the boundaries of their competence, based on their education, training, supervised experience, state and national professional credentials, and appropriate professional experience. Counselors will demonstrate a commitment to gain knowledge, personal awareness, sensitivity, and skills pertinent to working with a diverse client population.

b. New Specialty Areas of Practice. Counselors practice in specialty areas new to them only after appropriate education, training, and supervised experience. While developing skills in new specialty areas, counselors take steps to ensure the competence of their work and to protect others from possible harm.

c. Qualified for Employment. Counselors accept employment only for positions for which they are qualified by education, training, supervised experience, state and national professional credentials, and appropriate professional experience. Counselors hire for professional counseling positions only individuals who are qualified and competent.

d. Monitor Effectiveness. Counselors continually monitor their effectiveness as professionals and take steps to improve when necessary. Counselors in private practice take reasonable steps to seek out peer supervision to evaluate their efficacy as counselors.

e. Ethical Issues Consultation. Counselors take reasonable steps to consult with other counselors or related professionals when they have questions regarding their ethical obligations or professional practice. (See H.1.)

f. Continuing Education. Counselors recognize the need for continuing education to maintain a reasonable level of awareness of current scientific and professional information in their fields of activity. They take steps to maintain competence in the skills they use, are open to new procedures, and keep current with the diverse and/or special populations with whom they work.

g. Impairment. Counselors refrain from offering or accepting professional services when their physical, mental, or emotional problems are likely to harm a client or others. They are alert to the signs of impairment, seek assistance for problems, and, if necessary, limit, suspend, or terminate their professional responsibilities. (See A.11.c.)

C.3. Advertising and Soliciting Clients

a. Accurate Advertising. There are no restrictions on advertising by counselors except those that can be specifically justified to protect the public from deceptive practices. Counselors advertise or represent their services to the public by identifying their credentials in an accurate manner that is not false, misleading, deceptive, or fraudulent. Counselors may only advertise the highest degree earned which is in counseling or a closely related field from a college or university that was accredited when the degree was awarded by one of the regional accrediting bodies recognized by the Council on Postsecondary Accreditation.

b. Testimonials. Counselors who use testimonials do not solicit them from clients or other persons who, because of their particular circumstances, may be vulnerable to undue influence.

c. Statements by Others. Counselors make reasonable efforts to ensure that statements made by others about them or the profession of counseling are accurate.

d. Recruiting Through Employment. Counselors do not use their places of employment or institutional affiliation to recruit or gain clients, supervisees, or consultees for their private practices. (See C.5.e.)

e. Products and Training Advertisements. Counselors who develop products related to their profession or conduct workshops or training events ensure that the advertisements concerning these products or events are accurate and disclose adequate information for consumers to make informed choices.

f. Promoting to Those Served. Counselors do not use counseling, teaching, training, or supervisory relationships to promote their products or training events in a manner that is deceptive or would exert undue influence on individuals who may be vulnerable. Counselors may adopt textbooks they have authored for instruction purposes.

g. Professional Association Involvement. Counselors actively participate in local, state, and national associations that foster the development and improvement of counseling.

C.4. Credentials

a. Credentials Claimed. Counselors claim or imply only professional credentials possessed and are responsible for correcting any known misrepresentations of their credentials by others. Professional credentials include graduate degrees in counseling or closely related mental health fields, accreditation of graduate programs, national voluntary certifications, government-issued certifications or licenses, ACA professional membership, or any other credential that might indicate to the public specialized knowledge or expertise in counseling.

b. ACA Professional Membership. ACA professional members may announce to the public their membership status. Regular members may not announce their ACA membership in a manner that might imply they are credentialed counselors.

c. Credential Guidelines. Counselors follow the guidelines for use of credentials that have been established by the entities that issue the credentials.

d. Misrepresentation of Credentials. Counselors do not attribute more to their credentials than the credentials represent, and do not imply that other counselors are not qualified because they do not possess certain credentials.

e. Doctoral Degrees From Other Fields. Counselors who hold a master's degree in counseling or a closely related mental health field, but hold a doctoral degree from other than counseling or a closely related field, do not use the title "Dr." in their practices and do not announce to the public in relation to their practice or status as a counselor that they hold a doctorate.

C.5. Public Responsibility

a. Nondiscrimination. Counselors do not discriminate against clients, students, or supervisees in a manner that has a negative impact based on their age, color, culture, disability, ethnic group, gender, race, religion, sexual orientation, or socioeconomic status, or for any other reason. (See A.2.a.)

b. Sexual Harassment. Counselors do not engage in sexual harassment. Sexual harassment is defined as sexual solicitation, physical advances, or verbal or nonverbal conduct that is sexual in nature, that occurs in connection with professional activities or roles, and that either (1) is unwelcome, is offensive, or creates a hostile workplace environment,

and counselors know or are told this; or (2) is sufficiently severe or intense to be perceived as harassment to a reasonable person in the context. Sexual harassment can con-
sist of a single intense or severe act or multiple persistent or pervasive acts.

c. Reports to Third Parties. Counselors are accurate, honest, and unbiased in reporting
    their professional activities and judgments to appropriate third parties including courts,
    health insurance companies, those who are the recipients of evaluation reports, and oth-
    ers. (See B.1.g.)

d. Media Presentations. When counselors provide advice or comment by means of public
    lectures, demonstrations, radio or television programs, prerecorded tapes, printed arti-
    cles, mailed material, or other media, they take reasonable precautions to ensure that
    (1) the statements are based on appropriate professional counseling literature and prac-
    tice; (2) the statements are otherwise consistent with the Code of Ethics and the
    Standards of Practice; and (3) the recipients of the information are not encouraged to
    infer that a professional counseling relationship has been established. (See C.6.b.)

e. Unjustified Gains. Counselors do not use their professional positions to seek or receive
    unjustified personal gains, sexual favors, unfair advantage, or unearned goods or ser-
    vices. (See C.3.d.)

C.6. Responsibility to Other Professionals

a. Different Approaches. Counselors are respectful of approaches to professional counsel-
    ing that differ from their own. Counselors know and take into account the traditions
    and practices of other professional groups with which they work.

b. Personal Public Statements. When making personal statements in a public context,
    counselors clarify that they are speaking from their personal perspectives and that they
    are not speaking on behalf of all counselors or the profession. (See C.5.d.)

c. Clients Served by Others. When counselors learn that their clients are in a professional
    relationship with another mental health professional, they request release from clients to
    inform the other professionals and strive to establish positive and collaborative profes-
    sional relationships. (See A.4.)

Section D: Relationships With Other Professionals

D.1. Relationships With Employers and Employees

a. Role Definition. Counselors define and describe for their employers and employees the
    parameters and levels of their professional roles.

b. Agreements. Counselors establish working agreements with supervisors, colleagues, and
    subordinates regarding counseling or clinical relationships, confidentiality, adherence to
    professional standards, distinction between public and private material, maintenance and
    dissemination of recorded information, work load, and accountability. Working agree-
    ments in each instance are specified and made known to those concerned.

c. Negative Conditions. Counselors alert their employers to conditions that may be
    potentially disruptive or damaging to the counselor's professional responsibilities or that
    may limit their effectiveness.

d. Evaluation. Counselors submit regularly to professional review and evaluation by their
    supervisor or the appropriate representative of the employer.

e. In-Service. Counselors are responsible for in-service development of self and staff.

f. Goals. Counselors inform their staff of goals and programs.

g. Practices. Counselors provide personnel and agency practices that respect and enhance the rights and welfare of each employee and recipient of agency services. Counselors strive to maintain the highest levels of professional services.

h. Personnel Selection and Assignment. Counselors select competent staff and assign responsibilities compatible with their skills and experiences.

i. Discrimination. Counselors, as either employers or employees, do not engage in or condone practices that are inhumane, illegal, or unjustifiable (such as considerations based on age, color, culture, disability, ethnic group, gender, race, religion, sexual orientation, or socioeconomic status) in hiring, promotion, or training. (See A.2.a. and C.5.b.)

j. Professional Conduct. Counselors have a responsibility both to clients and to the agency or institution within which services are performed to maintain high standards of professional conduct.

k. Exploitative Relationships. Counselors do not engage in exploitative relationships with individuals over whom they have supervisory, evaluative, or instructional control or authority.

l. Employer Policies. The acceptance of employment in an agency or institution implies that counselors are in agreement with its general policies and principles. Counselors strive to reach agreement with employers as to acceptable standards of conduct that allow for changes in institutional policy conducive to the growth and development of clients.

D.2. Consultation (See B.6.)

a. Consultation as an Option. Counselors may choose to consult with any other professionally competent persons about their clients. In choosing consultants, counselors avoid placing the consultant in a conflict of interest situation that would preclude the consultant being a proper party to the counselor's efforts to help the client. Should counselors be engaged in a work setting that compromises this consultation standard, they consult with other professionals whenever possible to consider justifiable alternatives.

b. Consultant Competency. Counselors are reasonably certain that they have or the organization represented has the necessary competencies and resources for giving the kind of consulting services needed and that appropriate referral resources are available.

c. Understanding With Clients. When providing consultation, counselors attempt to develop with their clients a clear understanding of problem definition, goals for change, and predicted consequences of interventions selected.

d. Consultant Goals. The consulting relationship is one in which client adaptability and growth toward self-direction are consistently encouraged and cultivated. (See A.1.b.)

D.3. Fees for Referral

a. Accepting Fees From Agency Clients. Counselors refuse a private fee or other remuneration for rendering services to persons who are entitled to such services through the counselor's employing agency or institution. The policies of a particular agency may make explicit provisions for agency clients to receive counseling services from members of its staff in private practice. In such instances, the clients must be informed of other options open to them should they seek private counseling services. (See A.10.a., A.11.b., and C.3.d.)

b. Referral Fees. Counselors do not accept a referral fee from other professionals.

D.4. Subcontractor Arrangements

When counselors work as subcontractors for counseling services for a third party, they have a duty to inform clients of the limitations of confidentiality that the organization may place on counselors in providing counseling services to clients. The limits of such confidentiality ordinarily are discussed as part of the intake session. (See B.1.e. and B.1.f.)

Section E: Evaluation, Assessment, and Interpretation

E.1. General

a. Appraisal Techniques. The primary purpose of educational and psychological assessment is to provide measures that are objective and interpretable in either comparative or absolute terms. Counselors recognize the need to interpret the statements in this section as applying to the whole range of appraisal techniques, including test and nontest data.

b. Client Welfare. Counselors promote the welfare and best interests of the client in the development, publication, and utilization of educational and psychological assessment techniques. They do not misuse assessment results and interpretations and take reasonable steps to prevent others from misusing the information these techniques provide. They respect the client's right to know the results, the interpretations made, and the bases for their conclusions and recommendations.

E.2. Competence to Use and Interpret Tests

a. Limits of Competence. Counselors recognize the limits of their competence and perform only those testing and assessment services for which they have been trained. They are familiar with reliability, validity, related standardization, error of measurement, and proper application of any technique utilized. Counselors using computer-based test interpretations are trained in the construct being measured and the specific instrument being used prior to using this type of computer application. Counselors take reasonable measures to ensure the proper use of psychological assessment techniques by persons under their supervision.

b. Appropriate Use. Counselors are responsible for the appropriate application, scoring, interpretation, and use of assessment instruments, whether they score and interpret such tests themselves or use computerized or other services.

c. Decisions Based on Results. Counselors responsible for decisions involving individuals or policies that are based on assessment results have a thorough understanding of educational and psychological measurement, including validation criteria, test research, and guidelines for test development and use.

d. Accurate Information. Counselors provide accurate information and avoid false claims or misconceptions when making statements about assessment instruments or techniques. Special efforts are made to avoid unwarranted connotations of such terms as IQ and grade equivalent scores. (See C.5.c.)

E.3. Informed Consent

a. Explanation to Clients. Prior to assessment, counselors explain the nature and purposes of assessment and the specific use of results in language the client (or other legally authorized person on behalf of the client) can understand, unless an explicit exception to this right has been agreed upon in advance. Regardless of whether scoring and interpretation are completed by counselors, by assistants, or by computer or other outside services, counselors take reasonable steps to ensure that appropriate explanations are given to the client.

b. Recipients of Results. The examinee's welfare, explicit understanding, and prior agreement determine the recipients of test results. Counselors include accurate and appropriate interpretations with any release of individual or group test results. (See B.1.a. and C.5.c.)

E.4. Release of Information to Competent Professionals

a. Misuse of Results. Counselors do not misuse assessment results, including test results, and interpretations, and take reasonable steps to prevent the misuse of such by others. (See C.5.c.)

b. Release of Raw Data. Counselors ordinarily release data (e.g., protocols, counseling or interview notes, or questionnaires) in which the client is identified only with the consent of the client or the client's legal representative. Such data are usually released only to persons recognized by counselors as competent to interpret the data. (See B.1.a.)

E.5. Proper Diagnosis of Mental Disorders

a. Proper Diagnosis. Counselors take special care to provide proper diagnosis of mental disorders. Assessment techniques (including personal interview) used to determine client care (e.g., locus of treatment, type of treatment, or recommended follow-up) are carefully selected and appropriately used. (See A.3.a. and C.5.c.)

b. Cultural Sensitivity. Counselors recognize that culture affects the manner in which clients' problems are defined. Clients' socioeconomic and cultural experience is considered when diagnosing mental disorders.

E.6. Test Selection

a. Appropriateness of Instruments. Counselors carefully consider the validity, reliability, psychometric limitations, and appropriateness of instruments when selecting tests for use in a given situation or with a particular client.

b. Culturally Diverse Populations. Counselors are cautious when selecting tests for culturally diverse populations to avoid inappropriateness of testing that may be outside of socialized behavioral or cognitive patterns.

E.7. Conditions of Test Administration

a. Administration Conditions. Counselors administer tests under the same conditions that were established in their standardization. When tests are not administered under standard conditions or when unusual behavior or irregularities occur during the testing session, those conditions are noted in interpretation, and the results may be designated as invalid or of questionable validity.

b. Computer Administration. Counselors are responsible for ensuring that administration programs function properly to provide clients with accurate results when a computer or other electronic methods are used for test administration. (See A.12.b.)

c. Unsupervised Test Taking. Counselors do not permit unsupervised or inadequately supervised use of tests or assessments unless the tests or assessments are designed, intended, and validated for self-administration and/or scoring.

d. Disclosure of Favorable Conditions. Prior to test administration, conditions that produce most favorable test results are made known to the examinee.

E.8. Diversity in Testing

Counselors are cautious in using assessment techniques, making evaluations, and interpreting the performance of populations not represented in the norm group on which an instrument was standardized. They recognize the effects of age, color, culture, disability, ethnic group, gender, race, religion, sexual orientation, and socioeconomic status on test administration and interpretation and place test results in proper perspective with other relevant factors. (See A.2.a.)

E.9. Test Scoring and Interpretation

a. Reporting Reservations. In reporting assessment results, counselors indicate any reservations that exist regarding validity or reliability because of the circumstances of the assessment or the inappropriateness of the norms for the person tested.

b. Research Instruments. Counselors exercise caution when interpreting the results of research instruments possessing insufficient technical data to support respondent results. The specific purposes for the use of such instruments are stated explicitly to the examinee.

c. Testing Services. Counselors who provide test scoring and test interpretation services to support the assessment process confirm the validity of such interpretations. They accurately describe the purpose, norms, validity, reliability, and applications of the procedures and any special qualifications applicable to their use. The public offering of an automated test interpretations service is considered a professional-to-professional consultation. The formal responsibility of the consultant is to the consultee, but the ultimate and overriding responsibility is to the client.

E.10. Test Security

Counselors maintain the integrity and security of tests and other assessment techniques consistent with legal and contractual obligations. Counselors do not appropriate, reproduce, or modify published tests or parts thereof without acknowledgment and permission from the publisher.

E.11. Obsolete Tests and Outdated Test Results

Counselors do not use data or test results that are obsolete or outdated for the current purpose. Counselors make every effort to prevent the misuse of obsolete measures and test data by others.

E.12. Test Construction

Counselors use established scientific procedures, relevant standards, and current professional knowledge for test design in the development, publication, and utilization of educational and psychological assessment techniques.

Section F: Teaching, Training, and Supervision

F.1. Counselor Educators and Trainers

a. Educators as Teachers and Practitioners. Counselors who are responsible for developing, implementing, and supervising educational programs are skilled as teachers and practitioners. They are knowledgeable regarding the ethical, legal, and regulatory aspects of the profession, are skilled in applying that knowledge, and make students and supervisees aware of their responsibilities. Counselors conduct counselor education and training programs in an ethical manner and serve as role models for professional behavior. Counselor educators should make an effort to infuse material related to human diversity into all courses and/or workshops that are designed to promote the development of professional counselors.

b. Relationship Boundaries With Students and Supervisees. Counselors clearly define and maintain ethical, professional, and social relationship boundaries with their students and supervisees. They are aware of the differential in power that exists and the student's or supervisee's possible incomprehension of that power differential. Counselors explain to students and supervisees the potential for the relationship to become exploitive.

c. Sexual Relationships. Counselors do not engage in sexual relationships with students or supervisees and do not subject them to sexual harassment. (See A.6. and C.5.b)

d. Contributions to Research. Counselors give credit to students or supervisees for their contributions to research and scholarly projects. Credit is given through coauthorship, acknowledgment, footnote statement, or other appropriate means, in accordance with such contributions. (See G.4.b. and G.4.c.)

e. Close Relatives. Counselors do not accept close relatives as students or supervisees.

f. Supervision Preparation. Counselors who offer clinical supervision services are adequately prepared in supervision methods and techniques. Counselors who are doctoral students serving as practicum or internship supervisors to master's level students are adequately prepared and supervised by the training program.

g. Responsibility for Services to Clients. Counselors who supervise the counseling services of others take reasonable measures to ensure that counseling services provided to clients are professional.

h. Endorsement. Counselors do not endorse students or supervisees for certification, licensure, employment, or completion of an academic or training program if they believe students or supervisees are not qualified for the endorsement. Counselors take reasonable steps to assist students or supervisees who are not qualified for endorsement to become qualified.

F.2. Counselor Education and Training Programs

a. Orientation. Prior to admission, counselors orient prospective students to the counselor education or training program's expectations, including but not limited to the following: (1) the type and level of skill acquisition required for successful completion of the training, (2) subject matter to be covered, (3) basis for evaluation, (4) training components that encourage self-growth or self-disclosure as part of the training process, (5) the type of supervision settings and requirements of the sites for required clinical field experiences, (6) student and supervisee evaluation and dismissal policies and procedures, and (7) up-to-date employment prospects for graduates.

b. Integration of Study and Practice. Counselors establish counselor education and training programs that integrate academic study and supervised practice.

c. Evaluation. Counselors clearly state to students and supervisees, in advance of training, the levels of competency expected, appraisal methods, and timing of evaluations for both didactic and experiential components. Counselors provide students and supervisees with periodic performance appraisal and evaluation feedback throughout the training program.

d. Teaching Ethics. Counselors make students and supervisees aware of the ethical responsibilities and standards of the profession and the students' and supervisees' ethical responsibilities to the profession. (See C.1. and F.3.e.)

e. Peer Relationships. When students or supervisees are assigned to lead counseling groups or provide clinical supervision for their peers, counselors take steps to ensure that students and supervisees placed in these roles do not have personal or adverse relationships with peers and that they understand they have the same ethical obligations as counselor educators, trainers, and supervisors. Counselors make every effort to ensure that the rights of peers are not compromised when students or supervisees are assigned to lead counseling groups or provide clinical supervision.

f. Varied Theoretical Positions. Counselors present varied theoretical positions so that students and supervisees may make comparisons and have opportunities to develop their own positions. Counselors provide information concerning the scientific bases of professional practice. (See C.6.a.)

g. Field Placements. Counselors develop clear policies within their training program regarding field placement and other clinical experiences. Counselors provide clearly stated roles and responsibilities for the student or supervisee, the site supervisor, and the program supervisor. They confirm that site supervisors are qualified to provide supervision and are informed of their professional and ethical responsibilities in this role.

h. Dual Relationships as Supervisors. Counselors avoid dual relationships such as performing the role of site supervisor and training program supervisor in the student's or supervisee's training program. Counselors do not accept any form of professional services, fees, commissions, reimbursement, or remuneration from a site for student or supervisee placement.

i. Diversity in Programs. Counselors are responsive to their institution's and program's recruitment and retention needs for training program administrators, faculty, and students with diverse backgrounds and special needs. (See A.2.a.)

F.3. Students and Supervisees

a. Limitations. Counselors, through ongoing evaluation and appraisal, are aware of the academic and personal limitations of students and supervisees that might impede performance. Counselors assist students and supervisees in securing remedial assistance when needed, and dismiss from the training program supervisees who are unable to provide competent service due to academic or personal limitations. Counselors seek professional consultation and document their decision to dismiss or refer students or supervisees for assistance. Counselors ensure that students and supervisees have recourse to address decisions made to require them to seek assistance or to dismiss them.

b. Self-Growth Experiences. Counselors use professional judgment when designing training experiences conducted by the counselors themselves that require student and supervisee self-growth or self-disclosure. Safeguards are provided so that students and supervisees are aware of the ramifications their self-disclosure may have on counselors whose primary role as teacher, trainer, or supervisor requires acting on ethical obligations to the profession. Evaluative components of experiential training experiences explicitly delineate predetermined academic standards that are separate and do not depend on the student's level of self-disclosure. (See A.6.)

c. Counseling for Students and Supervisees. If students or supervisees request counseling, supervisors or counselor educators provide them with acceptable referrals. Supervisors or counselor educators do not serve as counselor to students or supervisees over whom they hold administrative, teaching, or evaluative roles unless this is a brief role associated with a training experience. (See A.6.b.)

d. Clients of Students and Supervisees. Counselors make every effort to ensure that the clients at field placements are aware of the services rendered and the qualifications of the students and supervisees rendering those services. Clients receive professional disclosure information and are informed of the limits of confidentiality. Client permission is obtained in order for the students and supervisees to use any information concerning the counseling relationship in the training process. (See B.1.e.)

e. Standards for Students and Supervisees. Students and supervisees preparing to become counselors adhere to the Code of Ethics and the Standards of Practice. Students and supervisees have the same obligations to clients as those required of counselors. (See H.1.)

Section G: Research and Publication

G.1. Research Responsibilities

a. Use of Human Subjects. Counselors plan, design, conduct, and report research in a manner consistent with pertinent ethical principles, federal and state laws, host institutional regulations, and scientific standards governing research with human subjects. Counselors design and conduct research that reflects cultural sensitivity appropriateness.

b. Deviation From Standard Practices. Counselors seek consultation and observe stringent safeguards to protect the rights of research participants when a research problem suggests a deviation from standard acceptable practices. (See B.6.)

c. Precautions to Avoid Injury. Counselors who conduct research with human subjects are responsible for the subjects' welfare throughout the experiment and take reasonable precautions to avoid causing injurious psychological, physical, or social effects to their subjects.

d. Principal Researcher Responsibility. The ultimate responsibility for ethical research practice lies with the principal researcher. All others involved in the research activities share ethical obligations and full responsibility for their own actions.

e. Minimal Interference. Counselors take reasonable precautions to avoid causing disruptions in subjects' lives due to participation in research.

f. Diversity. Counselors are sensitive to diversity and research issues with special populations. They seek consultation when appropriate. (See A.2.a. and B.6.)

G.2. Informed Consent

a. Topics Disclosed. In obtaining informed consent for research, counselors use language that is understandable to research participants and that (1) accurately explains the purpose and procedures to be followed; (2) identifies any procedures that are experimental or relatively untried; (3) describes the attendant discomforts and risks; (4) describes the benefits or changes in individuals or organizations that might be reasonably expected; (5) discloses appropriate alternative procedures that would be advantageous for subjects; (6) offers to answer any inquiries concerning the procedures; (7) describes any limitations on confidentiality; and (8) instructs that subjects are free to withdraw their consent and to discontinue participation in the project at any time. (See B.1.f.)

b. Deception. Counselors do not conduct research involving deception unless alternative procedures are not feasible and the prospective value of the research justifies the deception. When the methodological requirements of a study necessitate concealment or deception, the investigator is required to explain clearly the reasons for this action as soon as possible.

c. Voluntary Participation. Participation in research is typically voluntary and without any penalty for refusal to participate. Involuntary participation is appropriate only when it can be demonstrated that participation will have no harmful effects on subjects and is essential to the investigation.

d. Confidentiality of Information. Information obtained about research participants during the course of an investigation is confidential. When the possibility exists that others may obtain access to such information, ethical research practice requires that the possibility, together with the plans for protecting confidentiality, be explained to participants as a part of the procedure for obtaining informed consent. (See B.1.e.)

e. Persons Incapable of Giving Informed Consent. When a person is incapable of giving informed consent, counselors provide an appropriate explanation, obtain agreement for participation, and obtain appropriate consent from a legally authorized person.

f. Commitments to Participants. Counselors take reasonable measures to honor all commitments to research participants.

g. Explanations After Data Collection. After data are collected, counselors provide participants with full clarification of the nature of the study to remove any misconceptions. Where scientific or human values justify delaying or withholding information, counselors take reasonable measures to avoid causing harm.

h. Agreements to Cooperate. Counselors who agree to cooperate with another individual in research or publication incur an obligation to cooperate as promised in terms of punctuality of performance and with regard to the completeness and accuracy of the information required.

i. Informed Consent for Sponsors. In the pursuit of research, counselors give sponsors, institutions, and publication channels the same respect and opportunity for giving informed consent that they accord to individual research participants. Counselors are aware of their obligation to future research workers and ensure that host institutions are given feedback information and proper acknowledgment.

G.3. Reporting Results

a. Information Affecting Outcome. When reporting research results, counselors explicitly mention all variables and conditions known to the investigator that may have affected the outcome of a study or the interpretation of data.

b. Accurate Results. Counselors plan, conduct, and report research accurately and in a manner that minimizes the possibility that results will be misleading. They provide thorough discussions of the limitations of their data and alternative hypotheses. Counselors do not engage in fraudulent research, distort data, misrepresent data, or deliberately bias their results.

c. Obligation to Report Unfavorable Results. Counselors communicate to other counselors the results of any research judged to be of professional value. Results that reflect unfavorably on institutions, programs, services, prevailing opinions, or vested interests are not withheld.

d. Identity of Subjects. Counselors who supply data, aid in the research of another person, report research results, or make original data available take due care to disguise the identity of respective subjects in the absence of specific authorization from the subjects to do otherwise. (See B.1.g. and B.5.a.)

e. Replication Studies. Counselors are obligated to make available sufficient original research data to qualified professionals who may wish to replicate the study.

G.4. Publication

a. Recognition of Others. When conducting and reporting research, counselors are familiar with and give recognition to previous work on the topic, observe copyright laws, and give full credit to those to whom credit is due. (See F.1.d. and G.4.c.)

b. Contributors. Counselors give credit through joint authorship, acknowledgment, foot-note statements, or other appropriate means to those who have contributed significantly to research or concept development in accordance with such contributions. The principal contributor is listed first and minor technical or professional contributions are acknowl-edged in notes or introductory statements.

c. Student Research. For an article that is substantially based on a student's dissertation or thesis, the student is listed as the principal author. (See F.1.d. and G.4.a.)

d. Duplicate Submission. Counselors submit manuscripts for consideration to only one journal at a time. Manuscripts that are published in whole or in substantial part in another journal or published work are not submitted for publication without acknowl-edgment and permission from the previous publication.

e. Professional Review. Counselors who review material submitted for publication, research, or other scholarly purposes respect the confidentiality and proprietary rights of those who submitted it.

Section H: Resolving Ethical Issues

H.1. Knowledge of Standards

Counselors are familiar with the Code of Ethics and the Standards of Practice and other applicable ethics codes from other professional organizations of which they are member, or from certification and licensure bodies. Lack of knowledge or misunderstand-ing of an ethical responsibility is not a defense against a charge of unethical conduct. (See F.3.e.)

H.2. Suspected Violations

a. Ethical Behavior Expected. Counselors expect professional associates to adhere to the Code of Ethics. When counselors possess reasonable cause that raises doubts as to whether a counselor is acting in an ethical manner, they take appropriate action. (See H.2.d. and H.2.e.)

b. Consultation. When uncertain as to whether a particular situation or course of action may be in violation of the Code of Ethics, counselors consult with other counselors who are knowledgeable about ethics, with colleagues, or with appropriate authorities.

c. Organization Conflicts. If the demands of an organization with which counselors are affiliated pose a conflict with the Code of Ethics, counselors specify the nature of such conflicts and express to their supervisors or other responsible officials their commitment to the Code of Ethics. When possible, counselors work toward change within the orga-nization to allow full adherence to the Code of Ethics.

d. Informal Resolution. When counselors have reasonable cause to believe that another counselor is violating an ethical standard, they attempt to first resolve the issue infor-mally with the other counselor if feasible, providing that such action does not violate confidentiality rights that may be involved.

e. Reporting Suspected Violations. When an informal resolution is not appropriate or fea-sible, counselors, upon reasonable cause, take action such as reporting the suspected eth-ical violation to state or national ethics committees, unless this action conflicts with confidentiality rights that cannot be resolved.

f. Unwarranted Complaints. Counselors do not initiate, participate in, or encourage the filing of ethics complaints that are unwarranted or intend to harm a counselor rather than to protect clients or the public.

H.3. Cooperation With Ethics Committees

Counselors assist in the process of enforcing the Code of Ethics. Counselors cooperate with investigations, proceedings, and requirements of the ACA Ethics Committee or ethics committees of other duly constituted associations or boards having jurisdiction over those charged with a violation. Counselors are familiar with the ACA Policies and Procedures and use it as a reference in assisting the enforcement of the Code of Ethics.

ACA STANDARDS OF PRACTICE

All members of the American Counseling Association (ACA) are required to adhere to the Standards of Practice and the Code of Ethics. The Standards of Practice represent minimal behavioral statements of the Code of Ethics. Members should refer to the applicable section of the Code of Ethics for further interpretation and amplification of the applicable Standard of Practice.

Section A: The Counseling Relationship

Section B: Confidentiality

Section C: Professional Responsibility

Section D: Relationship With Other Professionals

Section E: Evaluation, Assessment and Interpretation

Section F: Teaching, Training, and Supervision

Section G: Research and Publication

Section H: Resolving Ethical Issues

Section A: The Counseling Relationship

Standard of Practice One (SP-1): Nondiscrimination. Counselors respect diversity and must not discriminate against clients because of age, color, culture, disability, ethnic group, gender, race, religion, sexual orientation, marital status, or socioeconomic status. (See A.2.a.)

Standard of Practice Two (SP-2): Disclosure to Clients. Counselors must adequately inform clients, preferably in writing, regarding the counseling process and counseling relationship at or before the time it begins and throughout the relationship. (See A.3.a.)

Standard of Practice Three (SP-3): Dual Relationships. Counselors must make every effort to avoid dual relationships with clients that could impair their professional judgment or increase the risk of harm to clients. When a dual relationship cannot be avoided, counselors must take appropriate steps to ensure that judgment is not impaired and that no exploitation occurs. (See A.6.a. and A.6.b.)

Standard of Practice Four (SP-4): Sexual Intimacies With Clients. Counselors must not engage in any type of sexual intimacies with current clients and must not engage in sexual intimacies with former clients within a minimum of 2 years after terminating the counseling relationship. Counselors who engage in such relationship after 2 years following termination have the responsibility to examine and document thoroughly that such relations did not have an exploitative nature.

Standard of Practice Five (SP-5): Protecting Clients During Group Work. Counselors must take steps to protect clients from physical or psychological trauma resulting from interactions during group work. (See A.9.b.)

Standard of Practice Six (SP-6): Advance Understanding of Fees. Counselors must explain to clients, prior to their entering the counseling relationship, financial arrangements related to professional services. (See A.10. a.-d. and A.11.c.)

Standard of Practice Seven (SP-7): Termination. Counselors must assist in making appropriate arrangements for the continuation of treatment of clients, when necessary, following termination of counseling relationships. (See A.11.a.)

Standard of Practice Eight (SP-8): Inability to Assist Clients. Counselors must avoid entering or immediately terminate a counseling relationship if it is determined that they are unable to be of professional assistance to a client. The counselor may assist in making an appropriate referral for the client. (See A.11.b.)

Section B: Confidentiality

Standard of Practice Nine (SP-9): Confidentiality Requirement. Counselors must keep information related to counseling services confidential unless disclosure is in the best interest of clients, is required for the welfare of others, or is required by law. When disclosure is required, only information that is essential is revealed and the client is informed of such disclosure. (See B.1. a.+f.)

Standard of Practice Ten (SP-10): Confidentiality Requirements for Subordinates. Counselors must take measures to ensure that privacy and confidentiality of clients are maintained by subordinates. (See B.1.h.)

Standard of Practice Eleven (SP-11): Confidentiality in Group Work. Counselors must clearly communicate to group members that confidentiality cannot be guaranteed in group work. (See B.2.a.)

Standard of Practice Twelve (SP-12): Confidentiality in Family Counseling. Counselors must not disclose information about one family member in counseling to another family member without prior consent. (See B.2.b.)

Standard of Practice Thirteen (SP-13): Confidentiality of Records. Counselors must maintain appropriate confidentiality in creating, storing, accessing, transferring, and disposing of counseling records. (See B.4.b.)

Standard of Practice Fourteen (SP-14): Permission to Record or Observe. Counselors must obtain prior consent from clients in order to record electronically or observe sessions. (See B.4.c.)

Standard of Practice Fifteen (SP-15): Disclosure or Transfer of Records. Counselors must obtain client consent to disclose or transfer records to third parties, unless exceptions listed in SP-9 exist. (See B.4.e.)

Standard of Practice Sixteen (SP-16): Data Disguise Required. Counselors must disguise the identity of the client when using data for training, research, or publication. (See B.5.a.)

Section C: Professional Responsibility

Standard of Practice Seventeen (SP-17): Boundaries of Competence. Counselors must practice only within the boundaries of their competence. (See C.2.a.)

Standard of Practice Eighteen (SP-18): Continuing Education. Counselors must engage in continuing education to maintain their professional competence. (See C.2.f.)

Standard of Practice Nineteen (SP-19): Impairment of Professionals. Counselors must refrain from offering professional services when their personal problems or conflicts may cause harm to a client or others. (See C.2.g.)

Standard of Practice Twenty (SP-20): Accurate Advertising. Counselors must accurately represent their credentials and services when advertising. (See C.3.a.)

Standard of Practice Twenty-One (SP-21): Recruiting Through Employment. Counselors must not use their place of employment or institutional affiliation to recruit clients for their private practices. (See C.3.d.)

Standard of Practice Twenty-Two (SP-22): Credentials Claimed. Counselors must claim or imply only professional credentials possessed and must correct any known misrepresentations of their credentials by others. (See C.4.a.)

Standard of Practice Twenty-Three (SP-23): Sexual Harassment. Counselors must not engage in sexual harassment. (See C.5.b.)

Standard of Practice Twenty-Four (SP-24): Unjustified Gains. Counselors must not use their professional positions to seek or receive unjustified personal gains, sexual favors, unfair advantage, or unearned goods or services. (See C.5.e.)

Standard of Practice Twenty-Five (SP-25): Clients Served by Others. With the consent of the client, counselors must inform other mental health professionals serving the same client that a counseling relationship between the counselor and client exists. (See C.6.c.)

Standard of Practice Twenty-Six (SP-26): Negative Employment Conditions. Counselors must alert their employers to institutional policy or conditions that may be potentially disruptive or damaging to the counselor's professional responsibilities, or that may limit their effectiveness or deny clients' rights. (See D.1.c.)

Standard of Practice Twenty-Seven (SP-27): Personnel Selection and Assignment. Counselors must select competent staff and must assign responsibilities compatible with staff skills and experiences. (See D.1.h.)

Standard of Practice Twenty-Eight (SP-28): Exploitative Relationships With Subordinates. Counselors must not engage in exploitative relationships with individuals over whom they have supervisory, evaluative, or instructional control or authority. (See D.1.k.)

Section D: Relationship With Other Professionals

Standard of Practice Twenty-Nine (SP-29): Accepting Fees From Agency Clients. Counselors must not accept fees or other remuneration for consultation with persons entitled to such services through the counselor's employing agency or institution. (See D.3.a.)

Standard of Practice Thirty (SP-30): Referral Fees. Counselors must not accept referral fees. (See D.3.b.)

Section E: Evaluation, Assessment and Interpretation

Standard of Practice Thirty-One (SP-31): Limits of Competence. Counselors must perform only testing and assessment services for which they are competent. Counselors must not allow the use of psychological assessment techniques by unqualified persons under their supervision. (See E.2.a.)

Standard of Practice Thirty-Two (SP-32): Appropriate Use of Assessment Instruments. Counselors must use assessment instruments in the manner for which they were intended. (See E.2.b.)

Standard of Practice Thirty-Three (SP-33): Assessment Explanations to Clients. Counselors must provide explanations to clients prior to assessment about the nature and purposes of assessment and the specific uses of results. (See E.3.a.)

Standard of Practice Thirty-Four (SP-34): Recipients of Test Results. Counselors must ensure that accurate and appropriate interpretations accompany any release of testing and assessment information. (See E.3.b.)

Standard of Practice Thirty-Five (SP-35): Obsolete Tests and Outdated Test Results. Counselors must not base their assessment or intervention decisions or recommendations on data or test results that are obsolete or outdated for the current purpose. (See E.11.)

Section F: Teaching, Training, and Supervision

Standard of Practice Thirty-Six (SP-36): Sexual Relationships With Students or Supervisees. Counselors must not engage in sexual relationships with their students and supervisees. (See F.1.c.)

Standard of Practice Thirty-Seven (SP-37): Credit for Contributions to Research. Counselors must give credit to students or supervisees for their contributions to research and scholarly projects. (See F.1.d.)

Standard of Practice Thirty-Eight (SP-38): Supervision Preparation. Counselors who offer clinical supervision services must be trained and prepared in supervision methods and techniques. (See F.1.f.)

Standard of Practice Thirty-Nine (SP-39): Evaluation Information. Counselors must clearly state to students and supervisees in advance of training the levels of competency expected, appraisal methods, and timing of evaluations. Counselors must provide students and supervisees with periodic performance appraisal and evaluation feedback throughout the training program. (See F.2.c.)

Standard of Practice Forty (SP-40): Peer Relationships in Training. Counselors must make every effort to ensure that the rights of peers are not violated when students and supervisees are assigned to lead counseling groups or provide clinical supervision. (See F.2.e.)

Standard of Practice Forty-One (SP-41): Limitations of Students and Supervisees. Counselors must assist students and supervisees in securing remedial assistance, when needed, and must dismiss from the training program students and supervisees who are unable to provide competent service due to academic or personal limitations. (See F.3.a.)

Standard of Practice Forty-Two (SP-42): Self-Growth Experiences. Counselors who conduct experiences for students or supervisees that include self-growth or self-disclosure must inform participants of counselors' ethical obligations to the profession and must not grade participants based on their nonacademic performance. (See F.3.b.)

Standard of Practice Forty-Three (SP-43): Standards for Students and Supervisees. Students and supervisees preparing to become counselors must adhere to the Code of Ethics and the Standards of Practice of counselors. (See F.3.e.)

Section G: Research and Publication

Standard of Practice Forty-Four (SP-44): Precautions to Avoid Injury in Research. Counselors must avoid causing physical, social, or psychological harm or injury to subjects in research. (See G.1.c.)

Standard of Practice Forty-Five (SP-45): Confidentiality of Research Information. Counselors must keep confidential information obtained about research participants. (See G.2.d.)

Standard of Practice Forty-Six (SP-46): Information Affecting Research Outcome. Counselors must report all variables and conditions known to the investigator that may have affected research data or outcomes. (See G.3.a.)

Standard of Practice Forty-Seven (SP-47): Accurate Research Results. Counselors must not distort or misrepresent research data, nor fabricate or intentionally bias research results. (See G.3.b.)

Standard of Practice Forty-Eight (SP-48): Publication Contributors. Counselors must give appropriate credit to those who have contributed to research. (See G.4.a. and G.4.b.)

Section H: Resolving Ethical Issues

Standard of Practice Forty-Nine (SP-49): Ethical Behavior Expected. Counselors must take appropriate action when they possess reasonable cause that raises doubts as to whether counselors or other mental health professionals are acting in an ethical manner. (See H.2.a.)

Standard of Practice Fifty (SP-50): Unwarranted Complaints. Counselors must not initiate, participate in, or encourage the filing of ethics complaints that are unwarranted or intended to harm a mental health professional rather than to protect clients or the public. (See H.2.f.)

Standard of Practice Fifty-One (SP-51): Cooperation With Ethics Committees. Counselors must cooperate with investigations, proceedings, and requirements of the ACA Ethics Committee or ethics committees of other duly constituted associations or boards having jurisdiction over those charged with a violation. (See H.3.)

REFERENCES

The following documents are available to counselors as resources to guide them in their practices. These resources are not a part of the Code of Ethics and the Standards of Practice.

American Association for Counseling and Development/Association for Measurement and Evaluation in Counseling and Development. (1989). The responsibilities of users of standardized tests (rev.). Washington, DC: Author.

American Counseling Association. (1988) (Note: This is ACA's previous edition of its ethics code). Ethical standards. Alexandria, VA: Author.

American Psychological Association. (1985). Standards for educational and psychological testing (rev.). Washington, DC: Author.

Joint Committee on Testing Practices. (1988). Code of fair testing practices in education. Washington, DC: Author.

National Board for Certified Counselors. (1989). National Board for Certified Counselors code of ethics. Alexandria, VA: Author.

Prediger, D. J. (Ed.). (1993, March). Multicultural assessment standards. Alexandria, VA: Association for Assessment in Counseling.

Appendix B

✳

CODE OF ETHICS
OF THE AMERICAN ASSOCIATION
OF MARRIAGE AND FAMILY THERAPY

AAMFT Code of Ethics
Revised July 1, 1998

The Board of Directors of the American Association for Marriage and Family Therapy (AAMFT) hereby promulgates, pursuant to Article 2, Section 2.013 of the Association's Bylaws, the Revised AAMFT Code of Ethics, effective July 1, 1998. The AAMFT Code of Ethics is binding on Members of AAMFT in all membership categories, AAMFT Approved Supervisors, and applicants for membership and the Approved Supervisor designation (hereafter, AAMFT Member). If an AAMFT Member resigns in anticipation of, or during the course of an ethics investigation, the Ethics Committee will complete its investigation. Any publication of action taken by the Association will include the fact that the Member attempted to resign during the investigation. Marriage and family therapists are strongly encouraged to report alleged unethical behavior of colleagues to appropriate professional associations and state regulatory bodies.

Contents

1. Responsibilty to clients
2. Confidentiality
3. Professional competence and integrity
4. Responsibility to students, employees, and supervisees
5. Responsibility to research participants
6. Responsibility to the profession
7. Financial arrangements
8. Advertising

SOURCE: Copyright © 2001. Reprinted by permission of the American Association for Marriage & Family Therapy..

1. Responsibility to Clients

Marriage and family therapists advance the welfare of families and individuals. They respect the rights of those persons seeking their assistance, and make reasonable efforts to ensure that their services are used appropriately.

1.1 Marriage and family therapists do not discriminate against or refuse professional service to anyone on the basis of race, gender, religion, national origin, or sexual orientation.

1.2 Marriage and family therapists are aware of their influential position with respect to clients, and they avoid exploiting the trust and dependency of such persons. Therapists, therefore, make every effort to avoid dual relationships with clients that could impair professional judgment or increase the risk of exploitation. When a dual relationship cannot be avoided, therapists take appropriate professional precautions to ensure judgment is not impaired and no exploitation occurs. Examples of such dual relationships include, but are not limited to, business or close personal relationships with clients. Sexual intimacy with clients is prohibited. Sexual intimacy with former clients for two years following the termination of therapy is prohibited.

1.3 Marriage and family therapists do not use their professional relationships with clients to further their own interests.

1.4 Marriage and family therapists respect the right of clients to make decisions and help them to understand the consequences of these decisions. Therapists clearly advise a client that a decision on marital status is the responsibility of the client.

1.5 Marriage and family therapists continue therapeutic relationships only so long as it is reasonably clear that clients are benefiting from the relationship.

1.6 Marriage and family therapists assist persons in obtaining other therapeutic services if the therapist is unable or unwilling, for appropriate reasons, to provide professional help.

1.7 Marriage and family therapists do not abandon or neglect clients in treatment without making reasonable arrangements for the continuation of such treatment.

1.8 Marriage and family therapists obtain written informed consent from clients before videotaping, audiorecording, or permitting third party observation.

2. Confidentiality

Marriage and family therapists have unique confidentiality concerns because the client in a therapeutic relationship may be more than one person. Therapists respect and guard confidences of each individual client.

2.1 Marriage and family therapists may not disclose client confidences except: (a) as mandated by law; (b) to prevent a clear and immediate danger to a person or persons; (c) where the therapist is a defendant in a civil, criminal, or disciplinary action arising from the therapy (in which case client confidences may be disclosed only in the course of that action); or (d) if there is a waiver previously obtained in writing, and then such information may be revealed only in accordance with the terms of the waiver. In circumstances where more than one person in a family receives therapy, each such family member who is legally competent to execute a waiver must agree to the waiver required by subparagraph (d). Without such a waiver from each family member legally competent to execute a waiver, a therapist cannot disclose information received from any family member.

2.2 Marriage and family therapists use client and/or clinical materials in teaching, writing, and public presentations only if a written waiver has been obtained in accordance with

Subprinciple 2.1(d), or when appropriate steps have been taken to protect client identity and confidentiality.

2.3 Marriage and family therapists store or dispose of client records in ways that maintain confidentiality.

3. Professional Competence and Integrity

Marriage and family therapists maintain high standards of professional competence and integrity.

3.1 Marriage and family therapists are in violation of this Code and subject to termination of membership or other appropriate action if they: (a) are convicted of any felony; (b) are convicted of a misdemeanor related to their qualifications or functions; (c) engage in conduct which could lead to conviction of a felony, or a misdemeanor related to their qualifications or functions; (d) are expelled from or disciplined by other professional organizations; (e) have their licenses or certificates suspended or revoked or are otherwise disciplined by regulatory bodies; (f) are no longer competent to practice marriage and family therapy because they are impaired due to physical or mental causes or the abuse of alcohol or other substances; or (g) fail to cooperate with the Association at any point from the inception of an ethical complaint through the completion of all proceedings regarding that complaint.

3.2 Marriage and family therapists seek appropriate professional assistance for their personal problems or conflicts that may impair work performance or clinical judgment.

3.3 Marriage and family therapists, as teachers, supervisors, and researchers, are dedicated to high standards of scholarship and present accurate information.

3.4 Marriage and family therapists remain abreast of new developments in family therapy knowledge and practice through educational activities.

3.5 Marriage and family therapists do not engage in sexual or other harassment or exploitation of clients, students, trainees, supervisees, employees, colleagues, research subjects, or actual or potential witnesses or complainants in investigations and ethical proceedings.

3.6 Marriage and family therapists do not diagnose, treat, or advise on problems outside the recognized boundaries of their competence.

3.7 Marriage and family therapists make efforts to prevent the distortion or misuse of their clinical and research findings.

3.8 Marriage and family therapists, because of their ability to influence and alter the lives of others, exercise special care when making public their professional recommendations and opinions through testimony or other public statements.

4. Responsibility to Students, Employees, and Supervisees

Marriage and family therapists do not exploit the trust and dependency of students, employees, and supervisees.

4.1 Marriage and family therapists are aware of their influential position with respect to students, employees, and supervisees, and they avoid exploiting the trust and dependency of such persons. Therapists, therefore, make every effort to avoid dual relationships that could impair professional judgment or increase the risk of exploitation. When a dual relationship cannot be avoided, therapists take appropriate professional precautions to ensure judgment is not impaired and no exploitation occurs. Examples of such dual relationships include, but are not limited to, business or close personal relationships with students, employees, or supervisees. Provision of therapy to students, employees, or supervisees is prohibited. Sexual intimacy with students or supervisees is prohibited.

4.2 Marriage and family therapists do not permit students, employees, or supervisees to perform or to hold themselves out as competent to perform professional services beyond their training, level of experience, and competence.

4.3 Marriage and family therapists do not disclose supervisee confidences except: (a) as mandated by law; (b) to prevent a clear and immediate danger to a person or persons; (c) where the therapist is a defendant in a civil, criminal, or disciplinary action arising from the supervision (in which case supervisee confidences may be disclosed only in the course of that action); (d) in educational or training settings where there are multiple supervisors, and then only to other professional colleagues who share responsibility for the training of the supervisee; or (e) if there is a waiver previously obtained in writing, and then such information may be revealed only in accordance with the terms of the waiver.

5. Responsibility to Research Participants

Investigators respect the dignity and protect the welfare of participants in research and are aware of federal and state laws and regulations and professional standards governing the conduct of research.

5.1 Investigators are responsible for making careful examinations of ethical acceptability in planning studies. To the extent that services to research participants may be compromised by participation in research, investigators seek the ethical advice of qualified professionals not directly involved in the investigation and observe safeguards to protect the rights of research participants.

5.2 Investigators requesting participants' involvement in research inform them of all aspects of the research that might reasonably be expected to influence willingness to participate. Investigators are especially sensitive to the possibility of diminished consent when participants are also receiving clinical services, have impairments which limit understanding and/or communication, or when participants are children.

5.3 Investigators respect participants' freedom to decline participation in or to withdraw from a research study at any time. This obligation requires special thought and consideration when investigators or other members of the research team are in positions of authority or influence over participants. Marriage and family therapists, therefore, make every effort to avoid dual relationships with research participants that could impair professional judgment or increase the risk of exploitation.

5.4 Information obtained about a research participant during the course of an investigation is confidential unless there is a waiver previously obtained in writing. When the possibility exists that others, including family members, may obtain access to such information, this possibility, together with the plan for protecting confidentiality, is explained as part of the procedure for obtaining informed consent.

6. Responsibility to the Profession

Marriage and family therapists respect the rights and responsibilities of professional colleagues and participate in activities which advance the goals of the profession.

6.1 Marriage and family therapists remain accountable to the standards of the profession when acting as members or employees of organizations.

6.2 Marriage and family therapists assign publication credit to those who have contributed to a publication in proportion to their contributions and in accordance with customary professional publication practices.

6.3 Marriage and family therapists who are the authors of books or other materials that are published or distributed cite persons to whom credit for original ideas is due.

6.4 Marriage and family therapists who are the authors of books or other materials published or distributed by an organization take reasonable precautions to ensure that the organization promotes and advertises the materials accurately and factually.

6.5 Marriage and family therapists participate in activities that contribute to a better community and society, including devoting a portion of their professional activity to services for which there is little or no financial return.

6.6 Marriage and family therapists are concerned with developing laws and regulations pertaining to marriage and family therapy that serve the public interest, and with altering such laws and regulations that are not in the public interest.

6.7 Marriage and family therapists encourage public participation in the design and delivery of professional services and in the regulation of practitioners.

7. Financial Arrangements

Marriage and family therapists make financial arrangements with clients, third party payors, and supervisees that are reasonably understandable and conform to accepted professional practices.

7.1 Marriage and family therapists do not offer or accept payment for referrals.

7.2 Marriage and family therapists do not charge excessive fees for services.

7.3 Marriage and family therapists disclose their fees to clients and supervisees at the beginning of services.

7.4 Marriage and family therapists represent facts truthfully to clients, third party payors, and supervisees regarding services rendered.

8. Advertising

Marriage and family therapists engage in appropriate informational activities, including those that enable laypersons to choose professional services on an informed basis.

General Advertising

8.1 Marriage and family therapists accurately represent their competence, education, training, and experience relevant to their practice of marriage and family therapy.

8.2 Marriage and family therapists assure that advertisements and publications in any media (such as directories, announcements, business cards, newspapers, radio, television, and facsimiles) convey information that is necessary for the public to make an appropriate selection of professional services. Information could include: (a) office information, such as name, address, telephone number, credit card acceptability, fees, languages spoken, and office hours; (b) appropriate degrees, state licensure and/or certification, and AAMFT Clinical Member status; and (c) description of practice. (For requirements for advertising under the AAMFT name, logo, and/or the abbreviated initials AAMFT, see Subprinciple 8.14 and 8.15, below).

8.3 Marriage and family therapists do not use a name which could mislead the public concerning the identity, responsibility, source, and status of those practicing under that name and do not hold themselves out as being partners or associates of a firm if they are not.

8.4 Marriage and family therapists do not use any professional identification (such as a business card, office sign, letterhead, or telephone or association directory listing) if it includes a statement or claim that is false, fraudulent, misleading, or deceptive. A statement is false, fraudulent, misleading, or deceptive if it (a) contains a material misrepresentation of fact; (b) fails to state any material fact necessary to make the statement, in light of all circumstances, not misleading; or (c) is intended to or is likely to create an unjustified expectation.

8.5 Marriage and family therapists correct, wherever possible, false, misleading, or inaccurate information and representations made by others concerning the therapist's qualifications, services, or products.

8.6 Marriage and family therapists make certain that the qualifications of persons in their employ are represented in a manner that is not false, misleading, or deceptive.

8.7 Marriage and family therapists may represent themselves as specializing within a limited area of marriage and family therapy, but only if they have the education and supervised experience in settings which meet recognized professional standards to practice in that specialty area.

Advertising Using AAMFT Designations

8.8 The AAMFT designations of Clinical Member, Approved Supervisor, and Fellow may be used in public information or advertising materials only by persons holding such designations. Persons holding such designations may, for example, advertise in the following manner:

> Jane Doe, Ph.D., a Clinical Member of the American Association for Marriage and Family Therapy. Alternately, the advertisement could read, Jane Doe, Ph.D., AAMFT Clinical Member.

> John Doe, Ph.D., an Approved Supervisor of the American Association for Marriage and Family Therapy. Alternately, the advertisement could read, John Doe, Ph.D., AAMFT Approved Supervisor.

> Jane Doe, Ph.D., a Fellow of the American Association for Marriage and Family Therapy. Alternately, the advertisement could read, Jane Doe, Ph.D., AAMFT Fellow.

More than one designation may be used if held by the AAMFT Member.

8.9 Marriage and family therapists who hold the AAMFT Approved Supervisor or the Fellow designation may not represent the designation as an advanced clinical status.

8.10 Student, Associate, and Affiliate Members may not use their AAMFT membership status in public information or advertising materials. Such listings on professional resumes are not considered advertisements.

8.11 Persons applying for AAMFT membership may not list their application status on any resume or advertisement.

8.12 In conjunction with their AAMFT membership, marriage and family therapists claim as evidence of educational qualifications only those degrees (a) from regionally accredited institutions or (b) from institutions recognized by states which license or certify marriage and family therapists, but only if such state regulation is recognized by AAMFT.

8.13 Marriage and family therapists may not use the initials AAMFT following their name in the manner of an academic degree.

8.14 Marriage and family therapists may not use the AAMFT name, corporate logo, and/or the abbreviated initials AAMFT or make any other such representation which would imply that they speak for or represent the Association. The Association is the sole owner of its name, corporate logo, and the abbreviated initials AAMFT. Its committees and divisions, operating as such, may use the name, corporate logo, and/or the abbreviated initials, AAMFT, in accordance with AAMFT policies.

8.15 Advertisements of Clinical Members may include the following:

> AAMFT Clinical Member Logo, Clinical Member's name, degree, license or certificate held when required by state law, name of business, address, and telephone number. If a business is listed, it must follow, not precede the Clinical Member's name. Such listings may not include AAMFT offices held by the Clinical Member, nor any specializations, since such a listing under the AAMFT name, Clinical Member logo, and/or the abbreviated initials AAMFT would imply that this specialization has been credentialed by AAMFT. The logo shall be used in accordance with stated guidelines.

8 .16 Marriage and family therapists use their membership in AAMFT only in connection with their clinical and professional activities.

8.17 Only AAMFT divisions and programs accredited by the AAMFT Commission on Accreditation for Marriage and Family Therapy Education, not businesses nor organizations, may use any AAMFT-related designation or affiliation in public information or advertising materials, and then only in accordance with AAMFT policies.

8.18 Programs accredited by the AAMFT Commission on Accreditation for Marriage and Family Therapy Education may not use the AAMFT name, corporate logo, and/or the abbreviated initials, AAMFT. Instead, they may have printed on their stationery and other appropriate materials a statement such as:

> The (name of program) of the (name of institution) is accredited by the AAMFT Commission on Accreditation for Marriage and Family Therapy Education.

8.19 Programs not accredited by the AAMFT Commission on Accreditation for Marriage and Family Therapy Education may not use the AAMFT name, corporate logo, and/or the abbreviated initials, AAMFT. They may not state in printed program materials, program advertisements, and student advisements that their courses and training opportunities are accepted by AAMFT to meet AAMFT membership requirements.

This Code is published by:
American Association for Marriage and Family Therapy
1133 15th Street, NW Suite 300
Washington, DC 20005-2710
(202) 452-0109
(202) 223-2329 FAX
www.aamft.org

© Copyright 1998 by the AAMFT. All rights reserved. Printed in the United States of America. No part of this publication may be reproduced, stored in a retrieval system, or transmitted, in any form or by any means, electronic, mechanical, photocopying, recording, or otherwise, without the prior written permission of the publisher.

Violations of this Code should be brought in writing to the attention of the AAMFT Ethics Committee,1133 15th Street, NW, Suite 300, Washington, DC 20005-2710, (telephone 202/452-0109).

Index